DBKDA 2016

The Eighth International Conference on Advances in Databases, Knowledge, and Data Applications

GraphSM 2016

The Third International Workshop on Large-scale Graph Storage and Management

June 26 - 30, 2016

Lisbon, Portugal

DBKDA 2016 Editors

Friedrich Laux, Reutlingen University, Germany

Andreas Schmidt, Karlsruhe University of Applied Sciences | Karlsruhe Institute of Technology, Germany

Dimitar Hristovski, University of Ljubljana, Slovenia

Printed from e-media with permission by:

Curran Associates, Inc.
57 Morehouse Lane
Red Hook, NY 12571

Some format issues inherent in the e-media version may also appear in this print version.

Printed by Curran Associates, Inc. (2016)

International Academy, Research, and Industry Association (IARIA)
412 Derby Way
Wilmington, DE 19810

Phone: (408) 893-6407
Fax: (408) 527-6351

petre@iaria.org

Additional copies of this publication are available from:

Curran Associates, Inc.
57 Morehouse Lane
Red Hook, NY 12571 USA
Phone: 845-758-0400
Fax: 845-758-2633
Email: curran@proceedings.com
Web: www.proceedings.com

Table of Contents

Database
Dimitar Hristovski, Andrej Kastrin, and Thomas C. Rindflesch

DBKDA 2016

Foreword

The Eighth International Conference on Advances in Databases, Knowledge, and Data Applications (DBKDA 2016), held between June 26 - 30, 2016 - Lisbon, Portugal, continued a series of international events covering a large spectrum of topics related to advances in fundamentals on databases, evolution of relation between databases and other domains, data base technologies and content processing, as well as specifics in applications domains databases.

Advances in different technologies and domains related to databases triggered substantial improvements for content processing, information indexing, and data, process and knowledge mining. The push came from Web services, artificial intelligence, and agent technologies, as well as from the generalization of the XML adoption.

High-speed communications and computations, large storage capacities, and load-balancing for distributed databases access allow new approaches for content processing with incomplete patterns, advanced ranking algorithms and advanced indexing methods.

Evolution on e-business, ehealth and telemedicine, bioinformatics, finance and marketing, geographical positioning systems put pressure on database communities to push the 'de facto' methods to support new requirements in terms of scalability, privacy, performance, indexing, and heterogeneity of both content and technology.

DBKDA 2016 also featured the following Workshop:

- GraphSM 2016: The Third International Workshop on Large-scale Graph Storage and Management

We take here the opportunity to warmly thank all the members of the DBKDA 2016 Technical Program Committee, as well as the numerous reviewers. The creation of such a high quality conference program would not have been possible without their involvement. We also kindly thank all the authors who dedicated much of their time and efforts to contribute to DBKDA 2016. We truly believe that, thanks to all these efforts, the final conference program consisted of top quality contributions.

Also, this event could not have been a reality without the support of many individuals, organizations, and sponsors. We are grateful to the members of the DBKDA 2016 organizing committee for their help in handling the logistics and for their work to make this professional meeting a success.

We hope that DBKDA 2016 was a successful international forum for the exchange of ideas and results between academia and industry and for the promotion of progress in the fields of databases, knowledge and data applications.

We are convinced that the participants found the event useful and communications very open. We also hope that Lisbon provided a pleasant environment during the conference and everyone saved some time for exploring this beautiful city.

DBKDA 2016 Chairs:

Friedrich Laux, Reutlingen University, Germany
Aris M. Ouksel, The University of Illinois at Chicago, USA
Serge Miranda, Université de Nice Sophia Antipolis, France

Andreas Schmidt, Karlsruhe University of Applied Sciences | Karlsruhe Institute of Technology, Germany
Maribel Yasmina Santos, University of Minho, Portugal
Filip Zavoral, Charles University Prague, Czech Republic
Maria Del Pilar Angeles, Universidad Nacional Autonoma de Mexico - Del Coyoacan, Mexico
Dimitar Hristovski, University of Ljubljana, Slovenia
Christian Krause, SAP Innovation Center Potsdam, Germany

DBKDA 2016

Committee

DBKDA Advisory Committee

Friedrich Laux, Reutlingen University, Germany
Aris M. Ouksel, The University of Illinois at Chicago, USA
Serge Miranda, Université de Nice Sophia Antipolis, France
Andreas Schmidt, Karlsruhe University of Applied Sciences | Karlsruhe Institute of Technology, Germany
Maribel Yasmina Santos, University of Minho, Portugal
Filip Zavoral, Charles University Prague, Czech Republic
Maria Del Pilar Angeles, Universidad Nacional Autonoma de Mexico - Del Coyoacan, Mexico

DBKDA 2016 Technical Program Committee

Nipun Agarwal, Oracle Corporation, USA
Suad Alagic, University of Southern Maine, USA
Abdullah Albarrak, University of Queensland, Australia
Toshiyuki Amagasa, University of Tsukuba, Japan
Bernd Amann, Université Pierre et Marie Curie (UPMC) - LIP6, France
Fabrizio Angiulli, University of Calabria, Italy
Masayoshi Aritsugi, Kumamoto University, Japan
Zeyar Aung, Masdar Institute of Science and Technology, United Arab Emirates
Ana Azevedo, Algoritmi R&D Center/University of Minho & Polytechnic Institute of Porto/ISCAP, Portugal
Gilbert Babin, HEC Montréal, Canada
Ilaria Bartolini, University of Bologna, Italy
Orlando Belo, University of Minho, Portugal
Fadila Bentayeb, University of Lyon 2, France
Arnab Bhattacharya, IIT Kanpur, India
Zouhaier Brahmia, University of Sfax, Tunisia
Francesco Buccafurri, University Mediterranea of Reggio Calabria, Italy
Erik Buchmann, Karlsruhe Institute of Technology (KIT), Germany
Martine Cadot, LORIA-Nancy, France
Ricardo Campos, Polytechnic Institute of Tomar / LIAAD - INESCT TEC Porto, Portugal
Michelangelo Ceci, University of Bari, Italy
Chin-Chen Chang, Feng Chia University Taiwan, Taiwan
Chi-Hua Chen, National Chiao Tung University - Taiwan, R.O.C.
Qiming Chen, HP Labs - Palo Alto, USA
Ding-Yuan Cheng, National Chiao Tung University, Taiwan , R.O.C.
Yangjun Chen, University of Winnipeg, Canada
Yung Chang Chi, National Cheng Kung University, Taiwan
Camelia Constantin, UPMC, France
Theodore Dalamagas, ATHENA Research and Innovation Center, Greece
Gabriel David, University of Porto, Portugal
Maria Del Pilar Angeles, Universidad Nacional Autonoma de Mexico - Del Coyoacan, Mexico

Taoufiq Dkaki, IRIT - Toulouse, France
Cédric du Mouza, CNAM - Paris, France
Gledson Elias, Universidade Federal da Paraiba, Brazil
Markus Endres, University of Augsburg, Germany
Bijan Fadaeenia, Islamic Azad University- Hamedan Branch, Iran
Feroz Farazi, University of Trento, Italy
Manuel Filipe Santos, Algoritmi research centre / University of Minho, Portugal
Sergio Firmenich, CONICET and LIFIA - Facultad de Informática, Universidad Nacional de La Plata, Argentina
Ingrid Fischer, University of Konstanz, Germany
Robert Gottstein, Technische Universität Darmstadt, Germany
Michael Gowanlock, Massachusetts Institute of Technology, Haystack Observatory, USA
Jerzy Grzymala-Busse, University of Kansas, USA
Dirk Habich, TU Dresden, Germany
Phan Nhat Hai, University of Oregon, USA
Takahiro Hara, Osaka University, Japan
Bingsheng He, Nanyang Technological University, Singapore
Erik Hoel, Esri, USA
Tobias Hoppe, Ruhr-University of Bochum, Germany
Martin Hoppen, Institute for Man-Machine Interaction - RWTH Aachen University, Germany
Wen-Chi Hou, Southern Illinois University at Carbondale, USA
Hamidah Ibrahim, Universiti Putra Malaysia, Malaysia
Dino Ienco, Irstea Montpellier, France
Yasunori Ishihara, Osaka University, Japan
Vladimir Ivancevic, University of Novi Sad, Serbia
Savnik Iztok, University of Primorska, Slovenia
Wassim Jaziri, ISIM Sfax, Tunisia
Sungwon Jung, Sogang University - Seoul, Korea
Vana Kalogeraki, Athens University of Economics and Business, Greece
Konstantinos Kalpakis, University of Maryland Baltimore County, USA
Mehdi Kargar, York University, Toronto, Canada
Rajasekar Karthik, Geographic Information Science and Technology Group/Oak Ridge National Laboratory, USA
Nhien An Le Khac, University College Dublin, Ireland
Sadegh Kharazmi, RMIT University - Melbourne, Australia
Peter Kieseberg, SBA Research, Austria
Daniel Kimmig, Karlsruhe Institute of Technology, Germany
Christian Kop, University of Klagenfurt, Austria
Michal Kratky, VŠB - Technical University of Ostrava, Czech Republic
Jens Krueger, Hasso Plattner Institute / University of Potsdam, Germany
Bart Kuijpers, Hasselt University, Belgium
Fritz Laux, Reutlingen University, Germany
YoonJoon Lee, KAIST, South Korea
Carson Leung, University of Manitoba, Canada
Sebastian Link, The University of Auckland, New Zealand
Chunmei Liu, Howard University, USA
Corrado Loglisci, University of Bari, Italy
Qiang Ma, Kyoto University, Japan

Sebastian Maneth, University of Edinburgh, UK
Murali Mani, University of Michigan - Flint, USA
Gerasimos Marketos, University of Piraeus, Greece
Michele Melchiori, Università degli Studi di Brescia, Italy
Ernestina Menasalvas, Universidad Politécnica de Madrid, Spain
Antonio Messina, Italian National Research Council - High Performances Computing and Networking Institute, Italy
Elisabeth Métais, CEDRIC / CNAM - Paris, France
Cristian Mihaescu, University of Craiova, Romania
Serge Miranda, Université de Nice Sophia Antipolis, France
Mehran Misaghi, Educational Society of Santa Catarina – Joinville, Brazil
Mohamed Mkaouar, Sfax, Tunisia
Jacky Montmain, LGI2P - Ecole des Mines d'Alès, France
Yasuhiko Morimoto, Hiroshima University, Japan
Franco Maria Nardini, ISTI-CNR, Italy
Khaled Nagi, Alexandria University, Egypt
Shin-ichi Ohnishi, Hokkai-Gakuen University, Japan
Benoît Otjacques, LIST - Luxembourg Institute of Science and Technology, Luxembourg
Aris M. Ouksel, The University of Illinois at Chicago, USA
George Papastefanatos, Athena Research and Innovation Center, Greece
Francesco Parisi, University of Calabria, Italy
Alexander Pastwa, Ruhr-Universität Bochum, Germany
Dhaval Patel, IIT-Roorkee, Singapore
Przemyslaw Pawluk, York University - Toronto, Canada
Bernhard Peischl, Softnet Austria | Institut für Softwaretechnologie | Technische Universität Graz, Austria
Alexander Peter, AOL Data Warehouse, USA
Alain Pirotte, University of Louvain (Louvain-la-Neuve), Belgium
Pascal Poncelet, LIRMM, France
Philippe Pucheral, University of Versailles & INRIA, France
Ricardo Queirós, ESEIG-IPP, Portugal
Mandar Rahurkar, Yahoo! Labs, USA
Praveen R. Rao, University of Missouri-Kansas City, USA
Peter Revesz, University of Nebraska-Lincoln, USA
Mathieu Roche, TETIS, Cirad, France
Miguel Romero, University of Chile, Chile
Florin Rusu, University of California, Merced, USA
Gunter Saake, Otto-von-Guericke-University Magdeburg, Germany
Satya Sahoo, Case Western Reserve University, USA
Fatiha Saïs, LRI (CNRS & Paris Sud University), France
Emanuel Sallinger, University of Oxford, UK
Abhishek Sanwaliya, Indian Institute of Technology - Kanpur, India
Ismael Sanz, Universitat Jaume I - Castelló, Spain
Maria Luisa Sapino, Università degli Studi di Torino, Italy
M. Saravanan, Ericsson India Pvt. Ltd -Tamil Nadu, India
Idrissa Sarr, Université Cheikh Anta Diop, Senegal
Najla Sassi Jaziri, ISSAT Mahdia, Tunisia
Andreas Schmidt, Karlsruhe University of Applied Sciences | Karlsruhe Institute of Technology, Germany

Yong Shi, Kennesaw State University, USA
Damires Souza, Federal Institute of Education, Science and Technology of Paraiba (IFPB), Brazil
Lubomir Stanchev, California Polytechnic State University, San Luis Obispo, USA
Ahmad Taleb, Najran University, Saudi Arabia
Tony Tan, National Taiwan University, Taiwan
Maguelonne Teisseire, Irstea - UMR TETIS, France
Telesphore Tiendrebeogo, Polytechnic University of Bobo-Dioulasso, Burkina Faso
Gabriele Tolomei, CNR, Italy
Jose Torres-Jimenez, CINVESTAV 3C, Mexico
Nicolas Travers, CNAM-Paris, France
Thomas Triplet, Computer Research Institute of Montreal (CRIM), Canada
Marina Tropmann-Frick, Christian-Albrechts-University of Kiel, Germany
Robert Ulbricht, Robotron Datenbank-Software GmbH, Germany
Marian Vajtersic, University of Salzburg, Austria
Maurice van Keulen, University of Twente, Netherlands
Genoveva Vargas, Solar | CNRS | LIG-LAFMIA, France
Marcio Victorino, University of Brasília, Brazil
Fan Wang, Microsoft Corporation - Bellevue, USA
Zhihui Wang, Dalian University of Technology, China
Kesheng (John) Wu, Lawrence Berkeley National Laboratory, USA
Guandong Xu, Victoria University, Australia
Maribel Yasmina Santos, University of Minho, Portugal
Jin Soung Yoo, Indiana University-Purdue University - Fort Wayne, USA
Feng Yu, Youngstown State University, USA
Filip Zavoral , Charles University Prague, Czech Republic
Wei Zhang, Amazon.com, USA
Jiakui Zhao, State Grid Information & Telecommunication Gruop, China

GraphSM 2016 Advisory Committee

Dimitar Hristovski, University of Ljubljana, Slovenia
Andreas Schmidt, Karlsruhe University of Applied Sciences & Karlsruhe Institute of Technology, Germany
Christian Krause, SAP Innovation Center Potsdam, Germany

GraphSM 2016 Technical Program Committee

Khaled Ammar, University of Waterloo, Canada
Blaz Fortuna, Jozef Stefan Institute, Slovenia
Holger Giese, Hasso-Plattner-Institut, Germany
Dimitar Hristovski, University of Ljubljana, Slovenia
Yasunori Ishihara, Osaka University, Japan
Christian Krause, SAP Innovation Center Potsdam, Germany
Dejan Lavbic, University of Ljubljana, Slovenia
Khaled Nagi, Alexandria University, Egypt
Elena Ravve, Ort-Braude College - Karmiel, Israel
Andreas Schmidt, Karlsruhe University of Applied Sciences & Karlsruhe Institute of Technology, Germany
Jim Webber, Neo Technology, USA
Tatjana Wezler, University of Maribor, Slovenia

Kokou Yetongnon, Université de Bourgogne, France
Albert Zündorf, Kassel University, Germany

Copyright Information

Object-Relational Mapping in 3D Simulation

Ann-Marie Stapelbroek,
Martin Hoppen
and Juergen Rossmann

Institute for Man-Machine Interaction
RWTH Aachen University
D-52074 Aachen, Germany
Email: ann-marie.stapelbroek@rwth-aachen.de {hoppen, rossmann}@mmi.rwth-aachen.de

***Abstract*—Usually, 3D simulation models are based on complex object-oriented structures. To master this complexity, databases should be used. However, existing approaches for 3D model data management are not sufficiently comprehensive and flexible. Thus, we develop an approach based on the relational data model as the most widespread database paradigm. To successfully combine an object-oriented 3D simulation system and a relational database management system, a mapping has to be defined bridging the differences in between. These are summarized as the object-relational impedance mismatch. Theoretical foundations of object-relational mapping are researched and existing, semi-automatic object-relational mappers are evaluated. As it turns out, existing mappers are not applicable in the presented case. Therefore, a new object-relational mapper is developed based on the utilized simulation system's meta information system. Key aspects of the developed approach are a necessary adaptation of the theoretical object-relational mapping strategies, database independence in conjunction with data type mapping, schema mapping by schema synchronization, and strategies for saving and loading model data as well as for change tracking. The developed prototype is evaluated using two exemplary simulation models from the fields of industrial automation and space robotics.**

Keywords–Object-Oriented 3D Simulation System; Relational Data Model; Relational Database Management System; Object-Relational Mapper; Object-Relational Mapping; Object-Relational Impedance Mismatch.

I. INTRODUCTION

3D simulation systems are used in different areas like space robotics and industrial automation to derive properties – especially, spatial properties – of a planned or existing system's behavior. Usually, 3D simulations are based on complex and extensive models. Therefore, databases are appropriate for data management to master the complex object-oriented structures of 3D simulation models and to make simulation states persistent [1]. As a result, different simulation runs can be recorded and analyzed [2]. In comparison with flat file storage, the usage of databases has key advantages, in particular, if data independence, multi-user synchronization, data integrity, data security, reliability, efficient data access and scalability are required [3]. However, existing approaches for 3D model data management using databases are not sufficiently comprehensive and flexible, motivating the development of a new approach.

The most widespread database paradigm is the relational data model. If relational databases should be used as a persistence layer for object-oriented 3D simulation systems, a mapping has to be defined bridging the differences between both paradigms. These differences are summarized as the object-relational impedance mismatch. The term object-relational mapping (OR mapping) describes the process of mapping the objects of an application (here, a 3D simulation system) to table entries of a relational database and vice versa. A manual mapping between the object-oriented concept and the relational database model is complex and error-prone so that object-relational mappers (OR mappers) are used. An OR mapper is a tool that builds a translation layer between application logic and relational database to perform a semi-automatic object-relational mapping.

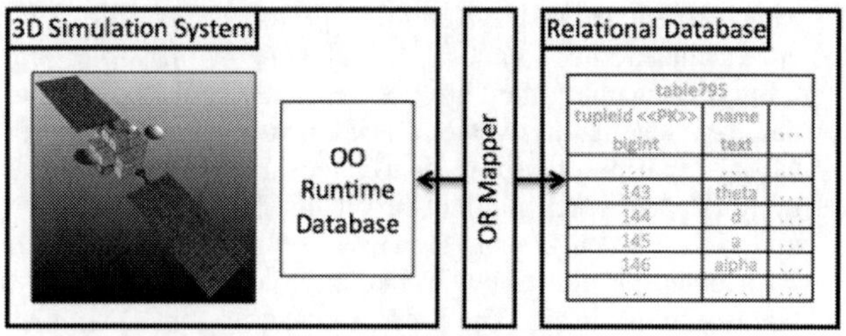

Figure 1. OR mapping for a 3D simulation system with an object-oriented runtime database (data: [4]).

In this paper, we present an OR mapper for 3D simulation systems with an object-oriented runtime database and a meta information system, see Figure 1. The work was conducted as a student project and is based on our previous work [1] [2]. A prototypical implementation is based on the 3D simulation system VEROSIM [5] and PostgreSQL [6] as a relational database management system (RDBMS). However, the underlying approach itself provides database independence allowing the usage of other RDBMSs. A key aspect of the presented OR mapping is the schema mapping that is build during a schema synchronization (based on [2]). The introduced concept considers both forward and reverse mapping. Furthermore, the OR mapper supports change tracking and resynchronization of changes. The OR mapper provides an eager and a lazy loading strategy. The prototype is evaluated using simulation models for industrial automation and space robotics (Figure 11).

The rest of this paper is organized as follows: In the next section, similar applications with a 3D context that integrate database technology are analyzed. Section III contains a short summary regarding the theoretical principals of OR mapping and Section IV introduces the utilized 3D simulation system VEROSIM and evaluates existing OR mappers. Subsequently, the newly developed concept for OR mapping is introduced in Section V and evaluated in Section VI. Finally, the paper is concluded in Section VII.

II. Related Work

In general, many applications with a 3D context have data management requirements similar to 3D simulation. Yet, the use of database technology is not widespread and files are still predominant. When databases are utilized at all, in many scenarios, they are used to store additional information (meta information, documents, films, positions, hierarchical structure ...) on scene objects or parts [7] [8] [9] [10] [11] [12] [13]. Yet, we need to manage the 3D model itself to obtain all the benefits from using database technology. Another important aspect for 3D simulation is arbitrary application schema support to be able to work with native data and avoid friction loss due to conversions. Many systems use a generic (scene-graph-like) geometric model, in most cases with attributes [7] [14] [15] [16] [17]. In such scenarios, schema flexibility can be achieved to a certain extent by providing import (and export) to different file formats [15] [18] [19] [20]. Some approaches support different or flexible schemata. For example in [14], schema alteration is realized by adding attributes to generic base objects. Other systems support a selection of different static [15] or dynamic [16] [21] schemata. However, most approaches focus on a specific field of application, thus, requiring and supporting only a corresponding fixed schema [22] [23] [24]. While Product Data Management (PDM) systems [8] [9] or similar file vaulting approaches for 3D data [25] [26] [27] in principle support arbitrary schemata they are not explicitly reflected within the database schema due to their "black box integration" approach. Most scenarios provide a distributed architecture in terms of multiuser support, a client-server model, or access control and rights management. However, only some build it on a Distributed Database (DDB)-like approach [21] [28] [17] with client-side databases. The latter is favorable for 3D simulation, e.g., to provide schema flexibility or a query interface on client-side, as well.

Altogether, while there are many existing approaches to use database technology in applications with a 3D context, none of them provides a comprehensive and flexible solution that fulfills all the requirements for 3D simulation.

III. Object-Relational Mapping

Some RDBMSs provide additional object-relational features. For example, PostgreSQL supports some object-oriented extensions like user defined types or inheritance. However, these features are not provided uniformly by all RDBMSs contradicting the desired database independence. Therefore, the OR mapping is realized with standard relational concepts only.

There are several references in literature dealing with the differences between object-oriented concepts and the relational data model. To solve the object-relational impedance mismatch and successfully generate an OR mapper, it is important to consider the properties of both paradigms and the consequent problems. For example, one main idea of object-orientation is inheritance [29]. However, the relational data model does not feature any comparable concept. Thus, rules have to be defined how inheritance can be mapped onto table structures. Further differences between both paradigms that contribute to the object-relational impedance mismatch are polymorphism, data types, identity, data encapsulation, and relationships.

The following subsections summarize the state-of-the-art of theoretical mapping strategies for inheritance, relationships and polymorphism.

A. Inheritance

The approaches to map objects onto tables differ in to how many tables one object is mapped. Most authors name three standard mapping strategies for inheritance. They are illustrated in Figure 3 regarding the exemplary inheritance hierarchy from Figure 2.

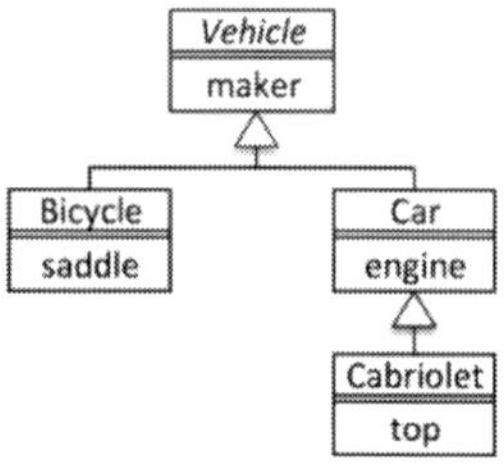

Figure 2. Exemplary inheritance hierarchy (adapted from [30, p. 62f]).

The first strategy is named *Single Table Inheritance* [30] and maps all classes of one inheritance hierarchy to one table, see Figure 3(a). A discriminator field is used to denote the type of each tuple [31]. An advantage is that all data is stored in one table preventing joins and allowing simple updates [30, p. 63]. Unfortunately, this strategy leads to a total denormalization, which is contrary to the concept of relational databases [31].

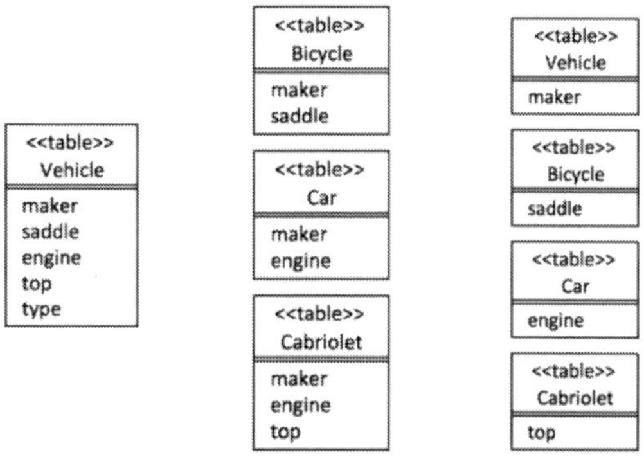

(a) Single Table Inheritance. (b) Concrete Table Inheritance. (c) Class Table Inheritance.

Figure 3. Standard mapping strategies for inheritance (adapted from [30, p. 62f]).

The *Concrete Table Inheritance* [30] strategy maps each concrete class to one table, see Figure 3(b). This mapping requires only few joins to retrieve all data for one object. A disadvantage is that schema changes in base classes are laborious and error-prone. [30, p. 62f]

The third standard mapping strategy for inheritance is named *Class Table Inheritance* [30] and uses one table for each class of the hierarchy, see Figure 3(c). It is the easiest approach to map objects onto tables [30, p. 62] and uses a normalized schema [31]. However, due to the use of foreign keys, this approach realizes an *is-a* relationship as a *has-a* relationship [31]. Thus, multiple joins are necessary if all data of one object is required. This aspect can have an effect on performance. [30, p. 62f] [32, p. 7]

Another possibility to map objects onto tables not mentioned in every reference on OR mapping is the generic approach [33]. It differs from the strategies mentioned above as it has no predefined structure. Figure 4 shows an exemplary set-up, which can be extended as required. The approach is particularly suitable for small amounts of data because it maps one object to multiple tables. It is advantageous if a highly flexible structure is required. Due to the generic table structure, elements can easily be added or rearranged. [33]

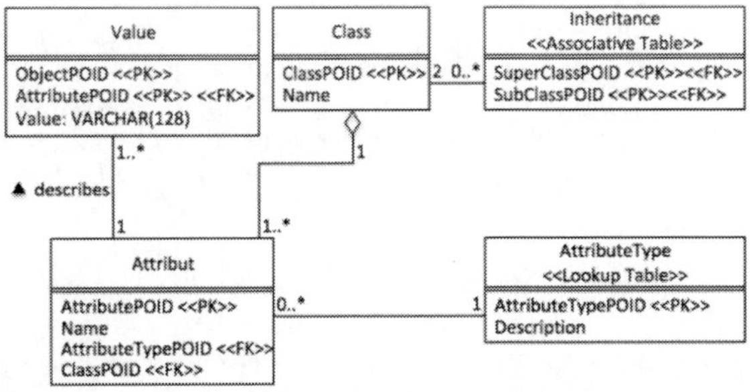

Figure 4. Map classes to generic table structure (adapted from [33, chapter 2.4]).

In conclusion, there is no single perfect approach to map objects onto tables yielding an optimal result in all situations. Instead, a decision has to be made from case to case depending on the most important properties. For this purpose, the three standard mapping strategies for inheritance can also be combined, however, to the disadvantage of more complexity. [30, p. 63]

B. Relationships

In contrast to relationships between two objects, which can be unidirectional, relationships between tables in a relational database are always bidirectional. In unidirectional relationships, associated objects do not know if and when they are referenced by another object [32]. Due to the mandatory mapping of unidirectional onto bidirectional relationships, information hiding cannot be preserved regardless of the relationship's cardinality, i.e., 1:1 (one-to-one), 1:n (one-to-many) or n:m (many-to-many) relationships.

1:1 relationships can simply be mapped onto tables using a foreign key. To map 1:n relationships, structures have to be reversed. [33] [30, p. 58f] In case of n:m relationships, additional tables are mandatory: A so-called association table is used to link the participating tables. [33] [30, p. 60] It is also possible to map an n:m relationship using multiple foreign keys in both tables if constant values for n and m are known. [33]

Several references describe the aforementioned mapping strategies for relationships. Besides, [34] describes an approach using an additional table regardless of the cardinality. Thus, objects can be mapped onto tables regardless of their relationships. Following [34], one disadvantage of the aforementioned approaches is the violation of the object-oriented principle of information hiding and abstraction. Furthermore, tables are cluttered by foreign key columns which reduce maintainability and performance. The authors prove (by a performance test) that their own approach shows no performance degradation. [34, p. 1446f]

C. Polymorphism

Polymorphism is an essential concept in object-orientation. However, relational databases do not have any feature to reference entries of different tables by one foreign key column. The target table and column have to be explicitly defined for each foreign key constraint. It is not possible to define a foreign key that references more than one table [35, p. 89]. Thus, a mapping is required to map polymorphic associations onto a relational database. Following [35], [36], there are three mapping approaches for polymorphic associations.

The first approach is named *Exclusive Arcs* and uses a separate foreign key column for each table that can be referenced by the polymorphic association, see Figure 5. This approach requires NULL values for foreign key columns. For each tuple, at most one of the foreign key columns may be unequal to NULL. Due to foreign key constraints, referential integrity can be ensured. However, the administrative effort for the aforementioned NULL rule is high. An advantage of this approach is that queries can easily be formulated.

Owner

ID<<PK>>	Name	Prename	Car<<FK>>	Cabriolet<<FK>>	Bicycle<<FK>>
1234	Müller	Hans	101	*null*	*null*
2456	Müller	Lieschen	112	*null*	*null*
5634	Meier	Ernst	*null*	*null*	87

Car

ID<<PK>>	Color	...
101	black	...
112	red	...

Bicycle

ID<<PK>>	Model	...
87	racer	...

Figure 5. Mapping of polymorphic associations using *Exclusive Arcs*.

Another approach is named *Reverse the Relationship* and is shown in Figure 6. It uses an intermediate table with two foreign key columns like the aforementioned approach for n:m relationships. Such an intermediate table has to be defined for each possible type (table) that can be referenced by the polymorphic association. [35], [36] The application has to ensure that only one entry of all subordinate tables is assigned to the entry of the superordinate table. [35, p. 96ff]

Owner

ID<<PK>>	Name	Prename
1234	Müller	Hans
2456	Müller	Lieschen
5634	Meier	Ernst

Cars

Owner<<FK>>	Car<<FK>>
1234	101
2456	112

Car

ID<<PK>>	Color	...
101	black	...
112	red	...

Bicycles

Owner<<FK>>	Bicycle<<FK>>
5634	87

Bicycle

ID<<PK>>	Model	...
87	racer	...

Figure 6. Mapping of polymorphic associations using *Reverse the Relationship*.

The third approach uses a super table (or "base table") and is named *Base Parent Table*. It is based on the basic idea of polymorphism where subtypes can be referenced using a common, often abstract supertype. In most cases, these supertypes themselves are not mapped to the relational database.

The strategy uses a table to represent a supertype for all its subtypes' tables as shown in Figure 7.

Owner

ID<<PK>>	Name	Prename	Vehicle<<FK>>
1234	Müller	Hans	101
2456	Müller	Lieschen	112
5634	Meier	Ernst	87

Vehicles

ID<<PK>>
101
112
87

Car

ID<<PK,FK>>	Color	...
101	black	...
112	red	...

Bicycle

ID<<PK,FK>>	Model	...
87	racer	...

Figure 7. Mapping of polymorphic associations using *Base Parent Table*.

Such a base table only consists of one column containing a primary key value. The assigned subordinate entry has the same primary key value as the entry of the base table. Thus, an unambiguous assignment is possible. This approach has the big advantage that base tables do not have to be considered in queries. They are only used to ensure referential integrity. [35, p. 100ff]

IV. Existing Solutions

For a long time, differences between both the object-oriented and relational paradigm were bridged by simple protocols like Java Database Connectivity (JDBC) and Open Database Connectivity (ODBC), which provide a general interface to different relational databases. These interfaces have the disadvantage that the programmer itself is responsible for data exchange between objects and tables. Due to the mixing of SQL statements and object-oriented commands, this usually leads to complex program code that is not easily maintained. [31]

OR mappers are used to realize a simpler and smarter mapping between objects and table entries on the one side and a clear separation between the object-oriented and relational layer on the other side. Thus, the application can be developed independently of the mapping and the database. As a consequence, different development teams can be deployed. [31]

There are several tools for OR mapping with different features and documentation. Examples are Hibernate (Java), NHibernate (.NET), ADO.NET Entity Framework (.NET), LINQ to SQL (.NET), Doctrine (PHP), ODB (C++), LiteSQL (C++), and QxOrm (C++). Not every existing mapper features all three standard mapping strategies for inheritance. Another main difference is how the mapping approach can be specified. In particular, OR mappers like Hibernate [37] and NHibernate [38] recommend an XML-based mapping while mappers like ODB [39] and QxORM [40] recommend the opposite.

The applicability of an OR mapper depends on the utilized application. In the presented scenario, this is the 3D simulation system VEROSIM, which is subsequently introduced before presenting the evaluation of existing OR mappers.

VEROSIM uses an in-memory runtime database called Versatile Simulation Database (VSD) for its internal data management. It is an object-oriented graph database providing the means to describe structure as well as behavior of a simulation model. Besides interfaces for data manipulation, it provides a change notification mechanism for updates, inserts and deletes. In VSD, objects are called instances and their classes are described by so-called meta instances representing the meta information system of VSD. Instances can have properties for simple values (e.g., integers or strings) or for referencing other instances – either a single target (1:1) or a list of targets (1:n). During runtime, instances can be identified by a unique id. VEROSIM and VSD are implemented in C++. [5]

Thus, an OR mapping is required that maps data of a runtime database like VSD onto a relational database. None of the existing OR mappers support a direct mapping of a runtime database's meta information system. They only map object-oriented classes and objects of a specific programming language. Similarly, the approach used in our previous work [2] maps a relational database to a generic object interface that is subsequently mapped to VSD. Thus, if one of these mappers is used, a second mapping is required to map between the meta information system and the object-oriented layer of the OR mapper.

Based on meta instances, any VSD instance can be classified during runtime. This is a key advantage for the OR mapping with regard to the generation and maintenance of all mappings. Thus, the decision was made to develop a new OR mapper. This allows the OR mapping to be tailored to the requirements of runtime simulation databases like VSD.

V. Object-Relational Mapper for 3D Simulation Systems

A basic decision criterion for OR mapping is the definition of the database schema. Given an existing object-oriented schema, *forward mapping* is used to derive a relational database schema. In contrast, if the initial situation is a given relational database schema, *reverse mapping* is used to derive an object-oriented schema. As already mentioned, database independence is a key aspect of OR mapping. In reverse mapping, this aspect is omitted as a specific database schema of a particular RDBMS is used as the basis for the mapping. [31] The focus of the presented OR mapper is forward mapping to map existing model data of the 3D simulation system onto an arbitrary relational database. Nevertheless, reverse mapping is supported in the concept as well to use the 3D simulation system for other existing databases (see the upper path in Figure 8).

The designed forward mapping of the presented OR mapper is briefly described in the following paragraph and the overall structure of the OR mapper is shown in Figure 8.

First of all, the database schema has to be generated to be able to store object-oriented simulation data in the relational database. Subsequently, a schema synchronization defines a schema mapping between the object-oriented and the relational schema. More details on this are given in [2]. The schema mapping defines which meta instance is mapped to which table. Based on this mapping, initial simulation model data can be stored. *Generate Schema Based on Meta Information* and *Export Model Data in Database* are performed only once and can be seen as the initialization of the OR mapping. Subsequently, model data can be loaded from the relational database and updated within the simulation database. A change tracking mechanism keeps track of changes within the simulation database and allows for their resynchronization to the relational database.

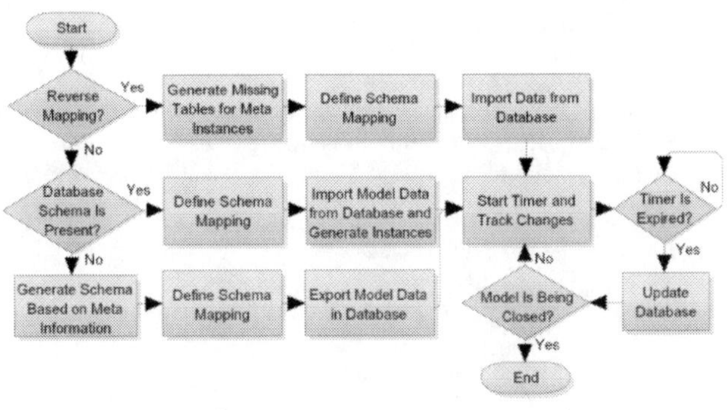

Figure 8. Sequence diagram of the presented OR mapping approach.

In most cases, structural aspects are associated with OR mapping. Behavioral and architectural aspects are often considered secondarily although they are not less important [30, p. 58]. All three aspects should be regarded when developing an OR mapper.

Architectural aspects define the communication between business logic and database. The basic principle is not to mix up the business logic with SQL statements, but rather to use separate classes for database access. These can be classified in four strategies: *Row Data Gateway*, *Table Data Gateway*, *Active Record* and *Data Mapper*. To completely isolate business logic, [30] recommends a Data Mapper. Although this is the most complex strategy, it is used for the developed OR mapper to realize an independent layer between the 3D simulation system and the selected relational database. As a result, both systems can independently be extended. Furthermore, Data Mapper is especially well suited for complex structures. [30, p. 49f]

Behavioral aspects define how data can be loaded from or saved to the relational database. With only a few instances to manage, it is easy to keep track of loaded, modified or removed instances and to synchronize these changes with the database. The more instances must be managed, the more complex this process gets. In addition, if various users or processes can access the database, it is even more complex. Here, it has to be ensured that a loaded instance contains valid and consistent data. Following [30], the pattern *Unit of Work* is indispensable to solve this behavioral and concurrency problem, see Figure 9. A Unit of Work can be seen as a control for OR mapping. It registers all loaded, removed or newly created instances as well as changes. A central concept of the Unit of Work is that it aggregates all changes and synchronizes them in their entirety rather than letting the application call separate stored procedures. Alternatives to a central Unit of Work are to immediately synchronize changes or to set dirty flags for each changed object. [30, p. 54f]

Given its many advantages, a Unit of Work is used in the presented OR mapper. To avoid repetitive loading of the same instances, the Unit of Work is combined with the pattern *Identity Mapping* as shown in Figure 9. An Identity Mapping records each instance loaded into the simulation database and maps it to the related tuple in the relational database. Before loading an instance from its tuple, the Unit of Work checks if there already is an Identity Mapping for this instance, which is especially important for lazy loading. [30, p. 55f] Compared

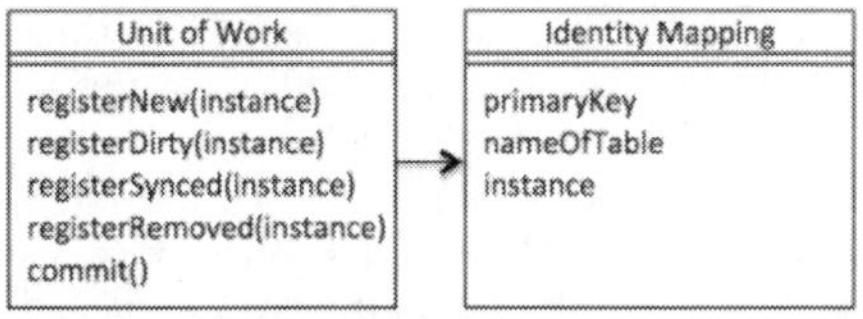

Figure 9. Combination of the patterns *Unit of Work* and *Identity Mapping* (adapted from [30]).

to literature [30] we extended the dirty mechanism. Instead of only registering whole instances as dirty, modified properties are registered as well. This allows to synchronize changes more efficiently.

The fundamentals of structural aspects are described in Section III. To minimize the overall number of joins, the Concrete Table Inheritance strategy was chosen for mapping inheritance. Furthermore, two strategies are selected to map relationships. 1:1 relationships are mapped to simple foreign key columns whereas 1:n relationships are mapped to association tables. However, this is only possible for monomorphic associations. For the polymorphic case, the strategies described in Subsection III-C have to be evaluated. Due to the high administrative effort, Exclusive Arcs is inapplicable. The other two strategies are compared regarding the formulation of queries. Base Parent Table allows for simpler queries. However, the theoretical mapping of this strategy (Figure 7) does not fit in combination with the aforementioned selected mappings for inheritance and monomorphic associations. In practice, a subordinated instance can be referenced by both a monomorphic and a polymorphic association of superordinated instances. As a consequence, the foreign key constraint could be violated. So the theoretical mapping of Base Parent Table is adapted to fit in combination with the aforementioned selected mappings for inheritance and monomorphic associations as shown in Figure 10. As an advantage, both the base table and the additional foreign key column do not need to be considered in queries. They are only used to ensure referential integrity.

Owner			
ID<<PK>>	Name	Prename	Vehicle<<FK>>
1234	Müller	Hans	101
2456	Müller	Lieschen	112
5634	Meier	Ernst	87

Vehicles
ID<<PK>>
101
112
87

Car		
ID<<PK>>	Color	base_Vehicle<<FK>>
101	black	101
112	red	112

Space in Bike Station		
ID<<PK>>	Space Number	Bicycle<<FK>>
307	1	87
308	2	89

Bicycle		
ID<<PK>>	Model	base_Vehicle<<FK>>
87	racer	87
89	e-bike	*null*

Figure 10. Adapted *Base Parent Table* mapping of polymorphic associations.

Another important part of an OR mapper is data type mapping. Data types of the object-oriented data model can differ from those of the relational data model. Thus, a data type mapping has to be defined. The developed OR mapper comprises an interface to use a dynamic data type mapping, which can be adapted for each database and its related data types. This is one main aspect of the supported database independence. Furthermore, the utilized Qt framework [41] (QSqlDatabase) allows for a vendor-independent database communication. Altogether, the developed OR mapper can easily support different RDBMSs.

After schema synchronization, model data can be loaded

from the relational database populating the simulation database with corresponding instances. A so-called *eager loading strategy* is used to immediately load and generate all model instances. The Unit of Work generates an identity mapping for each loaded instance. This provides an unambiguous mapping between each loaded instance and the corresponding tuple in the relational database. Furthermore, a so-called *lazy loading strategy* is specified for selectively loading model data from the database. It is based on the ghost strategy presented in [30, p. 227ff]. Here, typically necessary information, like primary key and table name, is determined for all tuples from all tables regardless whether the instance is loaded or not. Ghost instances are generated containing only this partially loaded data. [30, p. 227ff] The presented OR mapper uses a *Ghost Identity Mapping* (Figure 9). The advantage of this modified approach is that only "complete" instances are present in the 3D simulation system's runtime database.

VI. Application

As mentioned before, schema generation and synchronization work independently of the selected simulation model. All required structures are defined during schema generation. In the evaluated configuration of the 3D simulation system VEROSIM, 910 tables, 1,222 foreign key columns, and 2,456 association tables are generated to map all meta instances and 1:1 as well as 1:n relationships. The schema generation takes about 200 seconds on a local PostgreSQL 9.4 installation. The required schema mapping is built up during schema synchronization and takes about 2.7 seconds.

Due to its flexibility, the OR mapper can be used for any simulation model. The prototype is evaluated using two exemplary models from two different fields of application: industrial automation and space robotics. Given the current functional range of the presented prototype, further tests do not appear to provide any additional insights.

Figure 11(a) shows the first model from the field of industrial robotics. The robot model contains only a few objects so that only 173 primary keys have to be generated to map all objects to table entries. It takes about 0.43 seconds to store the whole robot into the relational database and about 4.7 seconds to load it.

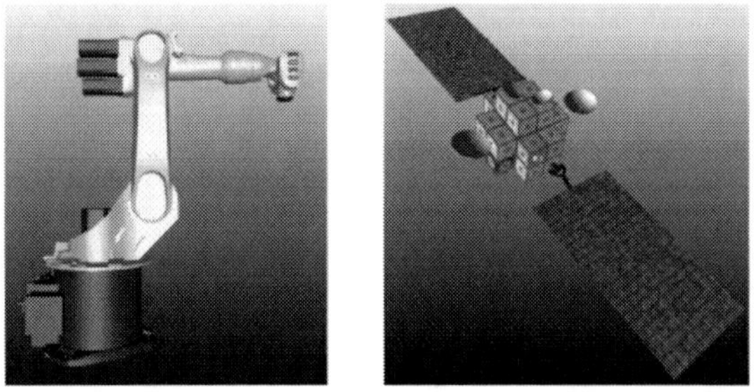

(a) Industrial robot simulation model.

(b) Modular satellite simulation model (data: [4]).

Figure 11. Evaluated simulation models.

The second model (Figure 11(b)) is a modular satellite. In comparison, it contains much more objects so that 19,463 primary keys are generated to map all objects to table entries. In this case, it takes about 22 seconds to store all objects of the satellite and about 7.1 seconds to load all of them from the relational database.

As mentioned in Section IV, a comparable interface to existing ORM solutions would be less efficient as well as more complex and time-consuming to realize due to the necessary second mapping. Thus, we refrain from performing such comparisons.

VII. Summary, Conclusion and Future Work

In contrast to flat files, database technology provides many advantages for managing 3D simulation models. However, existing approaches for database integration into applications with a 3D context do not provide a sufficiently comprehensive and flexible solution. Given the prevalence of relational DBMS and the preferred object-oriented modeling of 3D simulation models, an OR mapping approach is recommended. Using existing ORM solutions (including our previous work [2]), an intermediate layer cannot be avoided. Thus, in this work, we develop a direct OR mapping approach.

The presented OR mapper allows a flexible and generic mapping between an object-oriented runtime simulation database and a relational database. It is based on the meta information system so that an OR mapping can be performed for arbitrary simulation models. The mapper detects schema changes, i.e., new or modified meta instances, and automatically adapts the used mapping without the need for a manual definition of persistent elements. Hence, compared to existing OR mappers, a complex and error-prone manual maintenance of the defined mapping can be omitted. The presented OR mapper separates the 3D simulation system and the used relational database so that business logic is not mixed with SQL statements. As a result, the 3D simulation system can be developed independently from data storage. Future projects can profit by time saving as they do not have to realize persistent data storage separately. Following [42, p. 525], the programming effort for storing objects in relational databases accounts for 20-30% of the total project effort. Finally, the presented OR mapping is successfully evaluated using two simulation models from two different fields of application (industrial automation and space robotics).

In future, data type mapping can be extended by more specialized data types and further RDBMSs can be combined with the prototype. Furthermore, the currently generated structures within the relational database do not contain explicit information on the inheritance relationships as they are not needed by the simulation system itself (they can be retrieved from its meta information system). However, to allow third party applications to interpret the data, inheritance structures would be of interest. Another aspect to investigate is the mapping of queries and operations. For the former, an object-based query language meeting VSD's demands, e.g., XQuery or (a variation of) Java Persistence Query Language (JPQL) or Hibernate Query Language (HQL), needs to be mapped to proper SQL queries. Further performance optimizations and, with an extended functional range of the mapper, evaluations beyond the results from the student project could be performed, as well. Finally, we could examine further applications, e.g., from other fields like forestry.

REFERENCES

[1] M. Hoppen and J. Rossmann, "A Database Synchronization Approach for 3D Simulation Systems," in DBKDA 2014,The 6th International Conference on Advances in Databases, Knowledge, and Data Applications, A. Schmidt, K. Nitta, and J. S. Iztok Savnik, Eds., Chamonix, France, 2014, pp. 84–91.

[2] M. Hoppen, M. Schluse, J. Rossmann, and B. Weitzig, "Database-Driven Distributed 3D Simulation," in Proceedings of the 2012 Winter Simulation Conference, 2012, pp. 1–12.

[3] A. Kemper and A. Eickler, Database Systems – An Introduction (orig.: Datenbanksysteme–Eine Einführung), 9th ed. München: Oldenbourg Verlag, 2013.

[4] J. Weise et al., "An Intelligent Building Blocks Concept for On-Orbit-Satellite Servcing," in Proceedings of International Symposium on Artificial Intelligence, Robotics and Automation in Space (i-SAIRAS), 2012, pp. 1–8.

[5] J. Roßmann, M. Schluse, C. Schlette, and R. Waspe, "A New Approach to 3D Simulation Technology as Enabling Technology for eROBOTICS," in 1st International Simulation Tools Conference & EXPO 2013, SIMEX'2013, 2013, pp. 39–46.

[6] The PostgreSQL Global Development Group, "PostgreSQL: About," 2015, URL: http://www.postgresql.org/about/ [retrieved: May, 2016].

[7] B. Damer et al., "Data-Driven Virtual Environment Assembly and Operation," in Virtual Ironbird Workshop, 2004, p. 1.

[8] U. Sendler, The PLM Compendium: Reference book of Product Lifecycle Management (orig.: Das PLM-Kompendium: Referenzbuch des Produkt-Lebenszyklus-Managements). Berlin: Springer, 2009.

[9] Verein Deutscher Ingenieure (VDI), "VDI 2219 - Information technology in product development Introduction and economics of EDM/PDM Systems (Issue German/English)," Düsseldorf, 2002.

[10] Y. Zhao et al., "The research and development of 3D urban geographic information system with Unity3D," in Geoinformatics (GEOINFORMATICS), 2013 21st International Conference on, 2013, pp. 1–4.

[11] D. Pacheco and S. Wierenga, "Spatializing experience: a framework for the geolocalization, visualization and exploration of historical data using VR/AR technologies," in Proceedings of the 2014 Virtual Reality International Conference, 2014.

[12] A. Martina and A. Bottino, "Using Virtual Environments as a Visual Interface for Accessing Cultural Database Contents," in International Conference of Information Science and Computer Applications (ICISCA 2012), Bali, Indonesia, 2012, pp. 1–6.

[13] T. Guan, B. Ren, and D. Zhong, "The Method of Unity3D-Based 3D Dynamic Interactive Query of High Arch Dam Construction Information," Applied Mechanics and Materials, vol. 256-259, 2012, pp. 2918–2922.

[14] G. Van Maren, R. Germs, and F. Jansen, "Integrating 3D-GIS and Virtual Reality Design and implementation of the Karma VI system," in Proceedings of the Spatial Information Research Centre's 10th Colloquium. University of Otago, New Zealand, 1998, pp. 16–19.

[15] J. Haist and V. Coors, "The W3DS-Interface of Cityserver3D," in European Spatial Data Research (EuroSDR) u.a.: Next Generation 3D City Models. Workshop Papers : Participant's Edition, Kolbe and Gröger, Eds., Bonn, 2005, pp. 63–67.

[16] M. Kamiura, H. Oisol, K. Tajima, and K. Tanaka, "Spatial views and LOD-based access control in VRML-object databases," in Worldwide Computing and Its Applications, ser. Lecture Notes in Computer Science, T. Masuda, Y. Masunaga, and M. Tsukamoto, Eds. Springer Berlin / Heidelberg, 1997, vol. 1274, pp. 210–225.

[17] E. V. Schweber, "SQL3D - Escape from VRML Island," 1998, URL: http://www.infomaniacs.com/SQL3D/SQL3D-Escape-From-VRML-Island.htm [retrieved: May, 2016].

[18] T. Scully, J. Doboš, T. Sturm, and Y. Jung, "3drepo. io: building the next generation Web3D repository with AngularJS and X3DOM," in Proceedings of the 20th International Conference on 3D Web Technology, 2015.

[19] Z. Wang, H. Cai, and F. Bu, "Nonlinear Revision Control for Web-Based 3D Scene Editor," in Virtual Reality and Visualization (ICVRV), 2014 International Conference on, 2014, pp. 73–80.

[20] J. Doboš and A. Steed, "Revision Control Framework for 3D Assets," in Eurographics 2012 - Posters, Cagliari, Sardinia, Italy, 2012, p. 3.

[21] D. Schmalstieg et al., "Managing complex augmented reality models," IEEE Computer Graphics and Applications, vol. 27, no. 4, 2007, pp. 48–57.

[22] M. Nour, "Using Bounding Volumes for BIM based electronic code checking for Buildings in Egypt," American Journal of Engineering Research (AJER), vol. 5, no. 4, 2016, pp. 91–98.

[23] B. Domínguez-Martín, "Methods to process low-level CAD plans and creative Building Information Models (BIM)," Doctoral Thesis, University of Jaén, 2014.

[24] S. Hoerster and K. Menzel, "BIM based classification of building performance data for advanced analysis," in Proceedings of International Conference CISBAT 2015 Future Buildings and Districts Sustainability from Nano to Urban Scale, 2015, pp. 993–998.

[25] H. Eisenmann, J. Fuchs, D. De Wilde, and V. Basso, "ESA Virtual Spacecraft Design," in 5th International Workshop on Systems and Concurrent Engineering for Space Applications, 2012.

[26] M. Fang, X. Yan, Y. Wenhui, and C. Sen, "The Storage and Management of Distributed Massive 3D Models based on G/S Mode," in Lecture Notes in Information Technology, vol. 10, 2012.

[27] D. Iliescu, I. Ciocan, and I. Mateias, "Assisted management of product data: A PDM application proposal," in Proceedings of the 18th International Conference on System Theory, Control and Computing, Sinaia, Romania, 2014.

[28] H. Takemura, Y. Kitamura, J. Ohya, and F. Kishino, "Distributed Processing Architecture for Virtual Space Teleconferencing," in Proc. of ICAT, vol. 93, 1993, pp. 27–32.

[29] D. J. Armstrong, "The Quarks of Object-Oriented Development," Communications of the ACM, vol. 49, no. 2, 2006, pp. 123–128.

[30] M. Fowler, Patterns of Enterprise Application Architecture, 1st ed. Addison Wesley, 2002.

[31] A. Schatten, "O/R Mapper und Alternativen," 2008, URL: http://www.heise.de/developer/artikel/O-R-Mapper-und-Alternativen-227060.html [retrieved: May, 2016].

[32] T. Neward, "The Vietnam of Computer Science," 2006, URL: http://www.odbms.org/2006/01/the-vietnam-of-computer-science/ [retrieved: May, 2016].

[33] S. W. Ambler, "Mapping Objects to Relational Databases: O/R Mapping In Detail," 2013, URL: http://www.agiledata.org/essays/mappingObjects.html [retrieved: May, 2016].

[34] F. Lodhi and M. A. Ghazali, "Design of a Simple and Effective Object-to-Relational Mapping Technique," in Proceedings of the 2007 ACM symposium on Applied computing. ACM, 2007, pp. 1445–1449.

[35] B. Karwin, SQL Antipatterns: Avoiding the Pitfalls of Database Programming, 1st ed. Railegh, N.C.: Pragmatic Bookshelf, 2010.

[36] ——, "Practical Object Oriented Models in Sql," 2009, URL: http://de.slideshare.net/billkarwin/practical-object-oriented-models-in-sql [retrieved: May, 2016].

[37] Hibernate, HIBERNATE–Relational Persistence for Idiomatic Java, 2015, URL: http://docs.jboss.org/hibernate/orm/5.0/manual/en-US/html/index.html [retrieved: May, 2016].

[38] NHibernate Community, NHibernate–Relational Persistence for Idiomatic .NET, 2015, URL: http://nhibernate.info/doc/nhibernate-reference/index.html [retrieved: May, 2016].

[39] Code Synthesis Tools CC, ODB: C++ Object-Relational Mapping (ORM), 2015, URL: http://www.codesynthesis.com/products/odb/ [retrieved: May, 2016].

[40] L. Marty, QxOrm (the engine) + QxEntityEditor (the graphic editor) = the best solution to manage your data in C++/Qt !, 2015, URL: http://www.qxorm.com/qxorm_en/home.html [retrieved: May, 2016].

[41] The Qt Company, "Qt Documentation," 2016, URL: http://doc.qt.io/qt-5/index.html [retrieved: May, 2016].

[42] A. M. Keller, R. Jensen, and S. Agarwal, "Persistence Software: Bridging Object-Oriented Programming and Relational Databases," in ACM SIGMOD Record, vol. 22, no. 2. ACM, 1993, pp. 523–528.

A Text Analyser of Crowdsourced Online Sources for Knowledge Discovery

Ioannis Markou
Information and Communication Systems Engineering
University of the Aegean, Samos, Greece
e-mail: janis.markou@gmail.com

Efi Papatheocharous
Swedish Institute of Computer Science (SICS)
Kista, Stockholm, Sweden
e-mail: efi.papatheocharous@sics.se

Abstract—**In the last few years, Twitter has become the centre of crowdsourced-generated content. Numerous tools exist to analyse its content to lead to knowledge discovery. However, most of them focus solely on the content and ignore user features. Selecting and analysing user features such as user activity and relationships lead to the discovery of authorities and user communities. Such a discovery can provide an additional perspective to crowdsourced data and increase understanding of the evolution of the trends for a given topic. This work addresses the problem by introducing a dedicated software tool developed, the Text Analyser of Crowdsourced Online Sources (TACOS). TACOS is a social relationship search tool that given a search term, analyses user features and discovers authorities and user communities for that term. For knowledge representation, it visualises the output in a graph, for increased readability. In order to show the applicability of TACOS, we have chosen a real example and aimed through two case studies to discover and analyse a specific type of user communities.**

Keywords-User communities; Authorities; Social Network Analysis.

I. INTRODUCTION

Over the years, micro-blogging platforms have become a popular means of exchanging current crowdsourced information. Twitter, counting over 500 million tweets sent per day [1], holds a large share of that information traffic. One of Twitter's success factors is that the exchanged information is highly concentrated, as a tweet is limited to 140 characters in length. The unstructured nature of that information has led to the development of numerous content analysis methods. Such methods can be applied on tweet datasets to perform various tasks such as opinion mining and topic extraction. These tasks can be useful for various reasons, from discovering users' movie opinions to predicting voting outcomes [2].

Many of the available content analysis methods are quite accurate. However, they cannot evaluate comprehensively the credibility of the analysed information. Twitter, like all micro-blogging platforms, is challenged by the credibility of the information that is being exchanged [3]. In this work, we propose that the key to evaluating content lies in Twitter's second success factor, the open access to information. In particular, a Twitter user can access other users' feeds just by following them, requiring no approval from the user being followed. Additionally, a user can comment, like, reply and mention other users without the two-way friendship feature found in other social networks. This one-way relationship is the foundation of Twitter's rapid spread of information and it forms a unique way of evaluating a user's content by the Twitter community. As a result, users with higher evaluation have created more credible content. Consequently, it is imperative in order to discover credible information, to first focus on who creates content and then on what the content is about [4].

Most approaches analysing Twitter focus on the content rather than the users who create the content [5]. Even the few approaches that analyse user data [6]-[11], focus on identifying information about separate users and lack to provide information about the relationships between users. The importance of having relationship data lies in the need to understand people interactions and group effects over the Internet. Furthermore, by tracking relationships of authority users (i.e., users that influence the content and type of information spread), additional credible users can be discovered. Finally, relationship data can discover user communities, in which users share some features or communal goals.

Conclusively, analysing user data has become paramount to knowledge discovery, whether it targets building recommendation engines, marketing campaigns to specific audiences, predicting user trends or understanding buyers' behaviour. Based on the above mentioned reasoning, it is apparent that there is a need for approaches that are capable of complementing the current ways of analysing Twitter data in terms of content, by focusing on users and their relationships. In this work, we have targeted to address this gap and have developed an approach implemented in a software tool (named TACOS for Text Analyser of Crowdsourced Online Sources) that extracts user attributes from tweets and evaluates them to structure user and relationship data. We explain our approach and show the applicability of the tool developed through two explorative use cases.

The rest of this paper is structured as follows: in Section II, the related work is presented. In Section III, the steps taken in order to design and implement the TACOS tool are described. In Section IV, our approach is analysed in detail. In Section V, the tool is validated against two use cases and in Section VI, the results are discussed. Finally, in Section VII, some conclusions are drawn and future directions are suggested.

II. RELATED WORK

Numerous Twitter analysis tools have been around since the popular micro-blogging platform was founded. Even though their implementations provide several advantages, they come with some limitations (described in Table I). The lower part of the table contains three services that are recent approaches focusing on user attributes rather than the content of tweets. A significant benefit for targeting the analysis of Twitter users and their attributes is that it can offer insights on 'authorities' on a given topic as well as help discover user communities that are related to the topic.

In summary, all of these tools and services lack fundamental functionality related to the users, such as locating the most influential users, visualising their relations and community connections that could enable for example targeted advertising for businesses. These functionalities, can offer insights beyond who-follows-who and number of favourites. They can highlight users and user communities in a particular domain, by also pinpointing the closest users that authorities interact with. Such information can help identify reliable sources (i.e., authorities) that generate information related to a particular topic. The effect of acquiring this knowledge is particularly important, both for popular and not so popular topics. For not popular topics, the detection of even a single influential user is as valuable as finding numerous influential users for popular topics with thousands of daily generated tweets. The suggested approach, described in the rest of this paper, covers this limitation from the existing implementations and visualises the retrieved, analysed user data in user-relationship graphs, where authorities and user communities are easily distinguishable.

III. Approach

A. Requirements Collection

At the early stages of the project, we conducted a set of interviews with researchers and industrial practitioners. In the interviews, a total of 5 people were questioned about their perceived possible usage and usefulness of the developed tool. One of the interviewees was female and the rest were male. We performed two structured interviews with the two researchers and three semi-structured interviews with the three industrial practitioners. The structured interviews lasted for about an hour each and included open-ended questions, dichotomous questions as well as Likert questions. The semi structured interviews included an open discussion with practitioners in a small-to-medium start-up company working in social network analysis. The discussions took place during one of the authors' ex-job placement in the company and the interviewees were working in the field of linguistics for several years.

Both types of interviews gave a different flavour of opinions which served as valuable input to the requirements for the system developed. Researchers expressed an interest in detecting the users that post content related to a specific research domain. In Twitter, the homophily principle is observed [12], so discovering relationships between users for a specific domain could help researchers expand their contacts on that domain. Industrial practitioners stressed that customers were more interested in users that create trends rather than the actual trends. These observations directed our efforts in defining the requirements for the solution proposed, as well as understanding the arising challenges.

B. Challenges

Such challenges concerned mainly the process of structuring and analysing user data [13]. At first, 'users' in Twitter are abstract entities, since users might be individuals, groups or organisations. Additionally, according to a user's posted content and activity, the user can be considered, among others, an 'authority', a 'topic expert' or a 'spammer'. Another challenge is analysing, modelling, interpreting and quantifying abstract social phenomena such as 'authority', 'domain expertise' and 'influence' [14]. The challenge lies in defining the appropriate classifiers for labelling a user as an authority or a domain expert. A last challenge is that user analysis alone is not enough to provide actionable information to an end-user. In order to provide insights regarding users and their relationships, information needs to be represented in an intuitive manner. This can be achieved by creating visualisations of the analysed user data.

TABLE I. MOST POPULAR NON-COMMERCIAL TWITTER USER ANALYSIS TOOLS AND SERVICES

Name	Description	Limitation
Nokia Internet Pulse [6]	Detects the most popular words for a topic in Twitter and visualises them in word-clouds. Word-clouds can be used to find popular users.	Does not show relationships between users or user-communities. Optimised for Nokia-specific keywords, which can lead to bias.
CO GNOS [7]	Locates topic experts by analysing user generated lists. Improves upon Who To Follow ([9]) by focusing on all users related to a topic.	Ignores other relevant users on a subject. Does not analyse relationship attributes such as mentions, retweets and replies. Does not offer visualisation.
Twitter rank [8]	Measures users' influence for a given topic. First applies topic modelling. Then it analyses users' followers and friends lists to create relationship networks for each topic.	Uses only followers and friends attributes and ignores other relationship attributes such as favourites, mentions and replies. Does not offer visualisation.
Twitter Who to Follow (TWF) [9]	Detects suggested users to follow by analysing user-provided attributes such as e-mail, contacts and location.	Ignores topics and attributes such as followers, mentions and replies to suggest users.
Tweet Reach [10]	Analyses tweets relevant to a search term. It supports statistics for tweets' impressions as well as distribution of tweets through time and percentage of replies and retweets.	Does not provide a high level of user analysis, besides detecting top contributors for a term.
Tweet chup [11]	Analyses user, connections, keywords and hashtags. Offers a high level of detail to improve engagement between users.	User engagement is limited to retweets and mentions. Does not offer information on communities of users for a given search term.

C. Suggested Solution

In this work, we have considered and targeted to address all of these challenges mentioned, and we defined and quantified the abstract concepts (i.e., authority, domain expertise and influence) by assigning a set of classifiers to them. In order to accurately quantify these concepts, weights have been used to assign the contribution of each values used to the estimation of the classifiers. These weights are based on the importance of each contributing factor in the equations. Classifiers were created by studying the different tweet and user attributes. By understanding what each attribute represents and how it is used by the users, we were able to create the formulae for each classifier. Weights were assigned to the classifiers by applying a classification algorithm to retrieved datasets. The confidence of the predictions was taken into account in order to assess weights to the selected classifiers. By doing so, we were able to determine which of the classifiers were most important for classifying a user as influential.

Prior to the analysis of the equations, it is important to define tweet types. Tweet types include *original*, *retweets* and *replies*. Original tweets are authored by the user that posted them. Retweets refer to tweets that are forwarded by a user that did not create the original content. Lastly, replies are tweets that their content refer to other tweet's content.

In detail, the influence score (i) shows the degree in which a user's tweets make other users interact with the content. It is calculated by:

$$i = 0.5 * a + 0.5 * de. \quad (1)$$

In (1), i is influence, a is *authority* and de is *domain expertise*. We define authority as the degree that a user posts original content that is shared by a large audience. It is calculated by:

$$a = 0.05*ps+0.35*rr+0.35*orr+0.05*pprr+0.2*vs. \quad (2)$$

To calculate (2), equations (3) – (6) were defined.

$$ps = (followers - friends)/\max(followers, friends), \quad (3)$$

$$rr=(authT - nonAuthT)/\max(authT, nonAuthT), \quad (4)$$

$$orr = (original - retweets) / \max(original, retweets), (5)$$

$$pprr= (puR-prR) / \max(puR, prR). \quad (6)$$

In (3), ps is a user's popularity score and it is based on the observation that popular users have disproportionate number of followers and friends, with friends being a lot fewer than followers. *followers* is the number of the user's followers and *friends* is the number of the user's friends (i.e., the users that the user follows). In (4), rr is the retweet ratio of the user (i.e., the user's relevant-to-the-topic tweets that are retweeted). *authT* is the number of the user's authority tweets (i.e., tweets that are retweeted by other users) and *nonAuthT* is the number of non-authority tweets of the user. In (5), orr is the original to retweet ratio of the user and we defined it as a metric for tweets originality. *original* is the number of tweets that the user posted and *retweets* is the number of the tweets that user retweeted from other user profiles. Finally, in (6), $pprr$ refers to the public replies (puR) to private replies (prR) ratio (i.e., the replies that a user made and are viewed by anyone following either one of these two users). Based on our observation, many authority users reply publicly by adding a '.' symbol before they mention the username that they are replying to. As a result, this metric takes that behaviour into consideration for the influence score. Last but not least, vs is the verification status of a user and shows if the user is verified by Twitter. If yes, $vs = 1$, otherwise $vs = 0$.

Domain expertise (de) is defined as the degree that a user is involved in a topic as well as the quality of the content that the user shares. It is calculated by:

$$de=0.15*aes+0.1*rd+0.2*mr+0.25*tc+0.2*cq+0.1*ud. \quad (7)$$

To calculate (7), equations (8) – (16) were defined.

$$aes = 0.2 * rp + 0.8 * cp, \quad (8)$$

$$rp = (replies-repliesR) / \max(replies,repliesR), \quad (9)$$

$$cp= (convR-convNonR)/\max(convR, convNonR), (10)$$

$$rd=times\_retweeted/retweeters*tweets, \quad (11)$$

$$mr = total\_mentions / num\_of\_relevant\_tweets, \quad (12)$$

$$tc = user\_associated\_tweets / relevant\_tweets, \quad (13)$$

$$cq = \sum_{i=1}^{k} favouritesNum_k * turtnr, \quad (14)$$

$$ud = total\_user\_relevant\_tweets / total\_user\_tweets, \quad (15)$$

$$total\_U\_relevant\_T = U\_DB\_relevant\_T\_before\_retrieval + relevant\_retrieved\_tweets \quad (16)$$

In (8), aes refers to audience engagement score and shows the degree that a user responds to conversations. In (9), rp refers to the replies participation of a user which is defined by the ratio of replies (*replies*) and replies received (*repliesR*). In (10), cp refers to the conversation participation of a user. It is defined as the ratio of conversations replied (*convR*) and conversations non replied (*convNonR*). Equation (11) calculates a user's retweets dedication (rd) and shows the degree in which users' retweets are retweeted by all users. In (12), mr is the mentions rate of a user and represents how often a user is mentioned. The *num_of_relevant_tweets* includes only original tweets. This means that it does not include retweets, as these are taken into account in other metrics. In (13), tc stands for topic contribution and represents the activity of a user for a particular topic for a single retrieval. Every day, a single retrieval is performed for each topic. By using this metric, a user's activity for a particular topic can be monitored through time. The variable *user_associated_tweets* refers to the total number of a user's relevant tweets, plus retweets and tweets retweeted by other users. In (14), cq refers to the content quality of a user's relevant to a topic tweets. *turtnr* refers to the number of a user's relevant tweets, without including retweets. In (15), ud reflects a user's dedication by calculating how many of the user's total tweets are related to the particular term. *total_user_tweets* can be found in each user's attributes. Last but not least, in (16), *T* stands for tweet, *U* for user and *DB* for database.

The implemented tool (named TACOS for Text Analyser of Crowdsourced Online Sources) uses (1) – (16) to calculate these classifiers based on extracted user attributes from tweets. It then evaluates users in terms of authority, domain expertise and influence. The final influence score (*i*) is calculated using (1). Moreover, TACOS uses activity attributes to detect relationships between analysed users and evaluate them in terms of interactivity. By detecting relationships, user communities are discovered. The relationship score (*rs*) between two users is calculated as:

$$rs = max(A\_B\_Score, B\_A\_Score). \quad (17)$$

A_B_Score shows the degree in which user *A* interacts with user *B* and it is calculated by:

$$A\_B\_Score = 0.3 * A\_Mentions\_B + 0.3 * A\_Replies\_B + 0.05 * A\_Retweets\_B + 0.15 * A\_Favourites\_B + 0.2 * A\_Follows\_B. \quad (18)$$

A_Mentions_B shows the times that user *A* mentioned user *B* in relevant tweets and so on. Respectively, *B_A_Score* is similar with scores reflecting user B's activity. For example *B_Mentions_A* shows how many times user *B* mentioned user A in his/her tweets.

Interaction score *is* shows the degree that both users interact with each other. Let's assume that $A = A\_B\_Score$ and $B = B\_A\_Score$. Then, if A and B are 0, then $is = 0$. Otherwise,

$$is = max(A, B) - min(A, B) / max(A, B). \quad (19)$$

Finally, to offer intuitive analysis reports, TACOS presents results in the form of graph visualisations that show influential users and their communities. In that visualisation, nodes represent users and edges represent relationships between users. Influence score (*i*) is represented by the size of the node, with larger nodes belonging to more influential users. Authority and domain expertise are not apparent at first glance, but are available by clicking on a node, together with other information. The weight of an edge represents the relationship score between two users, with a thicker edge showing high activity, at least from one of the users towards the other. If there is activity from both users, then the relationship is considered as interactive, and the edge is shown in blue colour to represent that. Last but not least, relationship graphs in Twitter are not necessarily two-way, since a user might follow another user but not being followed by the second user. For our graphs, we wanted to emphasize on the flow of information, according to the HITS – hubs and authorities algorithm [15] [16]. For that reason, edges in our graphs don't show following status but influence, so the edges point towards the more influential between two users.

IV. SYSTEM DESCRIPTION

In this section, our approach's system design is described. TACOS consists of 7 modules. In Figure 1, our approach's system design is illustrated. The front end interacting with the user includes the Query Validator (QV) and Graph Visualisation (GV) modules. The QV consumes the user's input as a query. The query can consist of one or more words, it may contain hashtags, at-signs and special symbols to limit the search results, following the rules of the Twitter Search API [17]. The GV module is responsible for the graph visualisation, i.e., the final result produced. The user can interact with the result by zooming in and out, panning and clicking on nodes and edges to reveal information about users and their relationships. The GV module is using JavaScript frameworks and so the graph has the same functionalities in desktops, smartphones and tablets.

Moving on to the back end, the Gavagai Lexicon Connector (GLC) module handles the transactions between the Gavagai Living Lexicon API and our tool. The Gavagai Living Lexicon [18] is a tool that finds semantically similar and associatively related terms for a given topic. These terms are then presented to the users where they can choose to include some, all or none of them to the retrieval process. The Data Retrieval (DR) module includes all methods responsible for the communication with the Twitter Search API in order to retrieve tweets and users from Twitter. The Data Analysis (DA) module is the core module of the tool and is responsible for analysing the output of the DR module. The DA module handles operations such as extracting features from the retrieved data and linking tweets to users. Moreover, it gathers additional information about each user concerning their activity and finally calculates the influence and relationship scores, which are the input of the GG module. The Graph Generator (GG) module is responsible for preparing analysed data for visualisation. The output of the GG module is the the input of the GV module.

The last module is the MongoDB no-SQL Database (MDB) which is responsible for handling transactions with the QV, DR, DA and GG modules. In detail, the database holds collections of tweet, user and search documents. Each search document contains the ids of the tweets and users that are associated with it, as well as sub-collections such as influence and relationship scores. After each search, new users and tweets are added to the respective collections and existing documents are updated. These updates also serve a purpose of reducing the amount of requests that our tool must make and thus, minimising the times where the request limit is exceeded.

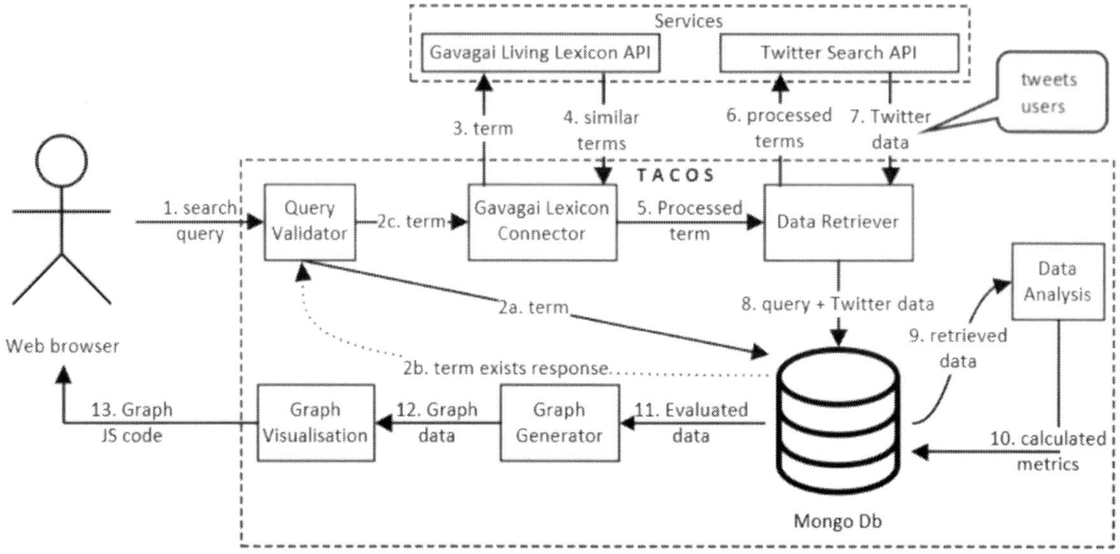

Figure 1. TACOS system design

V. VALIDATION

Due to the large amount of information posted on Twitter, it is challenging to aggregate tweet and user data for specific topics and events. In order to demonstrate our approach's ability to track the activity for specific events, we selected an event, the XP2015 conference on agile development practices, as an ideal scenario of use to validate our tool against, due to its manageable volume of data. With TACOS we retrieved about 500 users and 2100 tweets within a 25-day period, including the dates that the conference was held. We then analysed that data and detected that 'XPConf' was the most influential user of the event (something reasonable as it was the event organizer). Besides user activity, many trending terms linking to companies tweeting about using agile practices (Ericsson), blogs about agile development (42stc) and cities (Helsinki, which hosted the conference) were discovered. The term 'agile development' was one of the popular trends with a broader meaning. That motivated us to perform an additional analysis with the 'agile development' term. For that term, TACOS retrieved about 5000 users and 9500 tweets within a 25-day period. After analysing the retrieved data, the terms 'DevOps', 'cloud' and 'IoT' were discovered among the most popular trends. These results are valuable, since they describe the current state of agile development methodologies.

It is therefore evident from the above use case that our approach is performed well for following both specific and broad trends and understanding how trends are connected to through time.

Equally important to discovering popular trends is detecting influential users and relationships between users that post content related to those trends. Moreover, it is meaningful to present results in a readable way, such as graph visualisations, where user communities can be seen. In the generated graph, influential users and users with interactive relationships were easily distinguishable. By clicking on user nodes, additional information was available, including a link to the user's Twitter account. By visiting many accounts that our approach evaluated as influential, we realised that all of them had posted relevant content and that themselves were heavily involved in agile development practices and communities. As a result, our approach can successfully detect influential users and user communities for a given topic. At the same time, it can visualise that information in a readable and intuitive way.

VI. RESULTS AND DISCUSSION

Detailed results obtained from the use case example (described in the previous section) can be found in [19].

It is evident that our approach successfully identified top trending topics and users for both terms used for validation purposes. Moreover, it is important to highlight that our approach presents satisfactory results regardless of query type. As a scientific conference, '#XP2015' refers to a seasonal event – it has a narrow context, so this term is a navigational query – it seeks content of a single entity [20]. On the other hand, 'agile development' refers to a broader term and thus, it represents an informational query [20]. As indicated with the above use case, the type of the query affected both the dataset size and data type distribution in the results.

Specifically, regarding the dataset size, Figure 2 shows the amount of retrieved tweets for both terms for every day of retrieval. As expected, the first term ('#XP2015') refers to an event happening in a specific point in time, thus higher volume of tweets are retrieved around that time period. On the other hand, the second term ('agile development') is broader, and so the number of tweets retrieved is distributed more evenly across time. The total number of retrieved tweets

(9476) and users (5010) for the second term exceeds the respective numbers of the first (2106 and 496 respectively).

Data types can refer to tweets or users. Tweet types have been analysed in a previous chapter. User types include plain users, retweeters and domain experts. When a tweet is original but not retweeted, its user is classified as plain. Accordingly, when a tweet is original and retweeted, its user is classified as domain expert. Last but not least, if a user posts a non-original tweet, the user is classified as a retweeter. Figures 3 and 4 show tweet types (i.e., original, retweets and replies) and user types (i.e., plain users, retweeters and domain experts) distribution for both terms of the use case.

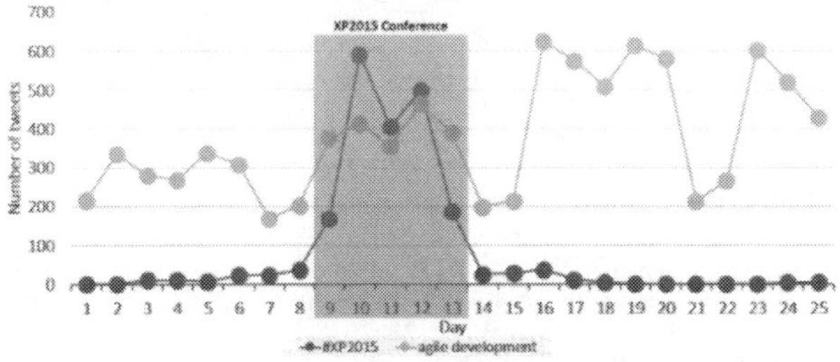

Figure 2. Retrieved tweets date distribution.

Figure 3. Retrieved tweets type distribution.

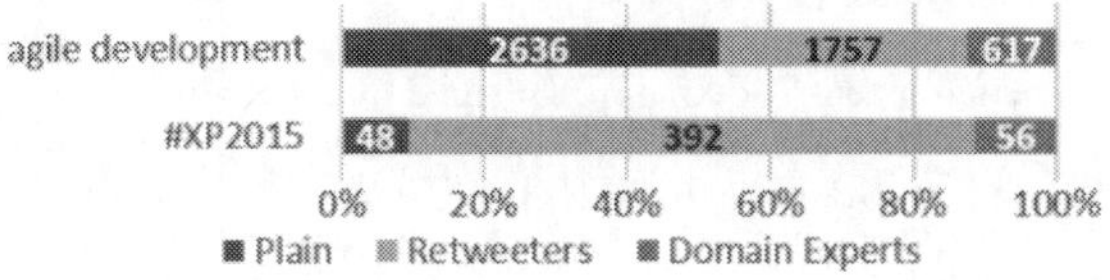

Figure 4. Retrieved users type distribution.

Seasonal events, such as the XP2015 conference, include fewer original tweets but a lot of retweets and replies. On the other hand, broader terms, such as 'agile development' include more original tweets and less retweets and replies. Consequently, from a user type perspective, seasonal terms include more retweeters and broad terms include more users posting original content. It can be therefore assumed that interaction between users is higher in seasonal terms than in broader ones. With our approach, the analysis and evaluation of tweets and users offered satisfactory results for both query types. Moreover, our approach visualises most popular users for the "#XP2015" term, in a clear way, as seen in Figure 5a. The produced graph is star-like, showing that all relationships have one user in common. However, this is rarely the case, especially for broad, not seasonal terms.

The second use case included the retrieval and analysis of data for the general term 'agile development' for a single day. We focused on a short timeframe in order to demonstrate our approach's ability to perform well, even when processing small datasets. In total, 100 tweets were retrieved and analysed, resulting in the evaluation of 125 users and the creation of 58 relationships between them.

For the produced graph, the most influential user is 'gclaps', as shown in Figure 5b. This user writes articles about agile development and start-ups. Several authority sources are also shown in the graph. Moreover, single-node and multi-node communities can be seen in the graph. Single-node communities are created because the analysis module checks for additional content for newly-retrieved users. Additionally, many of these single-node graphs represent new tweets that haven't been retweeted yet.

As can be observed, discovering influential users and their relationships with topic communities can be easily done with our approach. By using JavaScript, optional information is hidden for each node and edge, thus increasing graph readability considerably.

Regarding other data sources, our models can be modified to support other social networks as well. From the developer oriented StackOverflow to the topic-generic Reddit, it is possible to discover influential users by replacing Twitter attributes with the equivalent ones of each network and then assigning specific weights to them, based on the results of the classification algorithm. For LinkedIn the process should be easier since the attribute "Influencer" is already included in the social network's feature list.

VII. CONCLUSIONS

In this work, we described an approach for analysing Twitter data in order to model abstract social terms such as influence, authority and domain expertise, and apply that model to evaluate users and enhance knowledge discovery. We then validated our approach against two case studies that demonstrate the performance of our approach, regardless of the type of the search query, making it suitable for analysing Twitter data. Many approaches focus solely on tweets analysis or offer limited user data analysis features. Moreover, there is a need for proper visualisation of user communities in a way that can allow big datasets to be presented in a readable way. As it was demonstrated in our results section, our approach can successfully visualise users in terms of influence metrics so that user communities and relationships between users can be easily distinguished. Based on these results, we are confident that our approach can be used in many scenarios in industrial environments and academia. From gaining insights for a company's marketing campaign to complementing scientific material by supporting scoping studies [21], and other existing scientific research methods (such as mapping studies [22], literature reviews [23]). Scoping studies are concerned with contextualizing knowledge in terms of identifying the current state of understanding; identifying the sorts of things we know and do not know; and then setting this within policy and practice contexts.

We plan to continue carrying out work in this domain to further study the results and improve our models' accuracy. Moreover, we plan to conduct a user study in order to determine the best way to release our tool as an open-source web application. Lastly, we plan to target other audiences, like software developers [24], and thus, enhancing our retrieval and analysis modules to support a wider range of social networks, blogs and forums.

Figure 5. (a) Most popular users for the '#XP2015' term. (b) The most influential user for the second use case for the 'agile development' term.

REFERENCES

[1] S. Haustein, et al., "Tweets as impact indicators: Examining the implications of automated "bot" accounts on Twitter." Journal of the Association for Information Science and Technology 67.1, 2016, pp. 232-238.

[2] A. Tumasjan, T. O. Sprenger, P. G. Sandner, I. M. Welpe, "Predicting elections with twitter: What 140 characters reveal about political sentiment.", ICWSM, 10, May 2010, pp. 178-85.

[3] S. Ravikumar, R. Balakrishnan and S. Kambhampati, "Ranking tweets considering trust and relevance." In Proceedings of the Ninth International Workshop on Information Integration on the Web, ACM. Vancouver, 2012, May, p. 4.

[4] J. Brown, A. J. Broderick, N. Lee, "Word of mouth communication within online communities: Conceptualizing the online social network." Journal of interactive marketing, 21(3), 2007, pp. 2-20.

[5] My Top Tweet – https://mytoptweet.com, retrieved: May, 2016.

[6] J. J. Kaye, et al., "Nokia internet pulse: a long term deployment and iteration of a twitter visualization." In CHI'12 Extended Abstracts on Human Factors in Computing Systems, ACM, 2012, May, pp. 829-844.

[7] S. Ghosh, N. Sharma, F. Benevenuto, N. Ganguly, K. Gummadi, "Cognos: crowdsourcing search for topic experts in microblogs." In Proceedings of the 35th international ACM SIGIR conference on Research and development in information retrieval, ACM. Vancouver, 2012, August, pp. 575-590.

[8] J. Weng, E. P. Lim, J. Jiang, Q. He, "Twitterrank: finding topic-sensitive influential twitterers. In Proceedings of the third ACM international conference on Web search and data mining. ACM, Vancouver, 2010, February, pp. 261-270.

[9] About Twitter's suggestions for who to follow | Twitter Help Center – https://support.twitter.com/articles/227220?lang=en, retrieved: May, 2016.

[10] How Far Did Your Tweets Travel? | TweetReach – https://tweetreach.com/, retrieved: May, 2016.

[11] Twitter analytic tool | Tweetchup – http://tweetchup.com/, retrieved: May, 2016.

[12] D. Stojanova, M. Ceci, A. Appice, S. Džeroski, "Network regression with predictive clustering trees." Data Mining and Knowledge Discovery, 25(2), 2012, pp. 378-413.

[13] R. Zafarani, M. A. Abbasi, H. Liu, "Social media mining: an introduction." Cambridge University Press, 2014.

[14] F. H. Khan, S. Bashir, U. Qamar, "TOM: Twitter opinion mining framework using hybrid classification scheme." Decision Support Systems, 57, pp. 245-257, 2014.

[15] F. Fouss, M. Saerens, J.M. Renders, "Links between Kleinberg's hubs and authorities, correspondence analysis, and Markov chains." In Data Mining, 2003. ICDM 2003. Third IEEE International Conference on, IEEE, Vancouver, 2003, November, pp. 521-524.

[16] J.M. Kleinberg, "Authoritative sources in a hyperlinked environment." Journal of the ACM (JACM), 46(5), 1999, pp. 604-632.

[17] The Search API | Twitter Developers – https://dev.twitter.com/rest/public/search, retrieved: May, 2016.

[18] Gavagai Living Lexicon online - Gavagai – Next generation text analytics. – https://gavagai.se/blog/2015/05/01/gavagai-living-lexicon-online/, retrieved: May, 2016.

[19] TACOS – http://johnmarkou.com/tacos/agile_development/, retrieved: May, 2016.

[20] B. J. Jansen, D. L. Booth, A. Spink, "Determining the user intent of web search engine queries." In Proceedings of the 16th international conference on World Wide Web, ACM, 2007, May, pp. 1149-1150.

[21] H. Arksey and L. O'Malley, "Scoping studies: towards a methodological framework." International journal of social research methodology, 8(1), 2005, pp. 19-32.

[22] K. Petersen, R. Feldt, S. Mujtaba, M. Mattsson, "Systematic mapping studies in software engineering." In 12th international conference on evaluation and assessment in software engineering, 2008, June, Vol. 17, No. 1, pp. 1-10.

[23] S. Keele, et al., "Guidelines for performing systematic literature reviews in software engineering." In Technical report, Ver. 2.3 EBSE Technical Report. EBSE, 2007.

[24] A. Zagalsky, O. Barzilay, A. Yehudai, "Example overflow: Using social media for code recommendation." In Proceedings of the Third International Workshop on Recommendation Systems for Software Engineering, 2012, June, pp. 38-42, IEEE Press.

A Novel Reduced Representation Methodology for Provenance Data

Mehmet Gungoren[1], Mehmet S. Aktas[2]
Computer Engineering
Yildiz Technical University
İstanbul, Turkey
e-mail: [1]mehmet.gungoren@std.yildiz.edu.tr, [2]aktas@yildiz.edu.tr

Abstract— **Learning structure and concepts in provenance data have created a need for monitoring scientific workflow systems. Provenance data is capable of expanding quickly due to the catch level of granularity, which can be quite high. This study examines complex structural information based provenance representations, such as Network Overview and Social Network Analysis. Further examination includes whether such reduced provenance representation approaches achieve clustering effective for understanding the hidden structures within the execution traces of scientific workflows. The study applies clustering on a scientific dataset from a weather forecast to determine its usefulness, compares the proposed provenance representations against prior studies on reduced provenance representation, and analyzes the quality of clustering on different types of reduced provenance representations. The results show that, compared to prior studies on representation, the Social Network Analysis based representation is more capable of completing data mining tasks like clustering while maintaining more reduced provenance feature space.**

Keywords- scientific workflows; scientific data provenance; complex structural information; data provenance; provenance.

I. INTRODUCTION

Provenance can be used as a ground basis for various applications and use cases, such as identifying trust values for data or data fragments [1]. The scientific data provenance collected from the life cycle of a data product is a record of the actions that contribute to the existence of the product. In other words, it identifies the object: the measures that have been implemented, and how, where, and by whom these actions have been implemented. Data provenance determines the extent to which a data product results from raw data. Recording the lineage of a data product is the latest series of activities (or "workflow") applied [2].

Scientific digital data is an important component of metadata for a data object. It can be used to determine the allocation, to identify relationships between objects, and to trace the differences in similar results [3]. Furthermore, in a broader purpose, digital data can help a researcher determine whether a given acquired object can be reused in its work by providing lineage information to support the quality of the data set.

One model that represents such entities and relationships is the Open Provenance Model (OPM) [4]. OPM defines the historical dependencies between entities. The source may be very large, and the catch may be carried out at a high level of granularity. This may occur, for instance, in a workflow system that encourages grained nodes (ex: at a mathematical operation) instead of coarse grains (i.e., at a great work parallel computing.). Moreover, XML-based OPM representation makes it difficult to conduct data analytics tasks on data provenance.

Chen, Plale, and Aktas introduced an approach to deal with large volumes of OPM-based provenance by assuming that the volumes would be large, and then selectively reducing the feature space while simultaneously preserving interesting features so that data mining on the reduced space will yield useful information [5][6]. To do this, they used statistical feature space integrated with a temporal representation of provenance data. Simple structural features (such as the number of in-degree/out-degree) and attribute features (such as number of characters in node name) were also used.

This study takes a slightly different approach in providing a reduced provenance representation of scientific datasets by investigating various complex structural information based representations for scientific data provenance. Algorithms for Network Overview (NO)-metric and Social Network Analysis (SNA)-metric representations of provenance data are introduced. Similar to the work of Chen, Plale, and Aktas, the present study also uses data mining tasks such as clustering to evaluate the usability of the NO-metric and SNA-metric representations of the datasets [5][6]. Such clustering tasks include understanding structures that describe and distinguish the general properties of the datasets in provenance databases to help with detecting any defective provenance data.

This paper provides several new factors to the scientific community. First, it introduces algorithms that convert OPM compatible provenance graphs to Network Overview metrics and Social Network Analysis based reduced provenance representations. It also assesses these complex structural information based representations by using data mining techniques on scientific provenance datasets. The paper evaluates a large weather forecast scientific provenance dataset with provenance traces generated from a real-life workflow [7]. The results demonstrate that, compared with other representation approaches, the SNA-metric representation is more capable of achieving data mining tasks like clustering while maintaining more reduced provenance feature space without any information loss.

The remainder of the paper is organized as follows: Section II reviews related work. Section III introduces the complex structural information based representation approach. The methodology is explained in Section IV, followed by the experimental evaluation of a large database of provenance in Section V. Section VI concludes the paper and discusses future work.

II. Related Work

Extraction and representation of information about the data-sources has been a subject of research for many years. Many studies have been conducted to represent data sources with reduced representation models and to provide extensive survey studies on data representation methods [1][8]. Agrawal et al. provides one of the first surveys in the context of applied scientific data processing [8]. Antunes et al. offers, in a more general context, a taxonomy for understanding and comparing various data representation techniques [1]. Simmhan et al. first suggested the value that provenance brings to e-Science applications [9]. Davidson et al. introduced the problem of mining and extracting information from provenance for the first time [10].

Santos et al. use clustering techniques to organize collections of workflow graphs [11]. They discuss reduced representations using labeled graphs and multidimensional vectors. However, their representation becomes too large when the workflow is big, and the structural information is lost when using multidimensional vectors.

Bose and Frew introduce a comprehensive survey of lineage retrieval for scientific data processing [12]. In this study, they also introduce a meta-model to identify and assess the components of lineage retrieval systems.

Dealing with temporal data dependencies is yet another problem in discovering hidden information. The goal of temporal data mining is to find hidden relationships between sequences and subsequences [1]. Chen, Plale and Aktas investigate the use of statistical features in order to represent provenance graphs [5][6]. Their study uses non-structural features, such as the number of characters in node labels, and structural features, such as the number of in-degree/out-degree of a node. Chen et al. [5] proposed a temporal graph partitioning algorithm as the basis for an abstract provenance representation. Based on this approach, the non-structural and structural features for each node within each partition are calculated, processed (with statistical operations (average)), and converted into a reduced abstract provenance representation. Chen et al. [5] address the problem of extraction and knowledge discovery from graphs of origin while overcoming the problem of scalability by reducing the large graphic source to a small sequence of temporal representation.

The present study differs from previous work by investigating the use of complex structural information, such as network overview metrics or social network metrics, for the reduced representation of provenance datasets. With the use of temporal representation, the representation sequences of provenance graphs may not be the same length, as the number of partitions will differ between provenance graphs. For example, in large provenance graphs, the number of partitions is high. In return, this increases the size of the reduced temporal provenance representation. However, this study explores the use of network metrics based representation in which the representation sequence is always the same length, regardless of the size of graphs.

III. Network Metrics Based Reduced Provenance Representation

This study defines the complex structural information (network-metrics) feature space vector of a provenance graph. Then, a function that creates the feature vector of the provenance graph based on the network-metrics feature space is defined. In addition two different categories of network metrics are introduced: Network Overview Metrics and Social Network Analysis Metrics. The following definitions work with both categories.

Definition 1. *For a feature space (vector) $N = (V, F, D)$, $V = \{v_1, \ldots, v_n\}$ denotes all the nodes in the provenance graph, the function $F: V \rightarrow D_1 \times D_2 \times \ldots \times D_d$ is a feature function that assigns a feature vector to any node $v \in V$, and the set $D = \{D_1, D_2, D_3, \ldots, D_d\}$ is called the feature space of N. Here, each feature is a network metric and has a numerical value. For example, the diameter of a node within a provenance graph is a feature. For each node in the V, D needs to be calculated.*

Definition 2. *For a network metric based feature space (vector) $N = (V, F, G, D, S)$, a representation function $G: D_1 \times D_2 \times \ldots \times D_i \rightarrow S_i$ applies average operation to feature $D_i \in D$ of all nodes in V and the set $S = \{S_1, S_2, S_3, \ldots, S_d\}$ is called the feature space of N. Here, for a provenance graph, set S becomes the reduced provenance representation.*

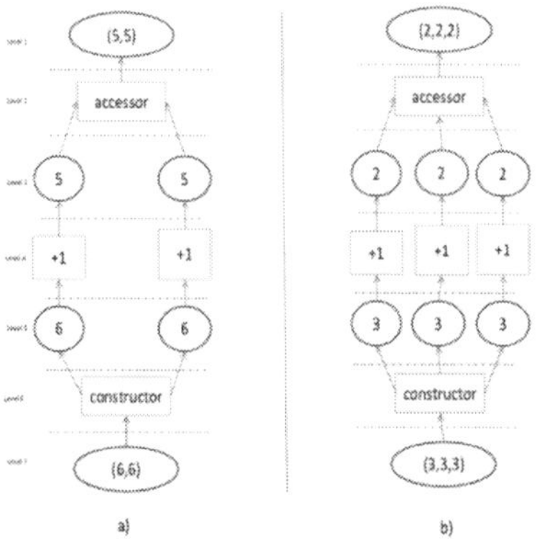

Figure 1. An example illustrating Temporal Partition [4].

A. Network Overview Based Reduced Provenance Representation

Networks have certain attributes that can be calculated to analyze the network's properties or characteristics. These attributes are often called network overview metrics. Due to the directed link structure of the provenance graphs, the present study investigates whether network overview metrics can be utilized as distinguishing features in provenance representation. For this investigation, six commonly used network properties are used: average degree is the degree of a node, or the number of edges that are adjacent to the node;

diameter is the maximal distance between all pairs of nodes; path length is the graph-distance between all pairs of nodes; density is the measurement of how completeness of the network; modularity is the measurement for how well a network decomposes into modular communities; connected component count is the measurement that determines the number of connected components in the network; and finally, giant component is a connected component of a given random graph that contains a constant fraction of the entire graph's vertices.

The pseudo code for the algorithm that creates the network overview metric based reduced representation is presented in Figure 6, and the process through which the NO-metric based representation of a provenance graph is generated is illustrated with an example. Each provenance graph has a link structure. Structural features such as NO-metrics are used as the representative features of a given provenance graph. To facilitate testing the use of NO-metrics, the commonly used NO-metrics were chosen as described above. Therefore, the feature space for each node in Figure 1(a) is D_i = {Average Degree, Diameter, Path Length, Density, Modularity, Connected Component Count, Giant}. For example, the resulting feature space values for the "accessor" node in Figure 1(a) is $D_{accessor}$ = {3.0, 2.0, 0.2, 0.111, 0.34, 0.0, 0.0}. After applying the average to D over all nodes belonging to Figure 1(a), the NO-metrics based reduced feature space is S = {1.0, 2.0, 1.2, 0.111, 0.34, 0.0, 0.0}. Note that, to facilitate testing the representation power of the NO-metrics, this study uses a statistical operation (average) to calculate the signature-representation of a given provenance graph. Other statistical operations may also be tested. Since this study's focus was mainly on the features, it only uses the average function.

B. *SNA-Metric based Reduced Provenance Representation*

This study also investigates the use of SNA-metrics in provenance representation. Social network analysis is the measurement of relationships between participating entities in a network. In general, the nodes in the network are the people and groups, while the links show relationships or flows between the nodes. To understand networks and their participants, SNA provides metrics to evaluate the location of participating actors in the network. The present research was aimed to find out whether SNA-metrics can capture enough information from provenance graphs to use them as feature space for reduced provenance representation. To do this, commonly used SNA metrics as described below are utilized. Degree centrality measures the "importance" or "influence" of a particular node within a network; betweenness centrality measures the influence over what flows in the network; and closeness centrality measures the visibility of nodes to monitor the information flow in the network. Eccentricity is a measurement that reflects how far, at most, each node is from every other node, and proximity prestige measures how close other actors are to a given actor. The pseudo code for the algorithm that creates the SNA-Metric based reduced representation is presented in Figure 7. In this representation, SNA-metrics are considered the representative features of a given provenance graph, so the feature space for each node in Figure 1(a) will be D_i = {Degree Centrality, Betweenness Centrality, Closeness Centrality, Density, Eccentricity}. For example, the resulting feature space values for "accessor" node in Figure 1(a) will be $D_{accessor}$ = {0.0, 0.0, 0.222, 2.0, 2.0, 0.0}. After applying the average to D over all nodes that belong to Figure 1(a), the SNA-metrics based reduced feature space is S = {0.012, 0.0, 0.049, 1.13, 1.086, 0.0}. Similar to the NO-Metric representation, to test the representation power of the SNA-metrics, a statistical operation (average) is used to calculate the signature-representation of a given provenance graph.

To further test the use of network-metrics based feature space as a representation, the researchers also apply the Temporal Representation approach introduced by Chen et al. [5][6]. Temporal Representation defines a strict, totally ordered partition that divides a provenance graph into a list of non-empty subsets. Given any provenance graph, Chen's Temporal Representation algorithm (Logical-P algorithm) generates a unique strict totally ordered partition. Figure 1 shows the temporal partitions obtained from three different provenance graphs. To test the usability of the Temporal Representation approach for feature space, simple structural feature sets were used in previous studies, including the node's in-degree and out-degree amounts [5][6]. In this study complex structural information based feature space is used for structural features.

C. *Temporal Representation with NO and SNA metrics Based Feature Spaces*

Chen et al. [5] define the feature space for a node subset and the statistical feature function that converts the provenance graphs, partitioned into subsets using Logical-P algorithm, into statistical feature space. Based on these definitions, the present study captures the following features for NO-metrics feature space from each subset Vi: <Average Degree, Diameter, Path Length, Density, Modularity, Connected Component Count, Giant>. The Temporal Representation with NO-metric based Feature Space is tested on the partitioned provenance graph shown in Figure 1. For example, the resulting provenance partition of Figure 1(a) is represented as: S={<1.0, 2.0, 0.2, 0.111, 0.34, 0.0, 0.0>, <3.0, 2.0, 0.2, 0.111, 0.34, 0.0, 0.0>, <2.0, 0.0, 0.0, 0.111, 0.34, 0.0, 0.0>, <2.0, 1.0, 0.1, 0.111, 0.34, 0.0, 0.0>, <2.0, 1.0, 0.1, 0.111, 0.34, 0.0, 0.0>, <3.0, 2.0, 0.2, 0.111, 0.34, 0.0, 0.0>, <1.0, 2.0, 0.2, 0.111, 0.34, 0.0, 0.0>}. Likewise, the following features for SNA-metrics feature space from each subset Vi are: <Degree Centrality, Betweenness Centrality, Closeness Centrality, Density, Eccentricity>. The Temporal Representation with SNA-Metric based Feature Space was tested on the partitioned provenance graph shown in Figure 1. The resulting provenance partition of Figure 1(a) is represented as: S={<0.111, 0.0, 0.111, 1.0, 1.0, 0.0>, <0.0, 0.0, 0.222, 2.0, 2.0, 0.0>, <0.0, 0.0, 0.0, 0.0, 0.0, 0.0>, <0.0,

0.0, 0.111, 1.0, 1.0, 0.0>, <0.0, 0.0, 0.111, 1.0, 1.0, 0.0>, <0.0, 0.0, 0.222, 2.0, 2.0, 0.0>, <0.111, 0.0, 0.111, 1.0, 1.0, 0.0>}.

D. Feature Selection Methodology

The selection of an optimal feature set depends upon both the mining targets and the nature of the provenance [5][6]. In this study, the target in unsupervised clustering is to group together provenance instances based on their original experiment. Therefore, the aim is to select a feature set that can discriminate between provenance instances of different experiments. In other words, the distance between two representations of provenance derived from the same experiment should be smaller than the distance between representations of provenance derived from different experiments. More features result in more distinguishing power while adding irrelevant features to a dataset often decreases the accuracy of the unsupervised clustering approaches. This study investigates whether network overview metrics or social network analysis metrics have enough discriminating power for unsupervised clustering tasks in scientific provenance datasets.

This study assumes that provenance graphs from related experiments have similar structure and similar attribute information, while provenance graphs from different experiments are either different in attribute information or in structural information. To this end, while using any feature set, Figure 1(a) and Figure 1(b) should be clustered together. To test this assumption, the Euclidean distance, calculated from the simple structural feature set (proposed by [5][6]), NO-metrics, and SNA-metrics based complex structural feature sets were investigated. The results of this investigation are shown in Table I. These distances show whether two graphs are relatively closer to each other for differing metrics. The results indicated that the distance between the provenance graphs in Figure 1(a) and Figure 1(b) turned out to be closer to each other for certain features more than others, meaning the distances calculated from complex structural information based feature space representations had more distinguishing power compared to other representations. It is important to note that the values of features were normalized before calculating the Euclidean Distance to make sure that all metrics contribute equally to the results. The normalized feature values scaled between 0 and 1.

TABLE I. EUCLIDEAN DISTANCE FOR DIFFERING FEATURE SETS AMONGST DIFFERENT REPRESENTATIONS

	Distance in Simple Structural Feature Set (from [5][6])
Figures 1(a) – 1(b)	0.7454
	Distance in NO-Metric Based Structural Feature Set
Figures 1(a) – 1(b)	0.5408
	Distance in SNA-Metric Based Structural Feature Set
Figures 1(a) – 1(b)	0.4429

Chen reported that the disadvantage of the simple structural feature set (i.e., amount of in-degree/out-degree) is that if two provenance graphs have the same structure but different node/edge information, it would be impossible to distinguish between the two through the structural feature set alone. To this end, Chen proposed an extension to the set by further splitting the edges into different types in OPM (i.e., used, wasGeneratedBy, wasControlledBy, wasTriggeredBy, wasDerivedFrom), so that one can discriminate graphs that have similar structure but are semantically different. The present study follows similar methodology, but assigns differing weights to each semantically different edge. In distinguishing the semantically different but structurally the same provenance graphs, the approach works with both network overview and social network analysis metrics.

IV. METHODOLOGY

This study addresses whether it is possible to detect failed workflows in a provenance dataset without the guidance of a workflow script or to detect provenance variants caused by either workflow execution failure or provenance capture failure. To answer these questions, the usability of complex structural information based reduced provenance representations is explored with a focus on finding variants to help detect faulty provenance data by checking cluster centroids in the case where correct and faulty provenances are naturally separated into different clusters.

Much like the study by Chen et al., the present study investigates the best unsupervised algorithm for the graph structure based provenance representation from several popular clustering algorithms: centroid-based (k-means), distribution-based (DBScan), and density-based (EM algorithm) [5][6]. Results indicated that the k-means algorithm produced the highest quality clusters. Hence, in this study, the k-means algorithm was selected to show the usefulness of the proposed representations.

Weka libraries and SimpleKmeans were used in the k-means algorithm. Using Euclidean distance as the similarity function in k-means limited the application of k-means to same-length representation. Since both NO-metric and SNA-metric based representations provide same-length representation for all provenance graphs, this was not problematic. However, when testing the temporal representation with network-metric based representation, this issue was limiting. To overcome this, the researchers followed the same approach as Chen et al., filling missing features with a special value of 0 to provide good performance in clustering results.

V. EXPERIMENTAL EVALUATION

To prove that the provenance representations using the graph partitioning approach can support scalable analysis while being resilient to errors in provenance data, the experiment is conducted using a 10GB provenance database with known failure patterns [7]. This 10GB database of provenance is populated from a workload of roughly 48,000 workflow instances that are modeled based on six real workflows. The LEAD NAM, SCOOP, and NCSF are weather and ocean modeling workflows, Gene2Life and MOTIF are bioinformatics and biomedical workflows, and the Animation workflow carries out computer animation rendering. Some of the workflows are small, having few nodes and edges, while others like Motif have a few hundred nodes and edges. In the 10GB database, each of the six workflow types has 2000 instances per failure mode, with the failure modes as following: No failures and dropped notifications (success case), 1% failure rate, 1% dropped notification rate, 1% failure rate, and 1% dropped notification rate.

The Karma provenance system is used to store the 10GB provenance dataset and to export the provenance in the form of OPM graphs [9]. From the provenance graphs, the adjacency matrix is generated. Then the complex network metrics and social network analysis metrics are calculated and stored.

The evaluation strategy used here follows the methodological analysis first described by Chen, Plale and Aktas [5][6]. No structural information is assumed in the representation of the provenance datasets within the 10GB database.

In order to help understand how the graph-structure based representations identify clusters, NAM workflow provenance datasets from weather forecast workflow were chosen, as Chen et al. identified that this is the best illustration of provenance capture from scientific workflows [5][6]. The temporal representation of the NAM provenance datasets has shown that NAM datasets include provenance graphs with varying numbers of partitions, ranging from 2 to 10. It turns out that a NAM provenance graph with 10 subsets is a complete graph, while provenance graphs with less than 10 partitions are incomplete and caused by dropped notifications. To test the usefulness of the graph structure based reduced representation approaches, a k-means clustering algorithm was applied to the provenance representations of NAM provenance datasets. Purity, Normalized Mutual Information (NMI), and Within-Cluster Sum of Squares (WCSS) were used to compare the performance of different clustering techniques.

The grouping of the NAM provenance dataset (based on the temporal length defined by Chen et al.) is shown in Figure 2. The grouping results indicate that 78% of the NAM provenance graphs have the largest possible number of partitions, and 6% of the graphs have small partitions ranging from 2 to 4. Small-partitioned provenance graphs indicate dropped notifications or early failures that might happen in the NAM workflow execution.

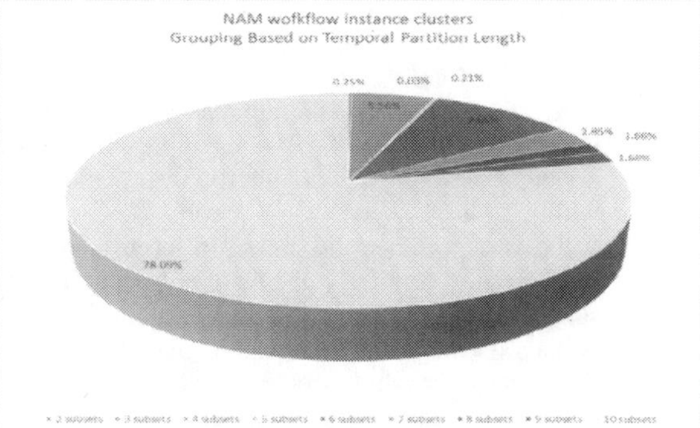

Figure 2. NAM workflow clusters - Grouping Based on Temporal Representation

To test the clustering on the reduced representations, the grouping results (shown in Figure 2) are used as the golden standard for Purity and NMI metrics. The clustering is evaluated on both NO-metric and SNA-metric based reduced provenance representations. The SimpleKMeans clustering algorithm with Euclidean Distance measurement is then applied to these representations. Unlike the temporal representation, the graph structure based representation has representation sequences of uniform length. Thus, the k-means clustering algorithm is applied without any limitations.

TABLE II. NAM WORKFLOW CLUSTERING RESULTS FOR K=9 AND VARYING REDUCED PROVENANCE REPRESENTATIONS

	Purity	NMI	WCCS
Network Overview	0.798375	0.503209	171.6229
SNA	0.922	0.516648	43.1794
TR+SNA	0.938625	0.555053	561.3776

Table II gives the summary of the quality of clustering results when k = 9. The results indicate that SNA-metric based representation and Temporal Partitioning with SNA representation lead to high quality clustering results. SNA metrics were better than NO metrics in capturing the complex structural information as features. Purity and NMI metrics were computed by calculating the correctly assigned workflow instances. To do this, the grouping results shown in Figure 2 were used as the golden standard. To further understand the behavior of clustering for varying reduced representation sizes, different k values were tested. To choose the number of cluster k, the quality of resulting clusters was plotted by computing Purity as an external evaluation criterion.

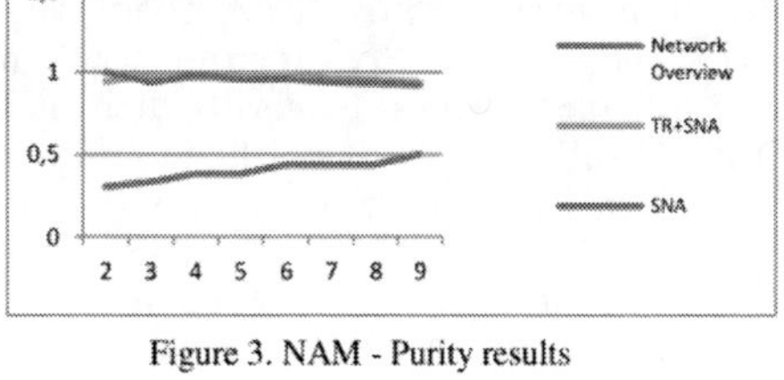

Figure 3. NAM - Purity results

Figure 3 shows that SNA-metrics based reduced provenance representation produced high quality clustering results for Purity Metric. This is because the link structure of the directed graphs contains enough information that can be used as features to differentiate the features and produce good clustering results. For example, an SNA-metric like prestige captures the popularity information of the nodes within a highly connected graph. The overall popularity value is expected to be higher in large graphs compared to small graphs. Similarly, the number of central nodes in large-scale linear provenance graphs is expected to be higher than in small-scale ones. Hence, the overall centrality value is expected to be high for large-scale graphs. The present investigation has shown that graph-structure based metrics can produce high quality clustering results while maintaining reduced provenance representation. The results also indicate that SNA metrics (such as centrality and prestige) capture the directed link structure of given provenance graphs better than network overview metrics based representation.

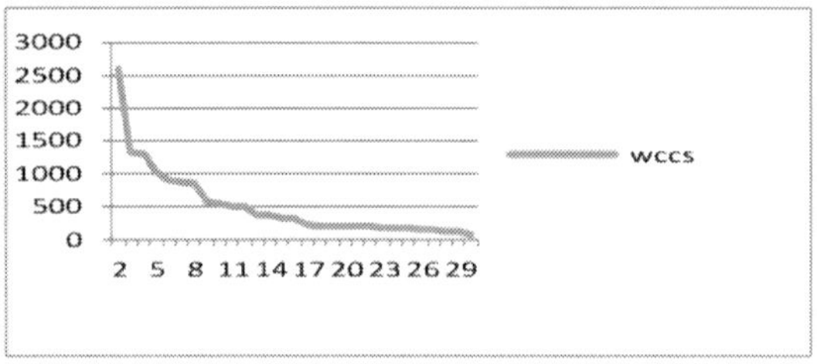

Figure 4. NAM – SNA k = [2,30] WCSS

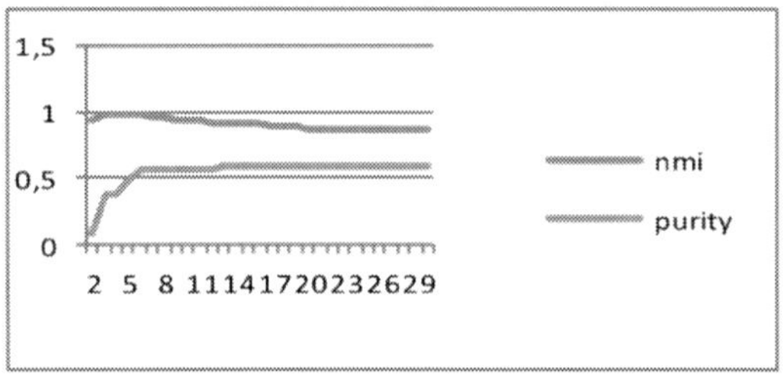

Figure 5. NAM - SNA k=[2,30] NMI Purity

Figure 4 and Figure 5 show the results of an experiment evaluating a k-means clustering algorithm on SNA-metric based representation by plotting the within cluster sum of squares and computing NMI and Purity for increasing values of k. The results indicated that after K reaches a value of 9, the Purity value is high and stable. This shows that the reduced representation in SNA-metric domain can lead to efficient unsupervised clustering.

As mentioned earlier, provenance graphs with few partitions indicate small provenance graphs. These graphs are often incomplete and may be caused by early failures in workflow execution or failures in provenance capture. Since the size of such graphs is small, their link structure information will not be enough to provide accurate clustering. Hence, if a provenance database contains a high number of small-size provenance graphs, graph structured based feature space is not expected to be effective in clustering. However, for scientific workflows where the number of nodes is high, such as NAM whether forecast workflow, such provenance representation can be useful. The present experiments indicated that, for a noisy large-scale scientific workflow dataset such as a NAM dataset, SNA-metric based representations provided high quality clustering.

VI. Conclusions and Future Work

This study investigates various graph structure based representations, such as Network Overview and Social Network Analysis metric representations for scientific data provenance. It also investigates whether such reduced provenance representation approaches lead to effective clustering on scientific data provenance for understanding the hidden structures within the execution traces of scientific workflows. Clustering was applied to the graph structure based representations on 10 GB scientific dataset to determine their usefulness. The graph structure based provenance representations were compared against other reduced provenance representation approaches. The quality of clustering on different types of reduced provenance representations was analyzed, and the results were reported. The results show that, compared with other representation approaches, the SNA-metric representation is more capable of data mining tasks like clustering while maintaining more reduced provenance feature space. In future work, the researchers plan to test the network-metrics based representations with a real-life dataset obtained from the AMSR-E satellite. They also plan to extend their work to combine both Network Overview metric and Social Network Analysis metric representations in one vector. Work remains to test whether complex structural information based provenance representation is useful in other data mining tasks, such as classification and association rule mining. The researchers plan to adapt state-of-the-art approaches for dimensionality reduction and high-contrast feature selection in future work, and to expand tests on the other scientific workflow datasets that are available in the 10GB provenance database introduced by Cheah et al. [7].

Acknowledgments

The authors would like to thank Dr. Beth Plale, the director of the Data to Insight Center (D2I) from Indiana University, for helping us throughout our studies, including but not limited to the use of Karma Service implementation, the computational facilities of the D2I Center, and the 10GB scientific provenance database. The authors also thank Dr. Peng Chen for his valuable insights on the use of temporal provenance representation. This study was supported by TUBITAK's (3501) National Young Researchers Career Development Program (Project No: 114E781, Project Title: Provenance Use in Social Media Software to Develop Methodologies for Detection of Information Pollution and Violation of Copyrights).

REFERENCES

[1] C. M. Antunes, and A. L. Oliveira, "Temporal data mining: An overview" KDD Workshop on Temporal Data Mining, 2001, pp. 1–13.

[2] M. Aktas, B. Plale, D. Leake and N. K. Mukhi, "Unmanaged Workflows: Their Provenance and Use", Q. Bai, Q. Liu eds. Data Provenance and Data Management in eScience, Studies in Computational Intelligence series, Springer, Vol 426, 2013, pp. 59-81.

[3] S. Bechhofer, D. D. Roure, M. Gamble, C. Goble and L. Buchan, "Research objects: Towards exchange and reuse of digital knowledge" The Future of the Web for Collaborative Science, 2010.

[4] L. Moreau, and et al., "The open provenance model core specification (v1. 1)" Future Generation Computer Systems. 27, 2011, pp. 743–756.

[5] P. Chen, and B. Plale, and M. Aktas, "Temporal representation for scientific data provenance" eScience 2012, pp. 1-8.

[6] P. Chen, and B. Plale, and M. Aktas, "Temporal Representation for Mining Scientific Data Provenance" Future Generation Comp. Syst. 36, 2014, pp. 363-378.

[7] Y. Cheah, B. Plale, J. Kendall-Morwick, D. Leake and L. Ramakrishnan, "A Noisy 10GB Provenance Database" 2nd Int'l Workshop on Traceability and Compliance of Semi-Structured Processes (TC4SP), co-located with Business Process Management (BPM), 2011, pp. 370-381.

[8] R. Agrawal and R. Srikant, "Fast algorithms for mining association rules" 20th Int. Conf. Very Large Data Bases, VLDB. 1215, pp. 487-499, 1994.

[9] Y. L. Simmhan, B. Plale, and D. Gannon, "A Survey of Data Provenance in e-Science" ACM SIGMOD Record. 34, 2005, pp. 31–36.

[10] S. B. Davidson and J. Freire, "Provenance and scientific workflows: challenges and opportunities" SIGMOD Conf., 2008, pp. 1345–1350.

[11] E. Santos, L. Lins, J. P. Ahrens, J. Freire, and C. T. Silva, "A first study on clustering collections of workflow graphs" IPAW, 2008, pp. 160-173.

[12] R. Bose and J. Frew., "Lineage retrieval for scientific data processing: a survey" ACM Comput. Surv. 37(1), March 2005, pp. 1-28.

```
assign 0 to total_avg, total_dia, total_pLen, total_dns, total_mdl, total_ccc, total_gia
for all nodes n in D do
        assign convertOPMtoAdjacencyMatrix(n) to adjacency_matrix
        assign averageDegree(adjacency _matrix) to avg
        assign diameter(adjacency _matrix) to dia
        assign pathLength(adjacency _matrix) to pLen
        assign density(adjacency_matrix) to dns
        assign modulartiy(adjacency_matrix) to mdl
        assign connectedComponentCount(adjacency_matrix) to ccc
        assign giant (adjacency_matrix) to gia
        assign total_avg + avg to total_avg; total_dia + dia to total_dia; total_pLen + pLen to  total_pLen;
total_dns + dns to total_dns; total_mdl + mdl to total_mdl; total_ccc + ccc to total_ccc; total_gia + gia to total_gia
end for
assign {total_avg/n, total_dia/n, total_pLen/n, total_dns/n, total_mdl/n, total_ccc/n, total_gia/n} to Feature_Space
```

Figure 6. Pseudo code for the algorithm CN metrics based reduced provenance representation

```
T <- set of all node in G
for all node k in T do
        assign empty to Stack(S)
        assign empty to LinkedList(Q)
        addLast k to LinkedListQ)
        while LinkedList(Q) is not empty do
                assign removeFirst from LinkedList(Q) to v
                add Stack(S) to v
                for all edge of v do
                        add opposite node to Linked(Q)
                end for
        end while
        for all nodes in T do
                if count of neighbour of s > 0 do
                        add count of neighbour of s to closenessCentrality
                        add count of neighbour of s to proximityPrestige
                        add max in count of neighbour of s or eccentricity of s to eccenricity
                end if
        end for
        for all out going edges from s do
                if count of neighbour of s > 0 do
                        add count of neighbour of s to degreeCenrality
                end if
        end for
        for all incoming edges from s do
                if count of neighbour of s > 0 do
                        add count of neighbour of s to degreePrestige
                end if
        end for
        if s is reachable from other nodes
                closenessCentrality /= reachableCount
                proximityPrestige /= reachableCount
        end if
        closenessCentrality /= All nodes count - 1
        degreeCentrality /= All nodes count - 1
        degreePrestige /= All nodes count - 1
end for
do normalization for all attributes of SNA
```

Figure 7. Pseudo code for the algorithm SNA metrics based reduced provenance representation

An Efficient Algorithm for Read Matching in DNA Databases

Yangjun Chen, Yujia Wu
Dept. Applied Computer Science
University of Winnipeg, Canada
email: y.chen@uwinnipeg.ca, wyj1128@yahoo.com

Jiuyong Xie
Dept. Physiology &Pathophysiology, College of Medicine
University of Manitoba, Canada
email: xiej@umanitoba.ca

***Abstract*—In this paper, we discuss an efficient and effective index mechanism to support the matching of massive reads (short DNA strings) in DNA databases. It is very important to the next generation sequencing in the biological research. The main idea behind it is to construct a trie structure over all the reads, and search the trie against a BWT-array *L* created for a genome sequence *s* to locate all the occurrences of every read in *s* once for all. In addition, we change a single-character checking against *L* to a multiple-character checking, by which multiple searches of *L* are reduced to a single scanning of *L*. In this way, high efficiency can be achieved. Experiments have been conducted, which show that our method for this problem is promising.**

Keywords—string matching; DNA sequences; tries; BWT-transformation

I. INTRODUCTION

The recent development of next-generation sequencing has changed the way we carry out the molecular biology and genomic studies. It has allowed us to sequence a *DNA* (Deoxyribonucleic acid) sequence at a significantly increased base coverage, as well as at a much faster rate. This facilitates building an excellent platform for the whole genome sequencing, and for a variety of sequencing-based analysis, including gene expressions, mapping *DNA-protein* interactions, whole-transcriptome sequencing, and RNA (Ribonucleic acid) splicing profiles. For example, the *RNA-Seq* protocol, in which processed *mRNA* is converted to *cDNA* and sequenced, is enabling the identification of previously unknown genes and alternative splice variants. The whole-genome sequencing of tumour cells can uncover previously unidentified cancer-initiating mutations.

The core and the first step to take advantage of the new sequencing technology is termed as *read aligning*, where a read is a short nucleotide sequence of 30 - 1000 base pairs (bp) generated by a high throughput sequencing machine made by Illumina, Roche, ABI/Life Technologies, which is in fact a sequence fragment fetched from a longer DNA molecule present in a sample that is fed into the machine. Most of the next-generation sequencing projects begin with a *reference sequence* which is a previously well studied, known *genome*. The process of a read aligning is to find the meaning of reads, or in other words, to determine their positions within a reference sequence, which will then be used for an effective statistical analysis.

Compared to the traditional pattern matching problems, the new challenge from the read aligning is its enormous volume, usually millions to billions of reads need to be aligned within a same reference sequence. For example, to sequence a human molecule sample with 15X coverage, one may need to align 1.5 billion reads of length about 100 characters (bps).

In general, three kinds of alignment algorithms are practically applied: *hash-based*, *string-matching-based*, as well as *inexact matching* (including *edit-distance* computation and *k-mismatching*). By the hash-based methods, short subsequences called *seeds* are extracted from a pattern sequence and their hash values are computed, which are used to search against a reference genome sequence. By the string-matching-based methods, different efficient algorithms are utilized, such as *Knuth-Morris-Pratt* [22], *Boyer-Moore* [9], and *Apostolico-Giancarlo* [3], as well as the algorithms based on different *indexes* like *suffix* trees [37][45], *suffix* arrays [35], and *BWT*-transformation (*Burrows-Wheeler* Transform) [10, 16, 40]. By the *edit-distance* computation, a *score* matrix to represent the relevance between characters is defined and an alignment with the highest total score is searched, for which the *dynamical programming* paradigm is typically employed. However, a recent research shows that the BWT can also be used as an index structure for the *k-mismatching* problem [30].

All the methods mentioned above are *single-pattern* oriented, by which a single string pattern is checked against an entire database to find all the alignments in all the sequences stored in the database. In the current research of the molecular biology, however, we need to check a bunch of string patterns each time and the size of all string patterns can be even much larger than the database itself. This requires us considering all the string patterns as a whole, rather than separately check them one by one. By the *Aho-Corasick* algorithm [1], the multiple patterns are handled. However, it cannot be utilized in an indexing environment since it has to search a target sequence linearly while by using indexes to expedite a search this is not expected.

In this paper, we address this issue and present a holistic string matching algorithm to handle million-billion reads. Our experiment shows that it can be more than 40% faster than single-pattern oriented methods when multi-million reads are checked. The main idea behind our method is:

1. Construct a trie *T* over all the pattern sequences, and check *T* against a BWT-array created as an index for a target (reference) sequence. This enables us to avoid repeated search of the same part of different reads.
2. Change a single-character checking to a multiple-character checking. (That is, each time a set of characters respectively from more than one read will be checked

against a BWT-array in one scan, instead of checking them separately one by one in multiple scans.)

In this way, high efficiency has been achieved.

The remainder of the paper is organized as follows. In Section II, we review the related work. In Section III, we briefly describe a string matching algorithm based on the BWT-transformation. In Section IV, we discuss our basic algorithm in great detail. In Section V, we improve the basic method by using multiple-character checkings. Section VI is devoted to the test results. Finally, a short conclusion is set forth in Section VII.

II. RELATED WORK

The matching of DNA sequences is just a special case of the general string matching problem, which has always been one of the main focuses in the computer science. All the methods developed up to now can be roughly divided into two categories: exact matching and inexact matching. By the former, all the occurrences of a pattern string p in a target string s will be searched. By the latter, a best alignment between p and s (i.e., a correspondence with the highest score) is searched in terms of a given score matrix M, which is established to indicate the relevance between characters (more exactly, the meanings represented by them).

A. Exact Matching

Scanning-based By this kind of algorithms, both pattern p and s are scanned from left to right, but often with an auxiliary data structure used to speed up the search, which is typically constructed by a pre-processor. The first of them is the famous *Knuth-Morris-Pratt* algorithm [22], which employs an auxiliary *next-table* (for p) containing the so-called shift information (or say, *failure function values*) to indicate how far to shift the pattern from right to left when the current character in p fails to match the current character in s. Its time complexity is bounded by $O(m + n)$, where $m = |p|$ and $n = |s|$. The *Boyer-Moore* approach [9] works a little bit better than the *Knuth-Morris-Pratt*. In addition to the next-table, a *skip-table* (also for p) is kept. For a large alphabet and small pattern, the expected number of character comparisons is about n/m, and is $O(m + n)$ in the worst case. Although these two algorithms have never been used in practice, they sparked a series of research on this problem, and improved by different researchers in different ways, such as the algorithms discussed in [1][27]. However, the worst-case time complexity remains unchanged. The idea of the 'shift information' has also been adopted by Aho and Corasick [1] for the *multiple-string* matching, by which s is searched for an occurrence of any one of a set of k patterns: $\{p_1, p_2, \ldots, p_k\}$. Their algorithm needs only $O(\sum_{i=1}^{k} m_i + n)$ time, where $m_i = |p_i|$ ($i = 1, \ldots, k$). However, this algorithm cannot be adapted to an index environment due its working fashion totally unsuitable for indexes.

Index-based In situations where a fixed string s is to be searched repeatedly, it is worthwhile constructing an index over s [46], such as suffix trees [37][45], suffix arrays [35], and more recently the *BWT*-transformation [10][16][30][31][40]. A suffix tree is in fact a *trie* structure [21] over all the suffixes of s; and by using the Weiner's algorithm it can be built in $O(n)$ time [37]. However, in comparison with suffix trees, the BWT-transformation is more suitable for DNA sequences due to its small alphabet Σ since the smaller Σ is, the smaller space will be occupied by the corresponding BWT index. According to a survey done by Li and Homer [30] on sequence alignment algorithms for next-generation sequencing, the average space required for each character is 12 - 17 bytes for suffix trees while only 0.5 - 2 byte for the BWT. Our experiments also confirm this distinction. For example, the file size of chromosome 1 of human is 270 Mb. But its suffix tree is of 26 Gb in size while its BWT needs only 390 Mb – 1 Gb for different compression rates of auxiliary arrays, completely handlable on PC or laptop machines. The huge size of a suffix tree may greatly affect the computation time. For example, for the Zebra fish and Rat genomes (sizes 1,464,443,456 pb, and 2,909,701,677 pb, respectively), we cannot finish the construction of their suffix trees within two days in a computer with 32GB RAM.

Hash-based Intrinsically, all hash-table-based algorithms [18, 20] extract short subsequences called 'seeds' from a pattern sequence p and create a *signature* (a bit string) for each of them. The search of a target sequence s is similar to that of the Brute Force searching, but rather than directly comparing the pattern at successive positions in s, their respective signatures are compared. Then stick each matching seed together to form a complete alignment. Its expected time is $O(m + n)$, but in the worst case, which is extremely unlikely, it takes $O(m \cdot n)$ time. The hash technique has also been extensively used in the DNA sequence research [19, 28, 29, 34, 39], and all experiments shows that they are generally inferior to the suffix tree and the BWT index in both running time and space requirements.

B. Inexact Matching

The inexact matching ranges from the score-based to the k-mismatching, as well as the k-error. By the score-based method, a score matrix M of size $|\Sigma| \times |\Sigma|$ is used to indicate the relevance between characters. The algorithm designed is to find the best alignment (or say, the alignment with the highest scores) between two given strings, which can be DNA sequences, protein sequences, or XML documents; and the *dynamic programming* paradigm is often utilized to solve the problem [14]. By the k-mismatching, we will find all those subsequences q of s such that $d(p, q) \leq k$, where $d(\ )$ is a distance function. When it is the *Hemming* distance, the problem is known as sequence matching with k *mismatches* [4]. When it is the *Levenshtein* distance, the problem is known as sequence matching with k *errors* [6]. There is a bunch of algorithms proposed for this problem, such as [4, 5, 24, 25, 42, 43] for the k-*mismatch*; and [6, 11, 15, 44] for the k-*error*. All the methods for the k-*mismatch* needs quadratic time $O(m \cdot n)$ in the worst case. However, the algorithm discussed in [2] has the best expected time complexity $O(n \cdot \sqrt{k} \cdot \log m)$. Especially, for small k and large Σ, the search requires sublinear time on average. In addition, the BWT can also be used as an index structure for this problem [30]. For the k-error, the worst case time complexity is the same as the k-mismatching. But the expected time can reach $O(k \cdot n)$ by an algorithm discussed in [11]. As a different kind of inexact matching, the string matching with *Don't-Cares* (or *wild-cards*) has also been an active research topic for decades, by which we may have wild-cards in p, in s, or in both of them. A wild card matches any character. Due to this property, the 'match' relation is no longer transitive, which precludes straightforward adaption of the *shift information* used by *Knuth-Morris-Pratt* and *Boyer-Moore*. All the methods proposed to solve this problem also needs quadratic time [38]. But using a suffix array as the index, however, the searching time can be reduced to O(log$n$) for some patterns, which contain only a sequence of consecutive Don't Cares [36].

III. BWT-TRANSFORMATION

In this section, we give a brief description of the BWT transformation to provide a discussion background.

A. BWT and String Compression

We use s to denote a string that we would like to transform. Assume that s terminates with a special character \$, which does not appear elsewhere in s and is alphabetically prior to all other characters. In the case of DNA sequences, we have $\$ < A < C < G < T$. As an example, consider s = *acagaca*\$. We can rotate s consecutively to create eight different strings as shown in Figure 1(a).

a	c	a	g	a	c	a	\$
c	a	g	a	c	a	\$	a
a	g	a	c	a	\$	a	c
g	a	c	a	\$	a	c	a
a	c	a	\$	a	c	a	g
c	a	\$	a	c	a	g	a
a	\$	a	c	a	g	a	c
\$	a	c	a	g	a	c	a

(a)

F	L
a_1	\$
c_1	a_1
a_2	c_1
g_1	a_2
a_3	g_1
c_2	a_3
a_4	c_2
\$	a_4

(b)

\$	a	c	a	g	a	c	a
a	\$	a	c	a	g	a	c
a	c	a	\$	a	c	a	g
a	c	a	g	a	c	a	\$
a	g	a	c	a	\$	a	c
c	a	\$	a	c	a	g	a
c	a	g	a	c	a	\$	a
g	a	c	a	\$	a	c	a

(c)

Figure 1. Rotation of a string

By writing all these strings stacked vertically, we generate an $n \times n$ matrix, where $n = |s|$ (see Figure 1(a).) Here, special attention should be paid to the first column, denoted as F, and the last column, denoted as L. For them, the following equation, called the *LF mapping*, can be immediately observed:

$$F[i] = L[i]\text{'s successor,} \qquad (1)$$

where $F[i]$ ($L[i]$) is the ith element of F (resp. L).

From this property, another property, the so-called *rank correspondence* can be derived, by which we mean that for each character, its ith appearance in F corresponds to its ith appearance in L, as demonstrated in Figure 1(b), in which the position of a character (in s) is represented by its subscript. (That is, we rewrite s as $a_1c_1a_2g_1a_3c_2a_4\$$.) For example, a_2 (representing the 2nd appearance of a in s) is in the second place among all the a-characters in both F and L while c_1 the first apperance in both F and L among all the c-characters. In the same way, we can check all the other appearances of different characters.

Now we sort the rows of the matrix alphabetically. We will get another matrix, called the *Burrow-Wheeler Matrix* [7][12][23] and denoted as $BWM(s)$, as demonstrated in Figure 1(c). Especially, the last column of $BWM(s)$, read from top to bottom, is called the BWT-transformation (or the BWT-array) and denoted as $BWT(s)$. So for s = *acagaca*\$, we have $BWT(s)$ = *acg*\$*caaa*.

By the BWM matrix, the LF-mapping is obviously not changed. Surprisingly, the rank correspondence also remains. Even though the ranks of different appearances of a certain character (in F or in L) may be different from before, their rank correspondences are not changed as shown in Figure 2(b), in which a_2 now appears in both F and L as the fourth element among all the a-characters, and c_1 the second element among all the c-characters.

rk_F	F	L	rk_L
–	\$	a_4	1
1	a_4	c_2	1
2	a_3	g_1	1
3	a_1	\$	–
4	a_2	c_1	2
1	c_2	a_3	2
2	c_1	a_1	3
1	g_1	a_2	4

By ranking the elements in F, each element in L is also ranked with the same number.

(a)

$F_\$ = <\$; 1, 1>$

$F_a = <a; 2, 5>$

$F_c = <c; 6, 7>$

$F_g = <g; 8, 8>$

(b)

Figure 2. LF-mapping and tank-correspondence

The first purpose of $BWT(s)$ is for the string compression since same characters with similar *right-contexts* in s tend to be clustered together in $BWT(s)$, as shown by the following example [10][16][40]:

BWT(tomorrow and tomorrow and tomorrow)

= wwwdd nnoooaatttmmmrrrrrrooo \$ooo

Such a transformed string can be effectively compressed and then decompressed. Due to the LF-mapping and the rank correspondence, it can also be easily restored to the original string.

The second purpose is for the string search, which will be discussed in the next subsection in great detail. We need this part of knowledge to develop our method.

B. String Search Using BWT

For the purpose of the string search, the character clustering in F has to be used. Especially, for any DNA sequence, the whole F can be divided into five or less segments: \$-segment, A-segment, C-segment, G-segment, and T-segment, denoted as $F_\$$, F_A, F_C, F_G, F_T, respectively. In addition, for each segment in F, we will rank all its elements from top to bottom, as illustrated in Figure 2(a). \$ is not ranked since it appears only once.

From Figure 2(a), we can see that the rank of a_4, denoted as $rk_F(a_4)$, is 1 since it is the first element in F_A. For the same reason, we have $rk_F(a_3) = 2$, $rk_F(a_1) = 3$, $rk_F(a_2) = 4$, $rk_F(c_2) = 1$, $rk_F(c_1) = 2$, and $rk_F(g_1) = 1$.

It can also be seen that each segment in F can be effectively represented as a triplet of the form: $<\alpha; x_\alpha, y_\alpha>$, where $\alpha \in \Sigma \cup \{\$\}$, and x_α, y_α are the positions of the first and last appearance of α in F, respectively. So the whole F

can be effectively compacted and represented as a set of $|\Sigma| + 1$ triplets, as illustrated in Figure 2(b).

Now, we consider α_j (the jth appearance of α in s). Assume that $rk_F(\alpha_j) = i$. Then, the position where α_j appears in F can be easily determined:

$$F[x_\alpha + i - 1] = \alpha_j. \qquad (2)$$

Besides, if we rank all the elements in L top-down in such a way that an α_j is assigned i if it is the ith appearance among all the appearances of α in L. Then, we will have

$$rk_F(\alpha_j) = rk_L(\alpha_j), \qquad (3)$$

where $rk_L(\alpha_j)$ is the rank assigned to α_j in L.

This equation is due to the rank correspondence between F and L. (See [10][16][40] for a detailed discussion. Also see Figure 2(a) for ease of understanding.)

With the ranks established, a string matching can be very efficiently conducted by using the formulas (2) and (3). To see this, let's consider a pattern string $p = aca$ and try to find all its occurrences in $s = acagaca\$$.

We work on the characters in p in the reverse order.

First, we check $p[3] = a$ in the pattern string p, and then figure out a segment in L, denoted as L', corresponding to $F_a = \langle a; 2, 5\rangle$. So $L' = L[2 .. 5]$, as illustrated in Figure 3(a), where we still use the non-compact F for explanation. In the second step, we check $p[2] = c$, and then search within L' to find the first and last c in L'. We will find $rk_L(c_2) = 1$ and $rk_L(c_1) = 2$. By using (3), we will get $rk_F(c_2) = 1$ and $rk_F(c_1) = 2$. Then, by using (2), we will figure out a sub-segment F' in F: $F[x_c + 1 - 1 .. x_c + 2 - 1] = F[6 + 1 - 1 .. 6 + 2 - 1] = F[6 .. 7]$. (Note that $x_c = 6$. See Figure 2(b) and Figure 3(b).) In the third step, we check $p[1] = a$, and find $L'' = L[6 .. 7]$ corresponding to $F' = F[6 .. 7]$. Repeating the above operation, we will find $rk_L(a_3) = 2$ and $rk_L(a_1) = 3$. See Figure 3(c). Since now we have exhausted all the characters in p and $F[x_a + 2 - 1, x_a + 3 - 1] = F[3, 4]$ contains only two elements, two occurrences of p in s are found. They are a_1 and a_3 in s, respectively.

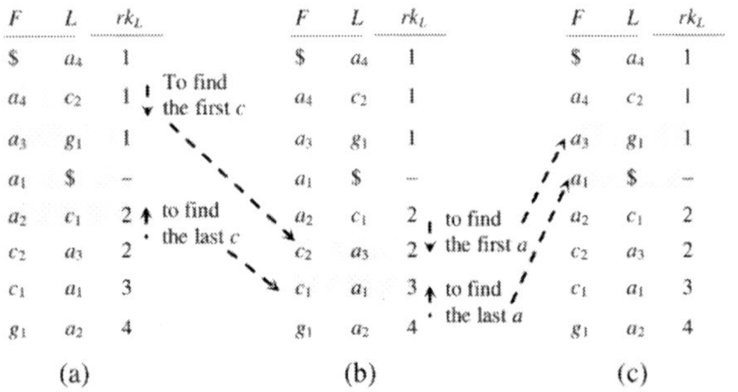

Figure 3. Sample trace

C. RankAll

The dominant cost of the above process is the searching of L in each step. However, this can be dramatically reduced by arranging $|\Sigma|$ arrays each for a character $\alpha \in \Sigma$ such that $\alpha[i]$ (the ith entry in the array for α) is the number of appearances of α within $L[1 .. i]$. See Figure 4(a) for illustration.

Now, instead of scanning a certain segment $L[x .. y]$ ($x \le y$) to find a subrange for a certain $\alpha \in \Sigma$, we can simply look up the array for α to see whether $\alpha[x - 1] = \alpha[y]$. If it is the case, then α does not occur in $L[x .. y]$. Otherwise, $[\alpha[x - 1] + 1, \alpha[y]]$ should be the found range. For example, to find the first and the last appearance of c in $L[2 .. 5]$, we only need to find $c[2 - 1] = c[1] = 0$ and $c[5] = 2$. So the corresponding range is $[c[2 - 1] + 1, c[5]] = [1, 2]$.

j	F	L	\$	a	c	g	t
1	\$	a_4	0	1	0	0	0
2	a_4	c_2	0	1	1	0	0
3	a_3	g_1	0	1	1	1	0
4	a_1	\$	1	1	1	1	0
5	a_2	c_1	1	1	2	1	0
6	c_2	a_3	1	2	2	1	0
7	c_1	a_1	1	3	2	1	0
8	g_1	a_2	1	4	2	1	0

(a)

i	A_a	A_c	A_g	A_t
0	0	0	0	0
1	1	1	1	0
2	4	2	1	0

For each $\beta = 4$ values in L, a *rankAll* value is stored.

(b)

Figure 4. *LF*-mapping and rank-correspondence

In this way, the searching of L can be saved and we need only a constant time to determine a subrange for a character encountered during a pattern searching.

The problem of this method is its high space requirement, which can be mitigated by replacing $\alpha[]$ with a compact array A_α for each $\alpha \in \Sigma$, in which, rather than for each $L[i]$ ($i \in \{1, \ldots, n\}$), only for some entries in L the number of their appearances will be stored. For example, we can divide L into a set of buckets of the same size and only for each bucket a value will be stored in A_α. Obviously, doing so, more search will be required. In practice, the size β of a bucket (referred to as a *compact factor*) can be set to different values. For example, we can set $\beta = 4$, indicating that for each four contiguous elements in L a group of $|\Sigma|$ integers (each in an A_α) will be stored. That is, we will not store all the values in Figure 4(a), but only store \$[4], a[4], c[4], g[4], t[4], and \$[8], a[8], c[8], g[8], t[8] in the corresponding compact arrays, as shown in Figure 4(b). However, each $\alpha[j]$ for $\alpha \in \Sigma$ can be easily derived from A_α by using the following formulas:

$$\alpha[j] = A_\alpha[i] + \rho, \qquad (4)$$

where $i = \lfloor j/\beta \rfloor$ and ρ is the number of α's appearances within $L[i \cdot \beta + 1 .. j]$, and

$$\alpha[j] = A_\alpha[i'] - \rho', \qquad (5)$$

where $i' = \lceil j/\beta \rceil$ and ρ' is the number of α's appearances within $L[j + 1 .. i' \cdot \beta]$.

Thus, we need two procedures: *sDown*(L, j, β, α) and *sUp*(L, j, β, α) to find ρ and ρ', respectively. In terms of whether $j - i \cdot \beta \le i' \cdot \beta - j$, we will call *sDown*($L$, j, β, α) or *sUp*(L, j, β, α) so that fewer entries in L will be scanned to find $\alpha[j]$.

Finally, we notice that the column for \$ can always be divided into two parts. In the first part, each entry is 0 while in the second part each entry is 1 (see Figure 4(a)). So we can simply keep a number to indicate where it is divided, instead of storing the whole column.

D. Construction of BWT arrays

For self-explanation, we describe how a BWT array is constructed [10][16][26][40] in this subsection.

As mentioned above, a string $s = a_0a_1 \dots a_{n-1}$ is always ended with \$ (i.e., $a_i \in \Sigma$ for $i = 0, \dots, n-2$, and a_{n-1} = \$). Let $s[i] = a_i$ ($i = 0,1, \dots, n-1$) be the ith character of s, $s[i..\ j] = a_i \dots a_j$ a substring and $s[i\ ..\ n-1]$ a suffix of s. Suffix array H of s is a permutation of the integers $0, \dots, n-1$ such that $H[i]$ is the start position of the ith smallest suffix. The relationship between H and the BWT array L can be determined by the following formulas:

$$\begin{cases} L[i] = \$, & \text{if } H[i] = 0; \\ L[i] = s[H[i]-1], & \text{otherwise.} \end{cases} \qquad (6)$$

Once L is determined, F can also be created immediately by using formula (1).

IV. MAIN ALGORITHM

In this section, we present our algorithm to search a bunch of reads against a genome s. Its main idea is to organize all the reads into a trie T and search T against L to avoid any possible redundancy. First, we present the concept of tries in Subsection *A*. Then, in Subsection *B*, we discuss our basic algorithm for the task. We improve this algorithm in Section V.

A. Tries over Reads

Let $\boldsymbol{D} = \{s_1, \dots, s_n\}$ be a DNA database, where each s_i ($i = 1, \dots, n$) is a genome, a very long string $\in \Sigma^*$ ($\Sigma = \{A, T, C, G\}$). Let $\boldsymbol{R} = \{r_1, \dots, r_m\}$ be a set of *reads* with each r_j being a short string $\in \Sigma^*$. The problem is to find, for every r_j's ($j = 1, \dots, m$), all their occurrences in an s_i ($i = 1, \dots, n$) in $\boldsymbol{D}$.

A simple way to do this is to check each r_j against s_i one by one, for which different string searching methods can be used, such as suffix trees [37][45], BW-transformation [10], and so on. Each of them needs only a linear time (in the size of s_i) to find all occurrences of r_j in s_i. However, in the case of very large m, which is typical in the new genomic research, one-by-one search of reads against an s_i is no more acceptable in practice and some efforts should be spent on reducing the running time caused by huge m.

Our general idea is to organize all r_j's into a trie structure T and search T against s_i with the BW-transformation being used to check the string matching. For this purpose, we will first attach \$ to the end of each s_i ($i = 1, \dots, n$) and construct $BWT(s_i)$. Then, attach \$ to the end of each r_j ($j = 1, \dots, m$) to construct $T = trie(\boldsymbol{R})$ over $\boldsymbol{R}$ as below.

If $|\boldsymbol{R}| = 0$, $trie(\boldsymbol{R})$ is, of course, empty. For $|\boldsymbol{R}| = 1$, $trie(\boldsymbol{R})$ is a single node. If $|\boldsymbol{R}| > 1$, $\boldsymbol{R}$ is split into $|\Sigma| = 5$ (possibly empty) subsets $\boldsymbol{R}_1, \boldsymbol{R}_2, \dots, \boldsymbol{R}_5$ so that each $\boldsymbol{R}_i$ ($i \in \{1, \dots, 5\}$) contains all those sequences with the same first character $\alpha_i \in \{A, T, C, G\} \cup \{\$\}$. The tries: $trie(\boldsymbol{R}_1)$, $trie(\boldsymbol{R}_2)$, ..., $trie(\boldsymbol{R}_5)$ are constructed in the same way except that at the kth step, the splitting of sets is based on the kth characters in the sequences. They are then connected from their respective roots to a single node to create $trie(\boldsymbol{R})$.

Example 1 As an example, consider a set of four reads:

r_1: ACAGA
r_2: AG
r_3: ACAGC
r_4: CA

For these reads, a trie can be constructed as shown in Figure 5(a). In this trie, v_0 is a virtual root, labeled with an *empty* character ε while any other node v is labeled with a *real* character, denoted as $l(v)$. Therefore, all the characters on a path from the root to a leaf spell a read. For instance, the path from v_0 to v_8 corresponds to the third read r_3 = ACAGC\$. Note that each leaf node v is labelled with \$ and associated with a *read identifier*, denoted as $\gamma(v)$.

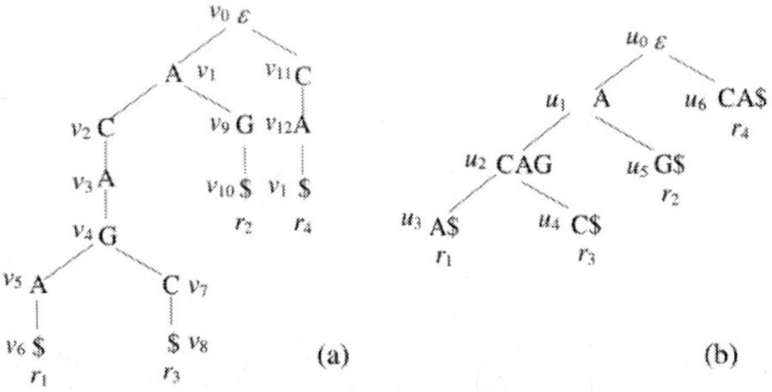

Figure 5. A trie and its compact version

The size of a trie can be significantly reduced by replacing each branchless path segment with a single edge. By a branchless path we mean a path P such that each node on P, except the starting and ending nodes, has only one incoming and one outgoing edge. For example, the trie shown in Figure 5(a) can be compacted to a reduced one as shown in Figure 5(b).

B. Integrating BWT Search with Trie Search

It is easy to see that exploring a path in a trie T over a set of reads $\boldsymbol{R}$ corresponds to scanning a read $r \in \boldsymbol{R}$. If we explore, at the same time, the L array established over a *reversed* genome sequence $\bar{s}$, we will find all the occurrences of r (without \$ involved) in s. This idea leads to the following algorithm, which is in essence a depth-first search of T by using a stack S to control the process. However, each entry in S is a triplet $<v, a, b>$ with v being a node in T and $a \le b$, used to indicate a subsegment in $F_{l(v)}[a\ ..\ b]$. For example, when searching the trie shown in Figure 5(a) against the L array shown in Figure 2(a), we may have an entry like $<v_1, 1, 4>$ in S to represent a subsegment $F_A[1\ ..\ 4]$ (the first to the fourth entry in F_A) since $l(v_1)$ = 'A'. In addition, for technical convenience, we use F_ε to represent the whole F. Then, $F_\varepsilon[a\ ..\ b]$ represents the segment from the ath to the bth entry in F.

In the algorithm, we first push $<root(T), 1, |s|>$ into stack S (lines 1 – 2). Then, we go into the main **while-loop** (lines 3 – 16), in which we will first pop out the top element from S, stored as a triplet $<v, a, b>$ (line 4). Then, for each child v_j of v, we will check whether it is a leaf node. If it is the case, a quadruple $<\gamma(v_i), l(v), a, b>$ will be added to the result $\Re$ (see line 7), which records all the occurrences of a read represented by $\gamma(v_i)$ in s. (In practice, we store compressed suffix arrays [35, 40] and use formulas (1) and (6) to calculate positions of reads in s.) Otherwise, we will determine a segment in L by calculating x' and y' (see lines 8 – 9). Then, we will use $sDown(L, x' - 1, \beta, \alpha)$ or $sUp(L, x' - 1, \beta, \alpha)$ to find $\alpha[x' - 1]$ as discussed in the previous section. (See line 10.) Next, we will find $\alpha[y']$ in a similar way. (See line 11.) If $\alpha[y'] > \alpha[x' - 1]$, there are some occurrences of α in $L[x' .. y']$ and we will push $<v_i, \alpha[x' - 1] + 1, \alpha[y']>$) into S, where $\alpha[x' - 1] + 1$ and $\alpha[y']$ are the first and last rank of α's appearances within $L[x' .. y']$, respectively. (See lines 12 – 13.) If $\alpha[y'] = \alpha[x' - 1]$, α does not occur in $L[x' .. y']$ at all and nothing will be done in this case. The following example helps for illustration.

ALGORITHM *readSearch*(*T*, *LF*, β)

```
begin
1.  v ← root(T); ℜ ← Φ;
2.  push(S, <v, 1, |s|>);
3.  while S is not empty do {
4.    <v, a, b> ← pop(S);
5.    let v_1, …, v_k be the children of v;
6.    for i = k downto 1 do {
7.      if v_i is a leaf then ℜ ← ℜ ∪ {<γ(v_i), l(v), a, b>};
8.      else{assume that F_l(v) = <l(v); x, y>;
9.          x' ← x + a - 1; y' ← x + b - 1; α ← l(v_i);
10.         find α[x' - 1] by sDown(L, x'-1, β, α) or sUp(L, x'-1, β, α);
11.         find α[y'] by sDown(L, y', β, α) or sUp(L, y', β, α);
12.         if α[ y'] > α[ x' - 1] then
13.            push(S, <v_i, α[x' - 1] + 1, α[y']>);
14.         }
15.   }
16. }
end
```

Figure 6. Algorithm *readSearch*( )

Example 2 Consider all the reads given in Example 1 again. The trie T over these reads are shown in Figure 5(a). In order to find all the occurrences of these reads in s = ACAGACA\$, we will run *readSearch*( ) on T and the LF of $\bar{s}$ shown in Figure 7(b). (Note that $s = \bar{s}$ for this special string, but the ordering of the subscripts of characters is reversed. In Figure 7(a), we also show the corresponding BWM matrix for ease of understanding.)

In the execution of *readSearch*( ), the following steps will be carried out.

Step 1: push $<v_0, 1, 8>$ into S, as illustrated in Figure 7(c).

Step 2: pop out the top element $<v_0, 1, 8>$ from S. Figure out the two children of v_0: v_1 and v_{11}. First, for v_{11}, we will use A_c to find the first and last appearances of $l(v_{11})$ = 'C' in $L[1 .. 8]$ and their respective ranks: 1 and 2. Assume that $\beta = 4$ (i.e., for each 4 consecutive entries in L a *rankAll* value is stored.) Further assume that for each A_α ($\alpha \in \{a, c, g, t\}$) $A_\alpha[0] = 0$. The ranks are calculated as follows.

(a)	j	F	L
$\$ \ A_4 C_2 A_3 G_1 A_2 C_1 A_1$	1	\$	A_4
$A_1 \$ \ A_4 C_2 A_3 G_1 A_2 C_1$	2	A_4	C_2
$A_2 C_1 A_1 \$ \ A_4 C_2 A_3 G_1$	3	A_3	G_1
$A_4 C_2 A_3 G_1 A_2 C_1 A_1 \$$	4	A_1	\$
$A_3 G_1 A_2 C_1 A_1 \$ \ A_4 C_2$	5	A_2	C_1
$C_1 A_1 \$ \ A_4 C_2 A_3 G_1 A_2$	6	C_2	A_3
$C_2 A_3 G_1 A_2 C_1 A_1 \$ \ A_4$	7	C_1	A_1
$G_1 A_2 C_1 A_1 \$ \ A_4 C_2 A_3$	8	G_1	A_2

(a) (b)

(c)

Figure 7. Illustration for Step 1

- To find the rank of the first appearance of 'C' in $L[1 .. 8]$, we will first calculate $C[0]$ by using formula (4) or (5) (i.e., by calling $sDown(L, 0, 4, C)$ or $sUp(L, 0, 4, C)$). Recall that whether (4) or (5) is used depends on whether $j - i \cdot \beta \le i' \cdot \beta - j$, where $i = \lfloor j/\beta \rfloor$ and $i' = \lceil j/\beta \rceil$. For $C[0]$, $j = 0$. Then, $i = i' = 0$ and (4) will be used:

  $$C[0] = A_c[\lfloor 0/4 \rfloor] + \rho.$$

  Since $A_c[\lfloor 0/4 \rfloor] = A_c[0] = 0$ and the search of $L[i \cdot \beta .. j] = L[0 .. 0]$ finds $\rho = 0$, $C[0]$ is equal to 0.
- To find the rank of the last appearance of 'C' in $L[1 .. 8]$, we will calculate $C[8]$ by using (4) for the same reason as above. For $C[8]$, we have $j = 8$ and $i = 2$. So we have

  $$C[8] = A_c[\lfloor 8/4 \rfloor] + \rho.$$

  Since $A_c[\lfloor 8/4 \rfloor] = A_c[2] = 2$, and the search of $L[i \cdot \beta .. j] = L[8 .. 8]$ finds $\rho = 0$, we have $C[8] = 2$.

So the ranks of the first and the last appearances of 'C' are $C[0] + 1 = 1$, and $C[8] = 2$, respectively. Push $<v_{11}, 1, 2>$ into S.

Next, for v_1, we will do the same work to find the first and last appearances of $l(v_1)$ = 'A' and their respective ranks: 1 and 4; and push $<v_1, 1, 4>$ into S. Now S contains two entries as shown in Figure 8(a) after step 2.

Step 3: pop out the top element $<v_1, 1, 4>$ from S. v_1 has two children v_2 and v_9. Again, for v_9 with $l(v_9)$ = 'G', we will use A_g to find the first and last appearances of G in $L[2 .. 5]$ (corresponding to $F_A[1 .. 4]$) and their respective ranks: 1 and 1. In the following, we show the whole working process.

- To find the rank of the first appearance of 'G' in $L[2 .. 5]$, we will first calculate $G[1]$. We have $j = 1$, $i = \lfloor j/\beta \rfloor = \lfloor 1/4 \rfloor = 0$ and $i' = \lceil 1/4 \rceil = 1$. Since $j - i \cdot \beta = 0 < i' \cdot \beta - j = 3$, formula (4) will be used:

  $$G[1] = A_g[\lfloor 1/4 \rfloor] + \rho.$$

  Since $A_g[\lfloor 0/4 \rfloor] = A_g[0] = 0$ and search of $L[i \cdot \beta .. j] = L[0 .. 0]$ finds $\rho = 0$, $G[1]$ is equal to 0.
- To find the rank of the last appearance of 'G' in $L[2 .. 5]$, we will calculate $G[5]$ by using (4) based on an analysis similar to above. For $G[5]$, we have $j = 5$ and $i = \lfloor j/\beta \rfloor = 1$. So we have

  $$G[5] = A_g[\lfloor 5/4 \rfloor] + \rho.$$

Since $A_g[\lfloor 5/4 \rfloor] = A_g[1] = 1$, and search of $L[i \cdot \beta \ .. \ j] = L[4 \ .. \ 5]$ finds $\rho = 0$, we have $G[5] = 1$.

We will push $<v_9, G[1] + 1, G[5]> = <v_9, 1, 1>$ into S.

For v_2 with $l(v_2) = $ 'C', we will find the first and last appearances of C in $L[2 \ .. \ 5]$ and their ranks: 1 and 2. Then, push $<v_2, 1, 2>$ in to S. After this step, S will be changed as shown in Figure 8(b).

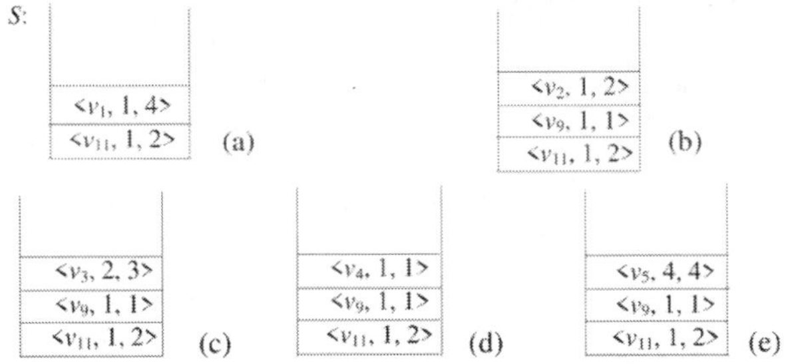

Figure 8. Illustration for stack changes

In the subsequent steps 4, 5, and 6, S will be consecutively changed as shown in Figure 8(c), (d), and (e), respectively.

In step 7, when we pop the top element $<v_5, 4, 4>$, we meet a node with a single child v_6 labeled with \$. In this case, we will store $<\gamma(v_6), l(v_5), 4, 4> = <r_1, A, 4, 4>$ in $\Re$ as part of the result (see line 7 in *searchRead*( ).) From this we can find that $rk_L(A_3) = 4$ (note that the same element in both F and L has the same rank), which shows that in $\bar{s}$ the substring of length $|r_1|$ staring from A_3 is an occurrence of r_1. □

C. *Time Complexity and Correctness Proof*

In this subsection, we analyze the time complexity of *readSearch*(T, LF, β) and prove its correctness.

C.1 *Time complexity*

In the main **while**-loop, each node v in T is accessed only once. If the rankAll arrays are fully stored, only a constant time is needed to determine the range for $l(v)$. So the time complexity of the algorithm is bounded by $O(|T|)$. If only the compact arrays (for the rankAll information) are stored, the running time is increased to $O(|T| \cdot \beta)$, where β is the corresponding compact factor. It is because in this case, for each encountered node in T, $O(\frac{1}{2} \cdot \beta)$ entries in L may be checked in the worst case.

C.2 *Correctness*

Proposition 1 Let T be a trie constructed over a collections of reads: $r_1, \ldots, r_m$, and LF a *BWT*-mapping established for a reversed genome $\bar{s}$. Let β be the compact factor for the *allRank* arrays, and $\Re$ the result of *readSearch*(T, LF, β). Then, for each r_j, if it occurs in s, there is a quadruple $\{<\gamma(v_i), l(v), a, b>\} \in \Re$ such that $\gamma(v_i) = r_j$, $l(v)$ is equal to the last character of r_j, and $F_{l(v)}[a], F_{l(v)}[a+1], \ldots, F_{l(v)}[b]$ show all the occurrences of r_j in s.

Proof. We prove the proposition by induction on the height h of T.

Basic step. When $h = 1$. The proposition trivially holds.

Induction hypothesis. Suppose that when the height of T is h, the proposition holds. We consider the case that the height of T is $h + 1$. Let v_0 be the root with $l(v_0) = \varepsilon$. Let $v_1, \ldots, v_k$ be the children of v_0. Then, $height(T[v_i]) \leq h$ $(i = 1, \ldots, k)$, where $T[v_i]$ stands for the subtree rooted at v_i and $height(T[v_i])$ for the height of $T[v_i]$. Let $l(v_i) = \alpha$ and $F_\alpha = <\alpha; a, b>$. Let $v_{i1}, \ldots, v_{il}$ be the children of v_i. Assume that x and y be the ranks of the first and last appearances of α in L. According to the induction hypothesis, searching $T[v_{ij}]$ against $L[a' \ .. \ b']$, where $a' = a + x - 1$ and $b' = a + y - 1$, the algorithm will find all the locations of all those reads with $l(v_i)$ as the first character. This completes the proof. □

V. IMPROVEMENTS

The algorithm discussed in the previous section can be greatly improved by rearranging the search of a segment of L when we visit a node v in T. Such a search has to be done once for each of its children by calling *sDown*( ) or *sUp*( ) (see lines 10 - 11 in *readSearch*( ).) Instead of searching the segment for each child separately, we can manage to search the segment only once for all the children of v. To this end, we will use integers to represent characters in Σ. For example, we can use 1, 2, 3, 4, 5 to represent A, C, G, T, \$ in a DNA sequence. In addition, two kinds of simple data structures will be employed:

- B_v: a Boolean array of size $|\Sigma| \cup \{\$\}$ associated with node v in T, in which, for each $i \in \Sigma$, $B_v[i] = 1$ if there exists a child node u of v such that $l(u) = i$; otherwise, $b_v[i] = 0$.
- c_i: a counter associated with $i \in \Sigma$ to record the number of i's appearances during a search of some segment in L.

See Figure 9 for illustration.

With these data structures, we change *sDown*(L, j, β, α) and *sUp*(L, j, β, α) to *sDown*(L, j, β, v) and *sUp*(L, j, β, v), respectively, to search L for all the children of v, but only in one scanning of L.

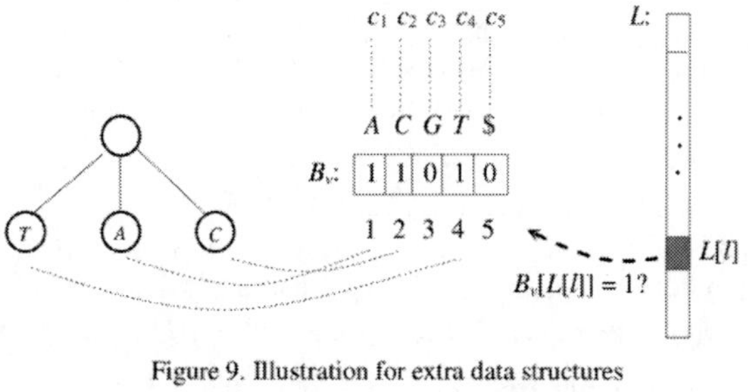

Figure 9. Illustration for extra data structures

In *sDown*(L, j, β, v), we will search a segment $L[\lfloor j/\beta \rfloor \cdot \beta + 1 \ .. \ j]$ from top to bottom, and store the result in an array D of length $|\Sigma|$, in which each entry $D[i]$ is the rank of i (representing a character), equal to $c_i + A_i[\lfloor j/\beta \rfloor]$, where c_i is the number of i's appearances within $L[\lfloor j/\beta \rfloor \cdot \beta + 1 \ .. \ j]$.

In the algorithm, $L[j' .. j]$ is scanned only once in the main **while**-loop (see lines 3 – 6), where $j' = \lfloor j/\beta \rfloor \cdot \beta + 1$ (see line 2.) For each encountered entry $L[l]$ ($j' \leq l \leq j$), we will check whether $B_v[L[l]] = 1$ (see line 4.) If it is the case, $c_{L[l]}$ will be increased by 1 to count encountered entries which are equal to $L[l]$. After the **while**-loop, we compute the ranks for all the characters respectively labeling the children of v (see lines 7 – 8).

FUNCTION *sDown*(L, j, β, v)

begin
1. $c_i \leftarrow 0$ for each $i \in \Sigma$;
2. $l \leftarrow \lfloor j/\beta \rfloor \cdot \beta + 1$;
3. **while** $l \leq j$ **do** {
4. **if** $B_v[L[l]] = 1$ **then** $c_{L[l]} \leftarrow c_{L[l]} + 1$;
5. $l \leftarrow l + 1$;
6. }
7. **for** $k = 1$ to $|\Sigma|$ **do** {
8. **if** $B_v[k] = 1$ **then** $D[k] \leftarrow A_k[\lfloor j/\beta \rfloor] + c_k$;
9. }
10. return D;

end

Figure 10. Algorithm *sDown*( )

sUp(L, j, β, v) is dual to *sDown*(L, j, β, v), in which a segment of L will be search bottom-up.

FUNCTION *sUp*(L, j, β, v)

begin
1. $c_i \leftarrow 0$ for each $i \in \Sigma$;
2. $l \leftarrow \lceil j/\beta \rceil \cdot \beta$;
3. **while** $l \geq j + 1$ **do** {
4. **if** $B_v[L[l]] = 1$ **then** $c_{L[l]} \leftarrow c_{L[l]} + 1$;
5. $l \leftarrow l - 1$; }
6. }
7. **for** $k = 1$ to $|\Sigma|$ **do** {
8. **if** $B_v[k] = 1$ **then** $D[k] \leftarrow A_k[\lceil j/\beta \rceil] - c_k$;
9. }
10. return D;

end

Figure 11. Algorithm *sUp*( )

See the following example for illustration.

Example 3 In this example, we trace the working process to generate ranges (by scanning $L[2 .. 5]$) for the two children v_2 and v_9 of v_1. For this purpose, we will calculate $C[1]$, $C[5]$ for $l(v_2)$ = *'C'*, and $G[1]$, $G[5]$ for $l(v_9)$ = *'G'*. First, we notice that $B_{v_1} = [0, 1, 1, 0, 0]$ and all the counters c_1, c_2, c_3, c_4, c_5 are set to 0.

By running *sDown*(L, 1, 4, v_1) to get $C[1]$ and $G[1]$, part of L will be scanned once, during which only one entry $L[1]$ = 'A' (represented by 1) is accessed. Since $B_{v_1}[L[1]] = B_{v_1}[1] = 0$, c_1 remains unchanged. Especially, both c_2 (for *'C'*) and c_3 (for *'G'*) remain 0. Then, $C[1] = A_c[\lfloor 1/4 \rfloor] + c_2 = 0$ and $G[1] = A_g[\lfloor 1/4 \rfloor] + c_3 = 0$.

By running *sDown*(L, 5, 4, v_1) to get $C[5]$ and $G[5]$, another part of L will be scanned, also only once, during which merely one entry $L[5]$ = *'C'* (represented by 2) is accessed. Since $B_{v_1}[L[5]] = B_{v_1}[2] = 1$, c_2 will be changed to 1. But c_3 (for *'G'*) remain 0. Then, we have $C[5] = A_c[\lfloor 5/4 \rfloor] + c_2 = 2$ and $G[5] = A_g[\lfloor 5/4 \rfloor] + c_3 = 1$.

Thus, the range for $l(v_2)$ = *'C'* is $[C[1] + 1, C[5]] = [1, 2]$, and the range for $l(v_9)$ = *'G'* is $[G[1] + 1, G[5]] = [1, 1]$. □

By using the above two procedures, our improved algorithm can be described as follows.

ALGORITHM *rS*(T, LF, β)

begin
1. $v \leftarrow root(T)$;
2. $push(S, \langle v, 1, |\Sigma|\rangle)$;
3. **while** S is not empty **do** {
4. $\langle v, a, b\rangle \leftarrow pop(S)$;
5. let $v_1, \ldots, v_k$ be all those children of v, which are labeled with \$;
6. let $u_1, \ldots, u_j$ be all the rest children of v;
7. **for** each $j \in \{1, \ldots, k\}$ **do** { $\mathfrak{R} \leftarrow \mathfrak{R} \cup \{\langle \gamma(v_j), l(v), a, b\rangle\}$;
8. assume that $F_{l(v)} = \langle l(v); x, y\rangle$;
9. $x' \leftarrow x + a - 1$; $y' \leftarrow x + b - 1$;
10. call *sDown*(L, x' - 1, β, v) or *sUp*(L, x' - 1, β, v) to find the ranks of the first appearances of all the labels of the children of v: $r(u_1), \ldots, r(u_j)$;
11. call *sDown*(L, y', β, v) or *sUp*(L, y', β, v) to find the ranks of the last appearances of all the labels of the children of v: $r'(u_1), \ldots, r'(u_j)$;
12. **for** $l = j$ **downto** 1 **do** { $push(S, \langle u_l, r(u_l), r'(u_l)\rangle)$ };
13. }

end

Figure 12. Algorithm *rR*( )

The main difference of the above algorithm from *readSearch*( ) consists in the different ways to search $L[a .. b]$. Here, to find the ranks of the first appearances of all the labels of the children of v, *sDown*( ) or *sUp*( ) is called to scan part of L only once (while in *readSearch*( ) this has to be done once for each different child.) See line 10. Similarly, to find the ranks of the last appearances of these labels, another part of L is also scanned only once. See line 11. All the other operations are almost the same as in *readSearch*( ).

VI. Experiments

In our experiments, we have tested altogether five different methods:

- *Burrows Wheeler Transformation* (BWT for short),
- *Suffix tree based* (Suffix for short),
- *Hash table based* (Hash for short),
- *Trie-BWT* (tBWT for short, discussed in this paper),
- *Improved Trie-BWT* (itBWT for short, discussed in this paper).

Among them, the codes for the suffix tree based and hash based methods are taken from the *gsuffix* package [7] while all the other three algorithms are implemented by ourselves. All of them are able to find all occurrences of every read in a genome. The codes are written in C++, compiled by GNU make utility with optimization of level 2. In addition, all of our experiments are performed on a 64-bit Ubuntu operating system, run on a single core of a 2.40GHz Intel Xeon E5-2630 processor with 32GB RAM.

The test results are categorized in two groups: one is on a set of synthetic data and another is on a set of real data. For both of them, five reference genomes are used:

TABLE I. CHARACTERISTICS OF GENOMES

Genomes	Genome sizes (bp)
Rat chr1 (Rnor_6.0)	290,094,217
C. merolae (ASM9120v1)	16,728,967
C. elegans (WBcel235)	103,022,290
Zebra fish (GRCz10)	1,464,443,456
Rat (Rnor_6.0)	2,909,701,677

A. *Tests on Synthetic Data Sets*

All the synthetic data are created by simulating reads from the five genomes shown in Table I, with varying lengths and amounts. It is done by using the *wgsim* program included in the *SAMtools* package [33] with default model for single reads simulation.

Over such data, the impact of five factors on the searching time are tested: number n of reads, length l of reads, size s of genomes, compact factors f_1 of *rankAlls* (see Subsection *C* in III) and compression factors f_2 of suffix arrays [35][40], which are used to find locations of matching reads (in a reference genome) in terms of formula (6) (see Subsection *D* in III).

A.1 Tests with varying amount of reads

In this experiment, we vary the amount n of reads with n = 5, 10, 15, … , 50 millions while the reads are 50 bps or 100 bps in length extracted randomly from *Rat chr1* and *C. merlae* genomes. For this test, the compact factors f_1 of *rankAlls* are set to be 32, 64, 128, 256, and the compression factors f_2 of suffix arrays are set to 8, 16, 32, 64, respectively. These two factors are increasingly set up as the amount of reads gets increased.

In Figures 13(a) and (b), we report the test results of searching the Rat chr1 for matching reads of 50 and 100 bps, respectively. From these two figures, it can be clearly seen that the hash based method has the worst performance while ours works best. For short reads (of length 50 bps) the suffix-based is better than the BWT, but for long reads (of length 100 bps) they are comparable. The poor performance of the hash-based is due to its inefficient brute-force searching of genomes while for both the BWT and the suffix-based it is due to the huge amount of reads and each time only one read is checked. In the opposite, for both our methods tBWT and itBWT, the use of tries enables us to avoid repeated checkings for similar reads.

In these two figures, the time for constructing tries over reads is not included. It is because in the biological research a trie can be used repeatedly against different genomes, as well as often updated genomes. However, even with the time for constructing tries involved, our methods are still superior since the tries can be established very fast as demonstrated in

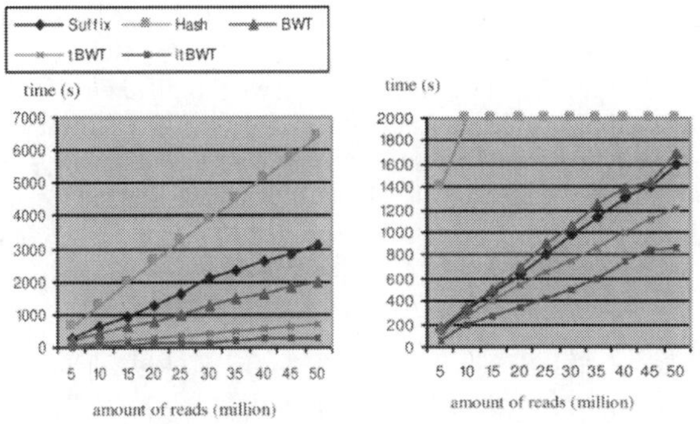

(a) (b)

Figure 13. Test results on varying amount of reads

Table II, in which we show the times for constructing tries over different amounts of reads.

TABLE II. TIME FOR TRIE CONSTRUCTION OVER READS OF LENGTH 100 BPS

No. of reads	30M	35M	40M	45M	50M
Time for Trie Con.	51s	63s	82s	95s	110s

The difference between tBWT and itBWT is due to the different number of BWT array accesses as shown in Table III. By an access of a BWT array, we will scan a segment in the array to find the first and last appearance of a certain character from a read (by tBWT) or a set of characters from more than one read (by itBWT).

TABLE III. NO. OF BWT ARRAY ACCESSES

No. of reads	30M	35M	40M	45M	50M
tBWT	47856K	55531K	63120K	70631K	78062K
itBWT	19105K	22177K	25261K	28227K	31204K

Figures 14(a) and (b) show respectively the results for reads of length 50 bps and 100 bps over the *C. merolae* genome. Again, our methods outperform the other three methods.

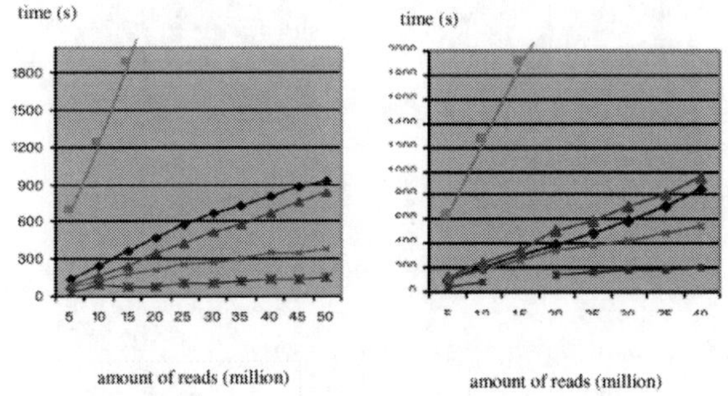

(a) (b)

Figure 14. Test results on varying amount of reads

A.2 Tests with varying length of reads

In this experiment, we test the impact of the read length on performance. For this, we fix all the other four factors but vary length l of simulated reads with $l = 35, 50, 75, 100, 125, \ldots, 200$. The results in Figure 15(a) shows the difference among five methods, in which each tested set has 20 million reads simulated from the Rat chr1 genome with $f_1 = 128$ and $f_2 = 16$. In Figure 15(b), the results show the the case that each set has 50 million reads. Figures 16(a) and (b) show the results of the same data settings but on C. merlae genome.

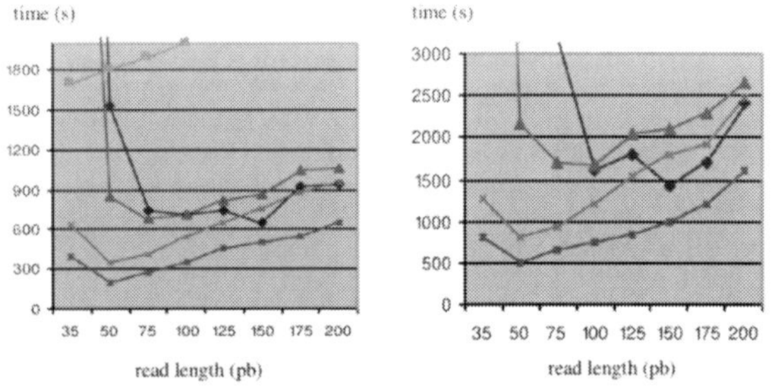

(a) (b)

Figure 15. Test results on varying length of reads

Again, in this test, the hash based performs worst while the suffix tree and the BWT method are comparable. Both our algorithms uniformally outperform the others when searching on short reads (shorter than 100 bps). It is because shorter reads tend to have multiple occurrences in genomes, which makes the trie used in tBWT and itBWT more beneficial. However, for long reads, the suffix tree beats the BWT since on one hand long reads have fewer repeats in a genome, and on the other hand higher possibility that variations occurred in long reads may result in earlier termination of a searching process. In practice, short reads are more often than long reads.

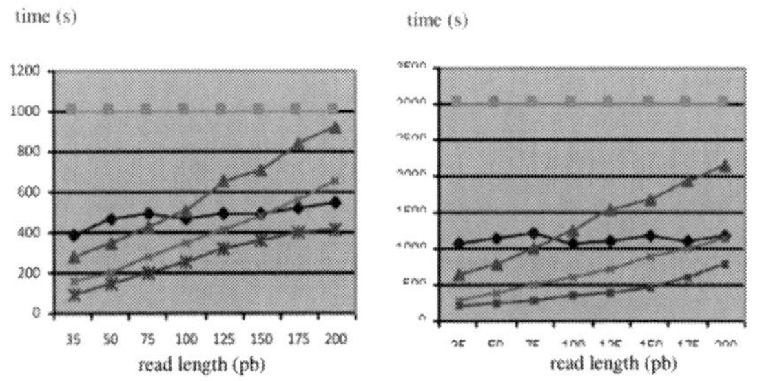

(a) (b)

Figure 16. Test results on varying length of reads

A.3 Tests with varying sizes of genome

To examine the impacts of varying sizes of genomes, we have made four tests with each testing a certain set of reads against different genomes shown in Table 1. To be consistent with foregoing experiments, factors except sizes of genomes remain the same for each test with $f_1 = 128$ and $f_2 = 16$. In Figure 17(a) and (b), we show the searching time on each genome for 20 million and 50 million reads of 50 bps, respectively. Figures 18(a) and (b) demonstrate the results of 20 million and 50 million reads but with each read being of 100 bps.

These figures show that, in general, as the size of a genome increases the time of read aligning for all the tested algorithms become longer. We also notice that the larger the size of a genome, the bigger the gaps between our methods and the other algorithms. The hash-based is always much slower than the others. For the suffix tree, we only show the matching time for the first three genomes. It is because the testing computer cannot meet its huge memory requirement for indexing the Zebra fish and Rat genomes (which is the main reason why people use the BWT, instead of the suffix tree, in practice.) Details for the 50 bp reads in Figure 17 and Figure 18 show that the tBWT and the itBWT are at least 30% faster than the BWT and the suffix tree, which happened on the *C. elegans* genome. For the Rat genome, our algorithms are even more than six times faster than the others.

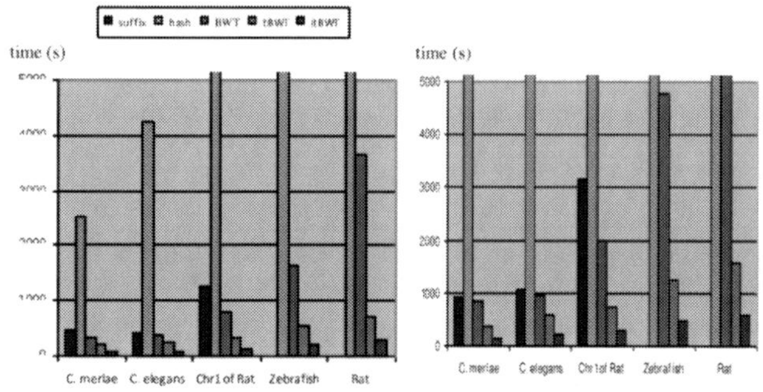

(a) (b)

Figure 17. Test results on varying sizes of genomes

Now let us have a look at Figures 18(a) and (b). Although our methods do not perform as good as for the 50 bp reads due to the increment of length of reads, they still gain at least 22% improvement on speed and nearly 50% acceleration in the best case, compared with the BWT.

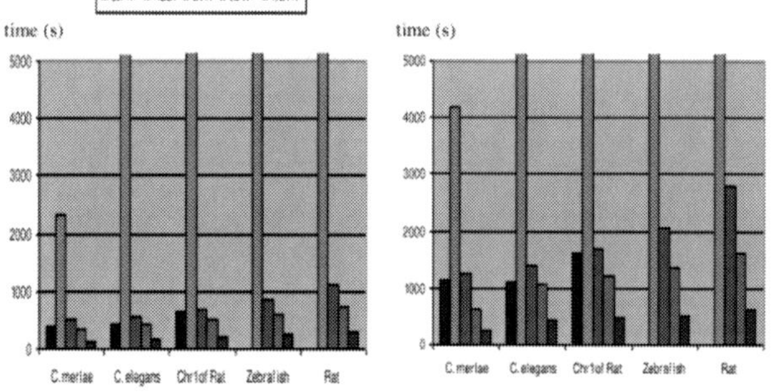

(a) (b)

Figure 18. Test results on varying sizes of genomes

A.4 Tests with varying compact and compression factors

In the experiments, we focus only on the BWT method, since there are no compressions in both the suffix tree and the hash-based method. The following test results are all for 20 million reads with 100 bps in length. We first show the impact of f_1 on performance with f_2 = 16, 64 in Figures 19(a) and (b), respectively. Then we show the effect when f_2 is set to 64, 256 in Figures 20(a) and (b).

From these figures, we can see that the performance of all three methods degrade as f_1 and f_2 increase. Another noticeable point is that both the itBWT and the tBWT are not so sensitive to the high compression rate. Although doubling f_1 or f_2 will slow down their speed, they become faster compared to the BWT. For example, in Figure 19, the time used by the BWT grows 80% by increasing f_1 from 8 to 64, whereas the growth of time used by the tBWT is only 50%. In addition, the factor f_1 has smaller impact on the itBWT than the BWT and the tBWT, since the extra data structure used in the itBWT effectively reduced the processing time of the trie nodes by half or more.

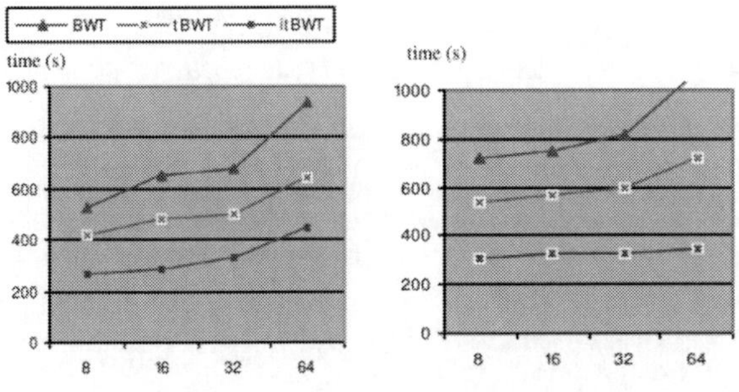

Figure 19. Test results on varying compact and compression factors

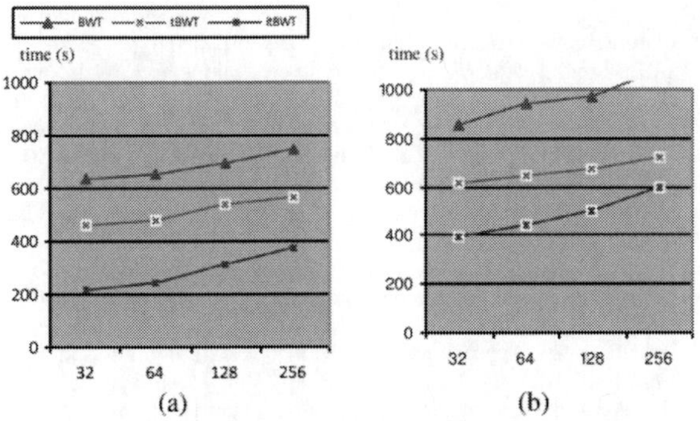

Figure 20. Test results on varying compact and compression factors

B. *Tests on Real Data Sets*

For the performance assessment on real data, we obtain RNA-sequence data from the project conducted in an RNA laboritary at University of Manitoba [23]. This project includes over 500 million single reads produced by Illumina from a rat sample. Length of these reads are between 36 bps and 100 bps after trimming using Trimmomatic [8]. The reads in the project are divided into 9 samples with different amount ranging between 20 million and 75 million. Two tests have been conducted. In the first test, we mapped the 9 samples back to rat genome of ENSEMBL release 79 [13]. We were not able to test the suffix tree due to its huge index size. The hash-based method was ignored as well since its running time was too high in comparison with the BWT. In order to balance between searching speed and memory usage of the BWT index, we set f_1 = 128, f_2 = 16 and repeated the experiment 20 times. Figure 17(a) shows the average time consumed for each algorithm on the 9 samples.

Since the source of RNA-sequence data is the transcripts, the expressed part of the genome, we did a second test, in which we mapped the 9 samples again directly to the Rat *transcriptome*. This is the assembly of all transcripts in the Rat genome. This time more reads, which failed to be aligned in the first test, are able to be exactly matched. This result is showed in Figure 21(b).

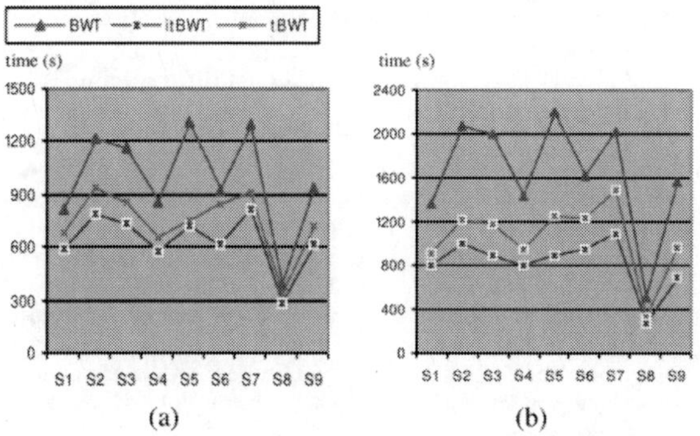

Figure 21. Test results on real data

From Figures 21(a) and (b), we can see that the test results for real data set are consistent with the simulated data. Our algorithms are faster than the BWT on all 9 samples. Counting the whole data set together, itBWT is more than 40% faster compared with the BWT. Although the performance would be dropped by taking tries' construction time into consideration, we are still able to save 35% time using itBWT.

VII. CONCLUSION AND FUTURE WORK

In this paper, a new method to search a large volume of pattern strings against a single long target string is proposed, aiming at efficient next-generation sequencing in DNA databases. The main idea is to combine the search of tries constructed over the patterns and the search of the BWT indexes over the target. Especially, the so-called multiple-character checking has been introduced, which reduces the multiple scanning of a BWT array to a single search of it. Extensive experiments have been conducted, which show that our method improves the running time of the traditional methods by an order of magnitude or more.

As a future work, we will extend the discussed method to handle inexact string matches, such as the string matching with k-mismatches and k-errors, as well as patterns containing 'don't-cares'. It is very challenging to integrate the existing techniques for treating mismatches into the BWT-transformation.

REFERENCES

[1] A.V. Aho and M.J. Corasick, "Efficient string matching: an aid to bibliographic search," Communication of the ACM, Vol. 23, No. 1, pp. 333 -340, June 1975.

[2] A. Amir, M. Lewenstein and E. Porat, "Faster algorithms for string matching with k mismatches," Journal of Algorithms, Vol. 50, No. 2, Feb.2004, pp. 257-275.

[3] A. Apostolico and R. Giancarlo, "The Boyer-Moore-Galil string searching strategies revisited," SIAM Journal on Computing, Vol. 15, No. 1, pp. 98 – 105, Feb. 1986.

[4] R.A. Baeza-Yates and G.H. Gonnet, "A new approach to text searching," in N.J. Belkin and C.J. van Rijsbergen (eds.) SIGIR 89, Proc. 12th Annual Intl. ACM Conf. on Research and Development in Information Retrieval, pp. 168 – 175, 1989.

[5] R.A. Baeza-Yates and G.H. Gonnet, "A new approach in text searching," Communication of the ACM, Vol. 35, No. 10, pp. 74 – 82, Oct. 1992.

[6] R.A. Baeza-Yates and C.H. Perleberg, "Fast and practical approximate string matching," in A. Apostolico, M. Crocchemore, Z. Galil, and U. Manber (eds.) Combinatorial Pattern Matching, Lecture Notes in Computer Science, Vol. 644, pp. 185 – 192, Springer-Verlag, Berlin.

[7] S. Bauer, M.H. Schulz, P.N. Robinson, gsuffix: http:://gsuffix. Sourceforge.net/, retrieved: April 2016.

[8] A.M.Bolger, M. Lohse and B. Usadel, "Trimmomatic Bolger: A flexible trimmer for Illumina Sequence Data," Bioinformatics, btu170, 2014.

[9] R.S. Boyer and J.S. Moore, "A fast string searching algorithm," Communication of the ACM, Vol. 20, No. 10, pp. 762 -772, Oct. 1977.

[10] M. Burrows and D.J. Wheeler, "A block-sorting lossless data compression algorithm," http://citeseer.ist.psu.edu/viewdoc/summary?doi=10.1.1.121.6177, retrieved: 2016.

[11] W.L. Chang and J. Lampe, "Theoretical and empirical compaisons of approximate string matching algorithms," in A. Apostolico, M. Crocchemore, Z. Galil, and U. Manber (eds.) Combinatorial Pattern Matching, Lecture Notes in Computer Science, Vol. 644, pp. 175 – 184, Springer-Verlag, Berlin, 1994.

[12] L. Colussi, Z. Galil, and R. Giancarlo, "On the exact complexity of string matching," Proc. 31st Annual IEEE Symposium of Foundation of Computer Science, Vol. 1, pp. 135 – 144, 1990.

[13] F. Cunningham, et al., "Nucleic Acids Research," 2015, 43, Database issue:D662-D669.

[14] S.R. Eddy, "What is dynamic programming?" Nature Biotechnology 22, 909 - 910, (2004) doi:10.1038/nbt0704-909.

[15] A. Ehrenfeucht and D. Haussler, "A new distance metric on strings computable in linear time," Discrete Applied Mathematics, Vol. 20, pp. 191 – 203, 1988.

[16] P. Ferragina and G. Manzini, "Opportunistic data structures with applications," In Proc. 41st Annual Symposium on Foundations of Computer Science, pp. 390 - 398. IEEE, 2000.

[17] Z. Galil, "On improving the worst case running time of the Boyer-Moore string searching algorithm," Communication of the ACM, Vol. 22, No. 9, pp. 505 -508, 1977.

[18] M.C. Harrison, "Implementation of the substring test by hashing," Communication of the ACM, Vol. 14, No. 12, pp. 777- 779, 1971.

[19] H. Jiang, and W.H. Wong, "SeqMap: mapping massive amount of oligonucleotides to the genome," Bioinformatics, **24**, 2395–2396, 2008.

[20] R.L. Karp and M.O. Rabin, "Efficient randomized pattern-matching algorithms," IBM Journal of Research and Development, Vol. 31, No. 2, pp. 249 – 260, March 1987.

[21] D.E. Knuth, The Art of Computer Programming, Vol. 3, Massachusetts, Addison-Wesley Publish Com., 1975.

[22] D.E. Knuth, J.H. Morris, and V.R. Pratt, "Fast pattern matching in strings," SIAM Journal on Computing, Vol. 6, No. 2, pp. 323 – 350, June 1977.

[23] lab website: http://home.cc.umanitoba.ca/~xiej/, retrieved: April 2016.

[24] G.M. Landau and U. Vishkin, "Efficient string matching in the presence of errors," Proc. 26th Annual IEEE Symposium on Foundations of Computer Science, pp. 126 – 136, 1985.

[25] G.M. Landau and U. Vishkin, "Efficient string matching with k mismatches," Theoretical Computer Science, Vol. 43, pp. 239 – 249, 1986.

[26] B. Langmead, "Introduction to the Burrows-Wheeler Transform," www.youtube.com/watch?v=4n7N Pk5lwbI, retrieved: April 2016.

[27] T. Lecroq, "A variation on the Boyer-Moore algorithm," Theoretical Computer Science, Vol. 92, No. 1, pp. 119 – 144, Jan. 1992.

[28] H. Li, et al., "Mapping short DNA sequencing reads and calling variants using mapping quality scores," Genome Res., **18**, 1851–1858, 2008.

[29] R. Li, et al., "SOAP: short oligonucleotide alignment program," Bioinformatics, 24, 713–714, 2008.

[30] H. Li and R. Durbin, "Fast and accurate short read alignment with Burrows–Wheeler Transform," Bioinformatics, Vol. 25 no. 14 2009, pp. 1754–1760.

[31] H. Li and R. Durbin, "Fast and accurate long-read alignment with Burrows–Wheeler Transform," Bioinformatics, Vol. 26 no. 5 2010, pp. 589–595.

[32] H. Li and. Homer, "A survey of sequence alignment algorithms for next-generation sequencing," Briefings in Bioinformatics. 2010;11(5):473-483. doi:10.1093/bib/bbq015.

[33] H. Li, "wgsim: a small tool for simulating sequence reads from a reference genome," https://github.com/lh3/wgsim/, 2014.

[34] H. Lin, et al., "ZOOM! Zillions of oligos mapped," Bioinformatics, 24, 2431–2437, 2008.

[35] U. Manber and E.W. Myers, "Suffix arrays: a new method for on-line string searches," Proc. the 1st Annual ACM-SIAM Symposium on Discrete Algorithms, pp. 319 – 327, SIAM, Philadelphia, PA, 1990.

[36] U. Manber and R.A. Baeza-Yates, "An algorithm for string matching with a sequence of don't cares," Information Processing Letters, Vol. 37, pp. 133 – 136, Feb. 1991.

[37] E.M. McCreight, "A space-economical suffix tree construction algorithm," Journal of the ACM, Vol. 23, No. 2, pp. 262 – 272, April 1976.

[38] R.Y. Pinter, "Efficient string matching with don't' care patterns," in A. Apostolico and Z. Galil (eds.) *Combinatorial Algorithms on Words*, NATO ASI Series, Vol. F12, pp. 11 – 29, Springer-Verlag, Berlin, 1985.

[39] M. Schatz, "Cloudburst: highly sensitive read mapping with mapreduce," Bioinformatics, **25**, 1363–1369, 2009.

[40] J. Seward, "bzip2 and libbzip2, version 1.0. 5: A program and library for data compression," URL http://www. bzip. org, 2007.

[41] A.D. Smith, et al, "Using quality scores and longer reads improves accuracy of Solexa read mapping," BMC Bioinformatics, **9**, 128, 2008.

[42] J. Tarhio and E. Ukkonen, "Boyer-Moore approach to approximate string matching," in J.R. Gilbert and R. Karlssion (eds.) SWAT 90, Proc. 2nd Scandinavian Workshop on Algorithm Theory, Lecture Notes in Computer Science, Vol. 447, pp. 348 – 359, Springer-Verlag, Berlin, 1990.

[43] J. Tarhio and E. Ukkonen, "Approximate Boyer-Moore String Matching," SIAM Journal on Computing, Vol. 22, No. 2, pp. 243 -260, 1993.

[44] E. Ukkonen, "Approximate string-matching with q-grams and maximal matches," Theoretical Computer Science, Vol. 92, pp. 191 – 211, 1992

[45] P. Weiner, "Linear pattern matching algorithm," Proc. 14th IEEE Symposium on Switching and Automata Theory, pp. 1 – 11, 1973.

[46] Y. Chen, D. Che and K. Aberer, "On the Efficient Evaluation of Relaxed Queries in Biological Databases," in Proc. 11th Int. Conf. on Information and Knowledge Management, Virginia, U.S.A.: ACM, Nov. 2002, pp. 227 – 236.

A Simplified Database Pattern for the Microservice Architecture

Antonio Messina, Riccardo Rizzo, Pietro Storniolo, Alfonso Urso
ICAR - CNR
Palermo, Italy
Email: {messina, ricrizzo, storniolo, urso}@pa.icar.cnr.it

Abstract—**Microservice architectures are used as alternative to monolithic applications because they are simpler to scale and more flexible. Microservices require a careful design because each service component should be simple and easy to develop. In this paper, a new microservice pattern is proposed: a database that can be considered a microservice by itself. We named this new pattern as *The Database is the Service*. The proposed simplified database pattern has been tested by adding ebXML registry capabilities to a noSQL database.**

***Keywords*–microservices, scalable applications, continuous delivery, microservices patterns, noSQL, database**

I. Introduction

The microservice architectural style [1] is a recent approach to build applications as suite of services, independently deployable, implementable in different programming languages, scalable and manageable by different teams.

Microservices architectures are opposed to monolithic applications. Monolithic applications are simpler to build and to deploy, but their structure forces the developers to work in team. Working in team the developers tends to deploy large applications that are difficult to understand and to modify.

Moreover, if a required service is implemented by a single application, the transactions volume can be increased only by running multiple copies of the same application, that has to access to the same database.

On the other side, developing a system based on microservices requires a special attention because it is a distributed system. In this case, even the team of developers can be distributed, it requires a special effort in coordination and communication.

In microservices based systems, one of the biggest challenge is the partition into separated services, each of them should be simple enough to have a small set of responsibilities. Data management require a special attention, because it can be one of the bottleneck of the system. So that it is convenient that only one or few microservices access the data, but this can affect the responsiveness of the whole system.

When a careful project solves all these issues, microservices became an effective architectural pattern, in fact studies have shown how this architectural pattern can give benefits when enterprise applications are deployed in cloud environments [2] and in containers [3], e.g., Docker [4]. Microservices are also considered the natural fit for the *Machine-to-Machine* (IoT) development [5].

The microservices pattern implies several important auxiliary patterns, such as, for example, those which concern how clients access the services in a microservices architecture, how clients requests are routed to an available service instance, or how each service use a database.

In the new microservice pattern proposed in this paper, a database, under certain circumstances and thanks to the integration of some business logic, can be considered a microservice by itself. It will be labeled as *The database is the service* pattern.

The remainder of the paper is organized as follows: Section 2 presents a brief overview about the *old* monolithic style and its drawbacks. The microservices architectures and the related pattern are described in Section 3. Section 4 presents the proposed pattern. In Section 5, we show a proof of concept of the pattern and its improved performances. Finally, conclusions are reported.

II. Background

To better understand the microservice style it is useful to compare it to the *monolithic style*: a monolithic application built as a single unit. Modern enterprise applications are typically built in three main parts: a client-side user interface, a server-side application, and a relational database. The server-side application handles the requests, executes domain logic, retrieves and updates data from the relational database, and selects and populates the views to be sent to the client-side. This server-side application can be defined as *monolith*, a single logical executable.

Essentially, a monolith application is the one where all its functionalities are packaged together as a single unit or application. This unit could be a JAR, WAR, EAR, or some other archive format, for which is all integrated in a single unit. This style of application is well known, because this is how applications have been built so far, it is easy to conceptualize and all the code is in one place. The most of existing tools, application servers, frameworks, scripts are able to deal with such kind of applications. In particular, IDEs are typically designed to easily develop, deploy, debug, and profile a single application. Stepping through the code base is easy because the codebase is all together.

Finally, a monolith is easy to share, to test and to deploy. A single archive, with all the functionality, can be shared between teams and across different stages of deployment pipeline. Once the application is successfully deployed, all the services, or features, are up and available. This simplifies testing as there are no additional dependencies to wait for in order to begin the test phase. Accessing or testing the application is simplified in either case. It is easy to deploy since, typically, a single archive needs to be copied to one directory. The deployment times could vary but the process is pretty straight forward. However, a monolithic application, no matter how modular, will eventually start to break down as the team grows, experienced developers leave and new ones join, application scope increases, new ways to access the applications are added, and so on. Moreover, it has a very limited agility, because every tiny change to the application means full redeployment of the archive. This means that developers will have to wait for the entire application to be deployed if they want to see the impact of quick change made in their workspace. Even if not intentional, but this may require tight coupling between different features of the application. This may not be possible all the time, especially if multiple developers are working on the application. This reduces agility of the team and the frequency by which new features can be delivered. If a single change to the application would require entire application to be redeployed, then this could become an obstacle to frequent deployments, and thus an important obstacle for continuous delivery.

Choice of technology for such applications are evaluated and decided before their development starts. Everybody in the team is required to use the same language, persistence stores, messaging system, and use similar tools to keep the team aligned. It is typically not possible to change technology stack mid stream without throwing away or rewriting significant part of existing application.

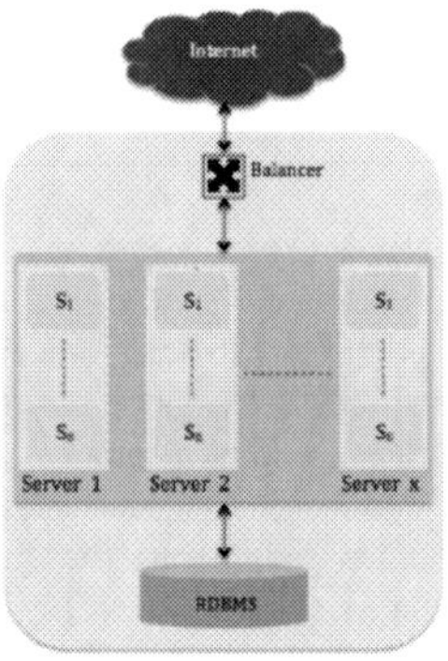

Figure 1. Services provided by horizontally scaled monolithic application

Monoliths can only scale in one dimension, i.e., they have to be entirely duplicated across a set of servers (see Figure 1). This way, each application instance will access all of the data. This makes caching less effective, increases memory consumption and i/o traffic.

Systems based on microservices present many advantages if compared to monolithic applications. Some of these advantages came from their distributed architecture and will be explained in the next section.

III. Microservices Architecture and Related Patterns

In the last years, several large Internet companies have used different mechanisms, strategies and technologies to address the limitations of the monolithic architecture: they can be referred as the *microservices architecture pattern*.

Microservices is a software architectural style that require functional decomposition of an application. A monolithic application is broken down into multiple smaller services, each deployed in its own archive, and then composed as a single application using standard lightweight communication, such as REST over HTTP (see Figure 2).

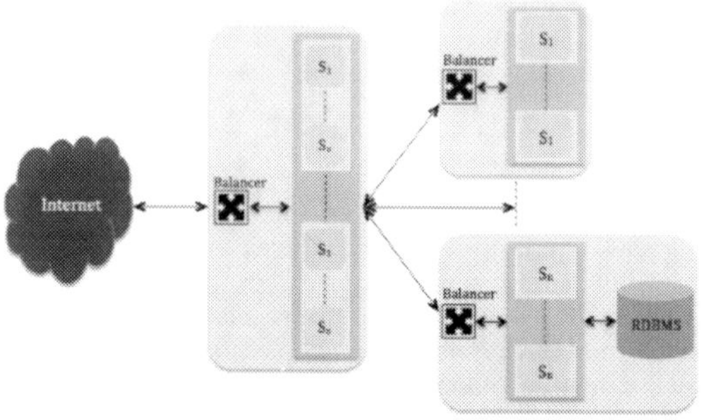

Figure 2. Tipical microservice-based application with lightweight frontend

The decomposition into a set of collaborating services is usually done applying the Y-axis scaling of the three dimension scalability model named the Scale Cube [6]:

- *X-axis scaling*: it is the simplest commonly used approach of scaling an application via horizontal duplication, namely running multiple cloned copies of an application behind a load balancer.
- *Y-axis scaling*: it represents an application's split by function, service or resource. Each service is responsible for one or more closely related functions. We can use a verb-based decomposition and define services that implement single use cases, or we can decompose the application by noun and create services responsible for all operations related to a particular entity.
- *Z-axis scaling*: it is commonly used to scale databases, because the data is partitioned across a set of servers. Each server runs an identical copy of the code and each service request is routed to the appropriate server according to a routing criteria.

Basically, the service design should be made by applying the *Single Responsibility Principle* [7], that defines a responsibility of a class as a reason to change, and states that a class should only have one reason to change.

There are several patterns [8] related to the microservices pattern. We mainly focus our attention on the following:

- The *API Gateway* pattern, that defines how clients access the services in a microservices architecture.
- The *Client-side Discovery* and *Server-side Discovery* patterns, used to route requests for a client to an available service instance in a microservices architecture.
- The *Service Registry* pattern, a critical component that tracks the instances and the locations of the services.
- The *Database per Service* pattern, that describes how each service has its own database.

A. The API Gateway Pattern

Microservices typically provide fine-grained APIs, which means that clients need to interact with multiple services. However, different clients need different data and network performance is different for different types of clients. Moreover, the number of service instances and their locations (host+port) changes dynamically and partitioning into services can change over time and should be hidden from clients.

An API gateway is the single entry point for all clients and handles requests in one of two ways. Some requests are simply proxied/routed to the appropriate service. It handles other requests by fanning out to multiple services. Rather than provide a one-size-fits-all style API, the API gateway can expose a different API for each client. It might also implement security, e.g., verify that the client is authorized to perform the request. There is a couple of obvious drawbacks, at least:

- *Increased complexity*, due to another moving part that must be developed, deployed and managed.
- *Increased response time*, due to the additional network hop through the API gateway. However, for most applications the cost of an extra roundtrip is insignificant.

B. The Discovery Patterns

In a monolithic application, services invoke one another through language-level method or procedure calls. In a traditional distributed system deployment, services run at fixed, well known locations (hosts and ports) and so they can easily call each using HTTP/REST or some RPC mechanism. However, a modern microservice-based application typically runs in a virtualized or containerized environments where the number of instances of a service and their locations changes dynamically. Consequently, the service clients must be enabled to make requests to a dynamically changing set of transient service instances.

- *Client-side*: The clients obtain the location of a service instance by querying a *Service Registry*, which knows the locations of all service instances. This implies fewer moving parts and network hops compared to *Server-side Discovery*, but clients are coupled to the *Service Registry* and you need to implement a client-side service discovery logic for each programming language/framework used by the application (see Figure 3).

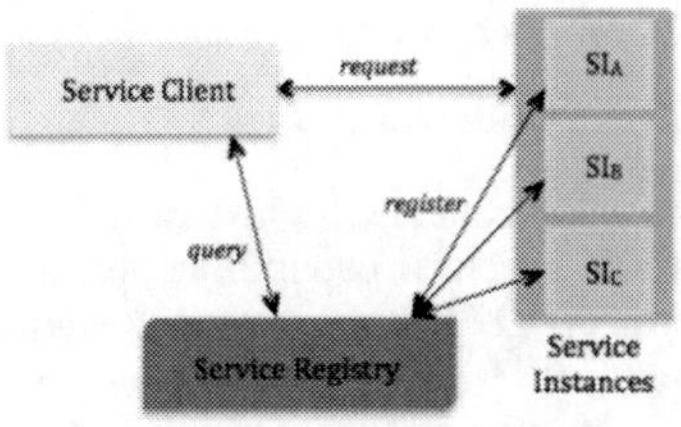

Figure 3. Client-side discovery pattern

- *Server-Side*: When making a request to a service, the client makes a request via a router (a.k.a. load balancer) that runs at a well known location. The router queries a service registry, which might be built into the router, and forwards the request to an available service instance. Compared to client-side discovery, the client code is simpler since it does not have to deal with discovery. Instead, a client simply makes a request to the router, but more network hops are required (see Figure 4).

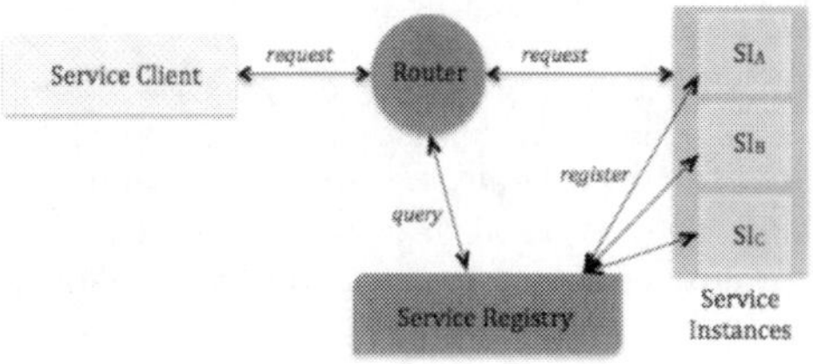

Figure 4. Server-side discovery pattern

C. The Service Registry Pattern

A service registry is a database of services, their instances and their locations. Service instances are registered with the service registry on startup and deregistered on shutdown. Client of the service and/or routers query the service registry to find the available instances of a service. Unless the service registry is built in to the infrastructure, it is yet another infrastructure component that must be setup, configured and managed. Moreover, the Service Registry is a critical system component. Although clients should cache data provided by the service registry, if the service registry fails that data will eventually become out of date. Consequently, the service registry must be highly available.

D. The Database per Service Pattern

According to this pattern, we should keep each microservice's persistent data private to that service and accessible only via its API. It means that the service's database is effectively part of the implementation of that service and it cannot be accessed directly by other services. There are a few different ways to keep a service's persistent data private:

- *Private-tables-per-service*: each service owns a set of tables that must only be accessed by that service.
- *Schema-per-service*: each service has a database schema that is private to that service
- *Database-server-per-service*: each service has its own database server. When the service has to be scaled, the database can be also scaled in a database cluster, no matter the service.

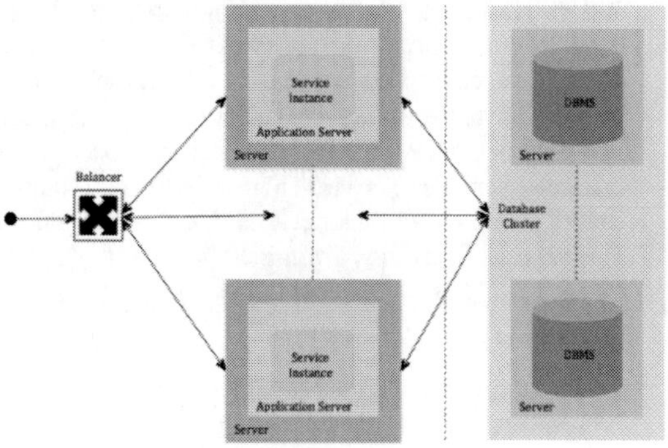

Figure 5. The Database per Service pattern applied to a scaled service using a database cluster

Figure 5 shows a typical architecture of a scaled service using its own database cluster.

IV. THE *Database is the Service* PATTERN

The granular nature of the microservice architectures may bring many benefits, but also comes with the cost of increased complexity.

Breaking a monolith into microservices simplifies each individual component, but the original complexity goes to surface when, at some point, someone has to put it all together [9]. Certainly, there is a sort of law of conservation of complexity in software and, if we break up big things into small pieces, then we push the complexity to their interactions [10].

Moreover, IT complexity in enterprise today continues to grow at a dizzying rate. Technology innovation, vendor heterogeneity, and business demands are major reasons why organizations are exposed to new risks, based on the gaps opened between the options and features of each IT element and product, and how they are implemented to support a well-defined policy and company strategy. The impact of such risks increases exponentially by failing to identify the handshakes and correlations of interrelated elements. Products, vendors, and IT layers must work together to prevent potential *black holes*: risks related to availability, resiliency and data loss.

It is not hard to understand how microservice architectures may amplify such risks, because their distributed nature. Moreover, in a monolithic application there was a method call acting as a subsystem boundary, in the microservice architecture we now introduce lots of remote procedure calls, REST APIs or messaging to glue components together across different processes and servers.

Once we have distributed a system, we have to consider a whole host of concerns that we didn't before. Network latency, fault tolerance, message serialisation, unreliable networks, asynchronicity, versioning, varying loads within our application tiers etc.

Starting from the *Database-Server per Service Pattern*, the addition of new behaviors and business logic at the database level may be a possible approach to reduce complexity, and thus the related risks, and also to gain improvements in terms of speed and scalability.

Problem: If each scalable service has its own database (cluster), as shown in Figure 5, is there any way to reduce the complexity of the architecture and the related risks, while also gaining more improvements in terms of speed and scalability?

Solution: Whenever the database has an open architecture and provides the necessary hooks to extend its capabilities, then it can embed the business logic that implements the desired service. The service is strictly coupled to the data, hence this pattern is even stronger than the *Database-Server per Service Pattern*, because the database itself acts as a business service. As shown in Figure 6, clients requests are routed via a load balancer, following the guidelines of the *Server-side Discovery Pattern*.

Some benefits of such approach are immediately clear at first sight:

a) the traditional service layer disappears, thanks to the whole removal of related hosts and application servers or containers;

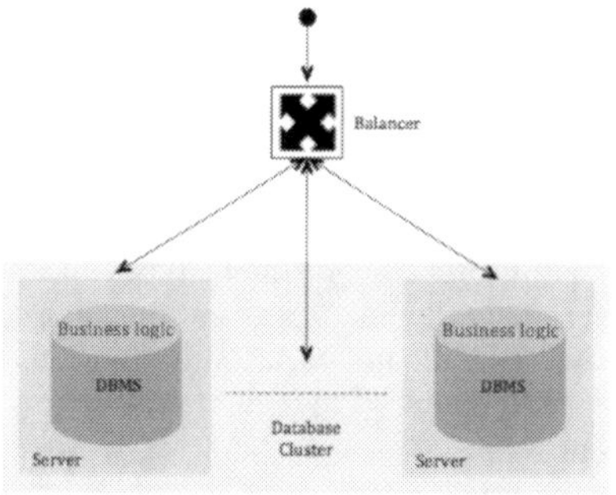

Figure 6. The Database is the Service pattern: DBMS with business logic

b) services deployed into the database have instant access to data, accessible at no cost (no third party libraries, no network issues, and so on);

c) less the involved components, less the complexity, the interactions and the potential risks.

If the database cluster layer is also available to clients, i.e., thanks to a specific library, we may achieve further simplification, because clients requests reach directly the service. Unlike *Client-side Discovery Pattern*, there's no need to implement a discovery logic into clients, there isn't any balancer, and the cluster layer supplies, at least, the same *Service Registry* capabilities. Figure 7 shows the way that super-simplified architecture looks.

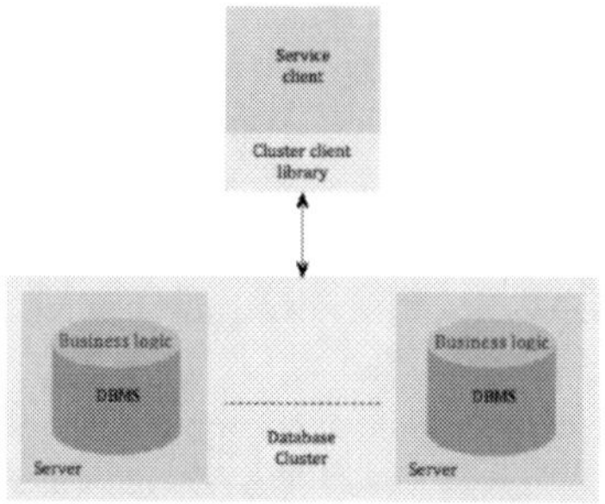

Figure 7. The Database is the Service pattern with client-side cluster support

Drawbacks are also obvious, first and foremost the dependency on the chosen database, because the service becomes integral to, and inseparable from, the database engine. Test and debug activities must also involve the database because of his primary role. For this reason, the database source code must be available, an open source product is the obvious choice.

V. PROOF OF CONCEPT

As a proof of concept for the proposed pattern, we have added ebXML registry capabilities to a noSQL database, starting from *EXPO* [19], a prototypal extension for OrientDB derived from *eRIC* [20], our previous SQL-based ebXML registry implemented as web service in Java.

An ebXML registry [15][16] is an open infrastructure based on XML that allows electronic exchange of business information in a consistent, secure and interoperable way.

The eXtensible Markup Language (ebXML) is a standard promoted by the Organization for the Advancement of Structured Information (OASIS) and was designed to create a global electronic market place where enterprises of any size, anywhere, can find each other electronically and conduct business using exchange of XML messages according to standard business process sequences and mutually agreed trading partner protocol agreements.

Nowadays, ebXML concepts and specifications are reused by the Cross-Enterprise Document Sharing (XDS) architectural model [17], defined by *Integrating the Healthcare Enterprise* (IHE) initiative [18], which is promoted by healthcare professionals and industries to improve the way computer systems in healthcare share informations.

In the following subsections, we introduce the noSQL database engine we have chosen and we briefly illustrate what we have done and some interesting performances results.

A. *Brief overview on OrientDB*

OrientDB [11] is an open source NoSQL DBMS developed in Java by Orient Technologies LTD and distributed under the Apache 2 license [14]. It collects features of document databases and graph databases, including object orientation. In graph mode, referenced relationships are like edges, accessible as first-class objects with a start vertex, end vertex, and properties. This interesting feature let us represent a relational model in document-graph model maintaining the relationships.

OrientDB supports an extended version of SQL, to allow all sort of CRUD (Create, Read, Update and Delete) and query operations, and ACID (Atomicity, Consistency, Isolation, Durability) transactions, helpful to recover pending document at the time of crash. It is easily embeddable and customizable and it handles HTTP Requests, RESTful protocols and JSON without any 3rd party libraries or components. It is also fully compliant with TinkerPop Blueprints [12], the standard of graph databases. Finally, his feature can be easily customized and it supports a multi-master distributed architecture, a 2nd level shared cache and the other features offered by embedded Hazelcast [13].

B. *A multi-model noSQL DBMS as an ebXML Registry*

OrientDB is also a customizable platform to build powerful server component and applications: since it contains an integrated web server, it is possible to create server side applications without the need to have a J2EE and Servlet container. The customizations can be obtained by developing new *Handlers*, to build plugins that start when OrientDB starts, or implementing *Custom Commands*, the suggested best way to add custom behaviors or business logic at the server side.

The multi-model nature of the OrientDB engine allows it to support Object data model, too. This model has been inherited by Object Oriented programming and supports the inheritance between types (sub-types extends the super-types), the polymorphism when you refer to a base class, and the direct binding from/to objects used in programming languages.

The OrientDB Object Interface works on top of the Document-Database and works like an Object Database: manages Java objects directly. This makes things easier for the Java developer, since the binding between Objects to Records is transparent. In that context, the Objects are referred as *POJOs*: Plain Old Java Objects. OrientDB uses Java reflection and Javassist [21] to bound POJOs to Records directly. Those proxied instances take care about the synchronization between a POJO and its underlying record. Every time you invoke a setter method against the POJO, the value is early bound into the record. Every time you call a getter method, the value is retrieved from the record if the POJO's field value is null. Lazy loading works in this way too.

The ebXML RIM objects are perfect POJOs, because they are serializable, have a no-argument constructor, and allow access to properties using getter and setter methods that follow a simple naming convention. They are also fully described by the standard set of Java XML annotation tags because they need to be transferred over the line properly encapsulated using the Java Architecture for XML Binding (JAXB) [22]. This means that we can add new custom properties preceded by the *@XMLTransient* tag without breaking things. We have used those new properties and the related getter and setter methods to add native OrientDB links between objects, which can be transparently serialized/deserialized by the OrientDB engine in their enriched form.

This approach has a great impact on the management of ebXML objects:

a) they are still used in the standard way within the client-server SOAP interactions;
b) the binding to the database records is transparent;
c) there is no need of extra data class object (DAO) hierarchy to manage the persistence;
d) we are able to make full use of the OrientDB capabilities.

An extension of the OrientdDB *OServerCommandAbstract* class has replaced the old Java servlet in the registry requests management. In particular, the *execute()* method is invoked at every HTTP request and let us to read the input HTTP stream and to write into the output HTTP stream. This is the place where we intercept, elaborate and reply to the incoming requests, by calling the real ebXML registry layer.

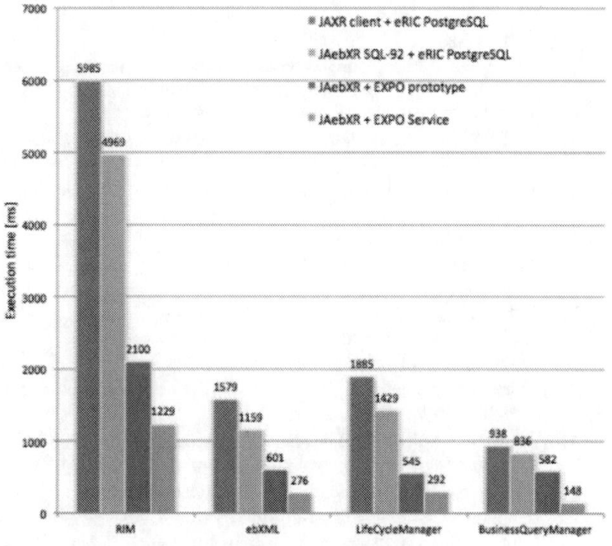

Figure 8. EXPO vs eRIC/PostgreSQL

To verify ebXML specifications compliance and to evaluate the performances, we have run the same ebXML test suite developed with the JAebXR API [23] and then we have compared the results in some different configurations. Figure 8 shows the interesting performance improvements obtained with EXPO service.

VI. Conclusions

While monoliths have been the norm for some time, microservices have emerged as an alternative to deal with certain limitation in monoliths. However, that doesn't mean that monoliths are completely obsolete. Just because others are gravitating to one more than the other, doesn't mean that it's going to be the best decision. Obviously, it's important to look at advantages and disadvantages of each and, as much information as possible, to make the aware decision. Keep also in mind that, due to the significant architectural differences, a direct comparative quantitative analysis is actually not easy to achieve, but we are working on it.

In this paper, we introduced a new microservice pattern where the database *is* the service. The proposed pattern has been tested adding ebXML registry capabilities to a noSQL database. Experimental tests have shown improved performances of the proposed simplified microservice architecture compared with SQL-based ebXML registry implemented as traditional Java web service.

References

[1] M. Fowler, "Microservices, a definition of this new architectural term", URL: http://martinfowler.com/articles/microservices.html [accessed: 2016-02-12].

[2] M. Villamizar, et al., "Evaluating the monolithic and the microservice architecture pattern to deploy web applications in the cloud", "Computing Colombian Conference (10CCC), 2015 10th", 2015, pp. 583–590, DOI: 10.1109/ColumbianCC.2015.7333476.

[3] M. Amaral, et al., "Performance Evaluation of Microservices Architectures Using Containers", "2015 IEEE 14th International Symposium on Network Computing and Applications (NCA)", 2015, pp. 27–34, DOI: 10.1109/NCA.2015.49.

[4] Docker Inc., "Docker, An open platform for distributed applications for developers and sysadmins", URL: https://www.docker.com [accessed: 2016-02-12].

[5] D. Namiot and M. Sneps-Sneppe, "On micro-services architecture", "International Journal of Open Information Technologies", 2014, vol. 2, no. 9, pp. 24–27, ISSN: 2307-8162.

[6] M. Abbott, T. Keeven, and M. Fisher, "Splitting Applications or Services for Scale", URL: http://akfpartners.com/techblog/2008/05/08/splitting-applications-or-services-for-scale/ [accessed: 2016-02-16].

[7] R. C. Martin, "Agile Software Development: Principles, Patterns, and Practices", Pearson Education, Nov. 2009, ISBN: 978-0-13597-444-5

[8] C. Richardson, "Microservice architecture patterns and best practices", URL: http://microservices.io/index.html [accessed: 2016-02-12].

[9] H. Hammer, "The Fallacy of Tiny Modules", URL: http://hueniverse.com/2014/05/30/the-fallacy-of-tiny-modules/ [accessed: 2016-02-28].

[10] M. Feathers, "Microservices Until Macro Complexity", URL: https://michaelfeathers.silvrback.com/microservices-until-macro-complexity [accessed: 2016-02-28].

[11] Orient Technologies LTD, "OrientDB", URL: http://orientdb.com [accessed: 2016-02-10].

[12] Apache Software Foundation, "Apache TinkerPop", URL: http://tinkerpop.incubator.apache.org [accessed: 2016-02-11].

[13] Hazelcast Inc., "Hazelcast, the Operational In-Memory Computing Platform", URL: http://hazelcast.com [accessed: 2016-02-10].

[14] Apache Software Foundation, "Apache License v2.0", Jan. 2004, URL: http://www.apache.org/licenses/LICENSE-2.0 [accessed: 2016-02-11].

[15] OASIS ebXML Registry Technical Committee, "Registry Information Model (RIM) v3.0", 2005, URL: http://docs.oasis-open.org/regrep/regrep-rim/v3.0/regrep-rim-3.0-os.pdf [accessed: 2016-02-10].

[16] OASIS ebXML Registry Technical Committee, "Registry Services and Protocols v3.0", 2005, URL: http://docs.oasis-open.org/regrep/regrep-rs/v3.0/regrep-rs-3.0-os.pdf [accessed: 2016-02-10].

[17] R. Noumeir, "Sharing Medical Records: The XDS Architecture and Communication Infrastructure", "IT Professional", Sep. 2010, Volume: 13, Issue: 4, ISSN: 1520-9202, DOI: 10.1109/MITP.2010.123.

[18] Integrating the Healthcare Enterprise (IHE), 2010, URL: http://ihe.net [accessed: 2016-02-17].

[19] A. Messina, P. Storniolo, and A. Urso, "Keep it simple, fast and scalable: a Multi-Model NoSQL DBMS as an (eb)XML-over-SOAP service", "The 30th IEEE International Conference on Advanced Information Networking and Applications (AINA-2016)", IEEE, in press.

[20] A. Messina and P. Storniolo, "eRIC v3.2: ebXML Registry by ICAR CNR", Technical Report: RT-ICAR-PA-13-03, Dec. 2013, DOI: 10.13140/RG.2.1.2108.9124.

[21] JBoss Javassist, "Javassist (Java Programming Assistant)", 2015, URL: http://jboss-javassist.github.io/javassist/ [accessed: 2016-02-29].

[22] Java Community Process, "JSR 222: Java Architecture for XML Binding (JAXB) 2.0", 2009, URL: https://jcp.org/en/jsr/detail?id=222 [accessed: 2016-02-29].

[23] A. Messina, P. Storniolo, and A. Urso, "JAebXR: a Java API for ebXML Registries for Federated Health Information Systems", "DBKDA 2015: The Seventh International Conference on Advances in Databases, Knowledge, and Data Applications", Rome, Italy, May 2015, pp. 33–39, ISBN: 978-1-61208-408-4.

Multidimensional Structures for Field Based Data

A Review of Models

Taher Omran Ahmed
IT Department, College of Applied Sciences,
Sultanate of Oman,
Computer Science Department, Faculty of Science
Aljabal Algharbi University, Azzentan, Libya
e-mail: taher.ibr@cas.edu.om, fenneer@yahoo.com

Abstract— **The growth in size of geographical data collected by different types of sensors and used in diverse applications have led to the adoption of spatial data warehouses (SDW) and spatial OLAP (SOLAP). Spatial data are represented as either discrete (objects) or continuous (raster), also called field-based data. The latter representation deals with data about natural phenomena that exist continuously in space and time. Continuity was not taken into account during the early days of SDW and SOLAP, however, during the last decade there were attempts to include this concept within SOLAP. In this paper, we present some of the concepts, issues and discuss the models proposed to represent spatiotemporal continuity in a decisional context and attempt to foresee where the research in this area is heading.**

Keywords-Data Warehousing; Field Based Data; Models; Multidimensional; SOLAP; Spatial Data.

I. INTRODUCTION

Data warehouses rely on multidimensional structures, which are based on the concept of facts or measures and dimensions. Facts are the subject of analysis and they are usually numeric values. Facts are defined by the combination of values (members) of dimensions if a corresponding value exists. Dimensions represent the context in which measures or facts are analyzed. Usually, dimensions are organized in hierarchies composed of several levels; each level represents a level of detail as required by the expected analysis. A hierarchy is a set of variables which represent different levels of aggregation of the same dimension and which are interlinked by a mapping [18]. Traditional data warehouses deal with alphanumeric data; however, most businesses take geographical location seriously when they seek good decisions and hence a large segment of data stored in corporate databases is spatial. It has been estimated that about 80% of data have a spatial component to it, like an address or a postal code [8]. In order to obtain maximum benefits of the spatial component of data, there had been important efforts that led, eventually, to the introduction and implementation of spatial data warehousing (SDW) and spatial OLAP (SOLAP).

Spatial data warehousing has been recognized as a key technology in enabling the interactive analysis of spatial data sets for decision-making support [11][19]. According to [22] a spatial data warehouse is a subject oriented, integrated, time-variant and non-volatile collection of both spatial data and non-spatial data in support of management's decision-making process. In plain terms, it is a conventional data warehouse that contains both spatial and non-spatial data where these two types of data complement each other in the support of the decision making process.

OLAP is a tool for analysis and exploration of conventional (alphanumeric) data warehouses. It can also be used for spatiotemporal analysis and exploration. However, the lack of cartographic representations leads to serious limitations (lack of spatial visualization, lack of map-based navigation, and so on) [19]. To overcome these limitations, visualization tools and map-based navigation tools have to be integrated within the conventional OLAP. The result would be a OLAP that can be seen as a client application on top of a spatial data warehouse [2]. The presence of these components would give specialists from multiple disciplines (forestry, public health, transport,...etc.) a new exploration and analysis potential known as Geographic Knowledge Discovery (GKD) [3].

This paper sheds a light on the research carried on spatial OLAP for continuous field data and the different models that have been proposed. In order to achieve our objective, a brief overview of spatial data warehousing is presented in Section 2. The rest of the paper is organized as follows: In Section 3, we discuss the major concepts of several multidimensional models for continuous field data that have been proposed. A comparison between models is presented in Section 4 and we conclude the paper in Section 5.

II. SPATIAL DATA WAREHOUSINGA AND SPATIAL OLAP

A spatial data warehouse contains three types of spatial dimensions; non-spatial, mixed and spatial dimensions.

The first type is a hierarchy containing members that are only located with place names (an address or a postal code) and not represented geometrically. The absence of geometrical representation handicaps the spatiotemporal exploration and analysis but it is still possible for the users to carry out the spatial cognition [13]. The second type is a hierarchy whose detailed level members have a geometric representation but general levels do not have one (at a certain level of aggregation). An example of this type of dimensions is using maps with polygons for cities and regions but neither for states nor country. In the last type of spatial dimensions, all members have a geometric representation.

In addition to spatial dimensions, two types of spatial measures are also distinguished, the first being a geometric shape or a set of shapes obtained by a combination of several geometric spatial dimensions. The second type is a result of spatial metric or topological operators [20].

A literature review of SOLAP shows an extensive amount of work, unfortunately most of the published research focused on the implementation side and on showing the advantages and potential uses of SOLAP. To the best of our knowledge, there is not enough solid attempts to go in-depth in the theory behind the concepts or to propose a sound mathematical model. Hence, SOLAP remained just an application that can be seen - by many - merely as a coupling between OLAP and GIS. Moreover, SOLAP solely deals with the discrete representation of GIS and hence it cannot grasp the essence of continuity in natural phenomena. Even when continuous field data are dealt with in a decisional context [14] they are treated as discrete and hence they lack their main characteristic that is, spatiotemporal continuity. For instance, [24] proposed a logical model to integrate spatial dimensions representing incomplete field data at different resolutions in a classical SOLAP architecture. Nonetheless, during the last ten or more years, serious attempts were made at integrating continuity in multidimensional structures.

III. Models

There is no consensus on one specific model to represent multidimensional structures for field-based data. In fact, even conventional multidimensional structures, which are more established, use different models. Over the last few years, several models were proposed for spatiotemporal multidimensional structures such as [21], where a logical multidimensional model to support spatial data on SDW is proposed. But, most of them concentrate on spatial continuity rather than spatiotemporal continuity.

In this section we present an overview of the main concepts of (four) major models.

A. *Ahmed and Miquel, 2005*

The model presented in [1] is one of the earliest models for multidimensional structures that attempts to include continuous field data as measures and dimensions. The researchers present the concepts, research issues and potentials of continuous multidimensional structures and propose a model for continuous field data. The model is based on the concept of basic cubes, which are used as the lowest level of detail of dimensions. To imitate the behavior of natural phenomena a continuous data warehouse will be treated as a second layer on top of the discrete data warehouse.

1) *Basic Definitions*

There are n dimensions with r being the rank of dimension levels starting from (*level 1*) all the way up to (*level r*) and k being the cardinality (number of members) of a given dimension level DL_i. The domain of values $dom(DL_i)$ for a given dimension level DL_i may contain two types of members: predefined members and any possible value between any two given members to give a continuous representation of the dimension level. A value x belonging to a specific dimension level DL_i can have ancestors and descendants which are specific instances related to x at higher and lower dimension levels respectively.

2) *Basic Cubes*

A basic cube is a cube at the lowest level of detail. The discrete basic cube $\boldsymbol{discC_b}$ is a 3-tuple $<\boldsymbol{D_b}, \boldsymbol{L_b}, \boldsymbol{R_b}>$ where $\boldsymbol{D_b}$ is a list of dimensions including a dimension measure M. L_b is the list of the lowest levels of each dimension and $\boldsymbol{R_b}$ is a set of cell data represented as a set of tuples containing level members and measures in the form of $x = [x_1, x_2, \ldots x_n, m]$ where m is the dimension that represents the measure.

To obtain a continuous representation of the basic cube, estimated measures related to the infinite members of a given spatial and temporal levels are calculated using actual cell values from $\boldsymbol{discC_b}$. This involves applying interpolation functions to a sample of $\boldsymbol{discC_b}$ values to calculate the measures corresponding to the new dimension members, which will result in continuous basic cube $\boldsymbol{contC_b}$.

A continuous basic cube contCb is 4-tuple $<\boldsymbol{D_b}, (\boldsymbol{D'_b}, \boldsymbol{F}), \boldsymbol{L_b}, \boldsymbol{R'_b}>$. Discrete and continuous dimensions are represented by $\boldsymbol{D_b}$, $\boldsymbol{D'_b}$ respectively. In addition, $\boldsymbol{F}$ is a set of interpolation functions associated with the continuous dimensions and has the same cardinality as $\boldsymbol{D'_b}$. The lowest levels of dimensions are represented by $\boldsymbol{L_b}$. The continuous representation is defined over a spatial and/or temporal interval. Hence, $\boldsymbol{R'_b}$ is a set of tuples of the form $x = [x_1, x_2, \ldots x_n, m]$ where $x_i \in [minDom(Lb_i) - \Delta, maxDom(Lb_i) + \Delta]$ with Δ being a small predefined value used to allow for continuous representation around the values of the domain of the dimension levels, and to predict values outside the specified interval. The measure m $\subseteq$ M can be either interpolated (approximated) or exact. When measures are interpolated m is defined as:

- $m = f(m_1, m_2, \ldots, m_k)$ where f is a spatial or temporal interpolation function,
- $m = f(m_1, m_2, \ldots, m_k)$ using values lying within a predefined spatial or temporal distance d, or
- $m = f_1 \circ f_2 (m_1, m_2, \ldots, m_k)$ or $m = f_2 \circ f_1 (m_1, m_2, \ldots, m_k)$. The order of applying interpolation functions.

It can be concluded that $discC_b \subseteq contC_b$

3) *Cubes*

Cubes at higher levels are built by applying a set of operations on data at the basic cube level. A cube C is defined as 4-tuple $<\boldsymbol{D}, \boldsymbol{L}, \boldsymbol{contC_b}, \boldsymbol{R}>$ where, D is a list of dimensions including M as defined before, L is the respective dimension level, R is cell data and $\boldsymbol{contC_b}$ is the basic cube from which C is built. Because of the nature of the continuous field data, different aggregation functions are used to build the cube at higher dimension hierarchies. For example, the sum of measures for a specific region or a specific period will be represented as an integral. Other aggregation functions like *min*, *max* or *average* will be performed on ***contCb*** and their results will be assigned to the higher levels of the hierarchy.

4) Aggregations

On a continuous field, two classes of operations are defined. The first deals with discrete operations and the second groups the continuous operations:

Discrete operations. Only the sample points are used.

DiscMax = v_i such that $v_i \geqslant f(s_k)\ \forall\ s_k \in S$

DiscMin = v_i such that $v_i \leqslant f(s_k)\ \forall\ s_k \in S$

$$\text{DiscSum} = \sum_{s_k \in E} f(S_k)$$

DiscCount = Card(S)

$$\text{DiscAvg} = {DiscSum}/{DiscCount}$$

Continuous operations. All values of the field are used.

ContMax = v_i such that $v_i \geqslant f(S_k)\ \forall\ S_k \in D \times T$

Cont Min = v_i such that $v_i \leqslant f(S_k)\ \forall\ S_k \in D \times T$

$$\text{ContSpatSum} = \int f(s)dp$$

$$\text{ContTempSum} = \int f(s)dt$$

$$\text{ContSpatAvg} = \int \frac{f(s)dt}{(region\ area)}$$

$$\text{ContTempAvg} = \int \frac{f(s)dt}{(t_2 - t_1)}$$

where $[t_1{:}t_2]$ *is a time interval*

B. *Vaisman and Zimányi, 2009*

Vaisman et al. [23] base their multidimensional model for continuous fields in spatial data warehouses on MultiDim model presented in [12]. A multidimensional schema consists of a finite set of dimensions and fact relationships. A dimension consists of at least one hierarchy, containing at least one level. A basic hierarchy is hierarchy with only one level. Several levels are related to each other through a binary relationship that defines a partial order $\preceq$ between levels. For any two consecutive related levels l_i, l_j, if $l_i \preceq l_j$ then l_i is called child and l_j is called parent. A level representing the less detailed data for a hierarchy is called a leaf level.

For spatial levels, the relationship can also be topological requiring a spatial predicate, e.g., intersection. A fact relationship may contain measures that can be spatial or thematic. The thematic measures are numeric that are analyzed quantifiably whereas the spatial measure can be represented by a geometry or field, or calculated using spatial operators, such as distance or area.

The dimension levels have two types of attributes (category and property). For parent level, the category attribute defines how child members are grouped. In the leaf level, the category attribute indicates the aggregation level of a measure in the fact relationship. The property attribute can be spatial (represented by geometry or field) or thematic (descriptive, alphanumeric data types). Hence, property attribute provides additional features of the level. A level is spatial if it has at least one spatial property attribute. Likewise, a hierarchy is spatial if it has at least one spatial level.

A *field type* is defined as a function from the spatial domain to a base type. Field types are obtained by applying the field(.). Therefore, the result of field(real) (e.g. representing a natural phenomenon) is a continuous function f : point → real. There are two types of fields (temporal and nontemporal). Field types are partial functions, i.e., they may be undefined for certain regions of space. Along with field types a set of operations over fields are defined and classified as in Table 1.

TABLE I. FIELDS AND OPERATION SETS

Class	Operations
Projection to Domain/Range	defspace, rangevalues, point, val
Interaction with Domain/Range	atpoint, atpoint, atline, atregion, at, atmin, atmax, defined, takes, concave, convex, flex
Rate of change	partialder_x, partialder_y
Aggregation operators	integral, area, surface, favg, fvariance, fstdev
Lifting	Operations on discrete types are generalized for field types

1) Relational Calculus

To express SOLAP queries [23], use a query language based on the tuple relational calculus (as in [7]) extended with aggregate functions and variable definitions. They show that this language expresses standard SOLAP queries and that, by extending the calculus with *field* types multidimensional, queries over fields can be expressed. The query language is introduced by example.

Figure 1 and Figure 2 show a query over discrete data and SOLAP operations respectively.

Query 1: Display the name and population of counties in California.
Answer: {c.name, c.population | County(c) ∧ ∃s (State(s) ∧ c.state = s.id ∧ s.name = `California')}

Query 1: Compute the total population of counties in California.
Answer: sum({c.population | County(c) ∧ ∃s (State(s) ∧ c.state = s.id ∧ s.name = `California')})

Figure 1. Query over discrete data

Query 3: Total area of land plots located within 10 km from Orange County that intersect San Diego County.
Answer: {c.name, nbLandPlots | County(c) ^nbLandPlots =
count({*l*.id | LandPlot(*l*)| ∧ ∃ *p* (Crop(*p*) ∧
sum$_2$({*y*.id, *y*.production | Yield(*y*) ∧ *y*.crop= *p*.id ∧
y.landPlot= *l*.id ∧ *l*.county = *c*.id ∧ ∃ *t* (Time(*t*) ∧
y.time= *t*.id ∧ *t*.date ≥ 1/3/2008 ∧ *t*.date ≤ 31/3/2008)})>100,000)})}

Figure 2. SOALP operations

2) Extending OLAP Operations with Continuous Fields

In addition to operations defined on fields specified in 3.2.1, they also define another set of operations that allows the interaction with domain and range. These operations are listed in Figure 3.

atpoint, atpoints, atline, atregion	restrict the function to a given subset of the space defined by a spatial value.
at :	restricts the function to a point or to a point set (a range) in the range of the function.
concave, convex:	restrict the function to the points where it is concave or convex, respectively
flex :	restricts the function to the points where convexity changes

Figure 3. Domain and range operators

There are also operators to compute how the field changes in space. Moreover, there are three aggregate operators defined as follows:

Field average favg : integral/area

Field variance fvariance : $\iint_s \frac{(f(x,y)-favg)^2}{area}\, dxdy$

Field Standard deviation fstdev : $\sqrt{fvariance}$

A class of multidimensional queries over fields denoted SOLAP-CF queries is also defined. Fields are classified as *temporal* identified by f(🌍,🕐) pictogram and *Non-temporal* identified by *f*(🌍) pictogram. In the Non-temporal field, each point in the space has a value (e.g., soil type) whereas for temporal field there is a value that changes with time instant at each point in the space (e.g. temperature). The model also supports field measures that can be pre-computed in the pre-processing stage as a function of many factors.

C. Bimonte and Kang, 2010

Prior to introducing their model, Bimonte et al. [4] define four requirements for definition of a formal model for field data as dimension and measures:

1. Measures as continuous field data
2. Hierarchy on continuous field data
3. Aggregation functions as Map Algebra functions
4. Independence of implementation

They argue that no existing model satisfies all 4 requirements.

1) Definitions

As in the previous models, Bimonte et al. [4] start by providing a uniform representation for field and vector data, which are used to define measures and dimensions members of the multidimensional model.

Real world entities are represented by 3 types of objects described by alphanumeric attributes. An object can represent levels and members of dimensions.

a) **An object**

An Object Structure S_e is a tuple $\langle a_1 \ldots an \rangle$ where $\forall\, i \in [1,\ldots n]$ a_i is an attribute defined on a domain $dom(a_i)$

An Instance of an Object Structure S_e is a tuple $\langle val(a_1),\ldots val(a_n)\rangle$ where $\forall i \in [1,\ldots n]$, $val(a_i) \in dom(a_i)$

'$I(S_e)$' denotes the set of instances of S_e

b) **Geographic Object**

A geographic object is a geometry (geom) and an optional set of alphanumeric attributes ($[a_1, \ldots a_n]$) whose values are associated to the whole geometry according to the vector model.

Let $g \subset R^2$. An Object Structure $S_e = \langle geom, [a_1,\ldots a_n]\rangle$ is a Geographic Object Structure if the domain of the attribute geom is a set of geometries: $dom(geom) \in 2^g$

geom is called 'geometric support'

c) **Field Object**

A Field Object extends a Geographic Object with a function that associates each point of the geometry to an alphanumeric value.

Let $S_e = \langle geom, field, [a_1,\ldots a_n]\rangle$ a Geographic Object Structure. S_e is a Field Object Structure if the domain of the attribute field is a set of functions defined on m sub-sets of points of geom having values in an alphanumeric domain dom_{field} : $dom(field) = \{f_1 \ldots f_m\}$

An Instance of a Field Object Structure S_e is a tuple $\langle g, f_j, val(a_1),\ldots val(a_n)\rangle$ where:

- $\forall i \in [1,\ldots n]$ $val(a_i) \in dom(a_i)$, $g \in dom(geom)$
- $f_j : g \rightarrow dom_{field}$ *and* $f_j \in \{f_1, \ldots, f_m\}$

'field support' is the input domain of f_j

2) Spatio-multidimensional Model for Field Data

A spatio-multidimensional model uses data as dimensions composed of hierarchies, and facts described by measures. A hypercube is an instance of the spatio-multidimensional model.

a) Hierarchies and facts

Vector objects are organized in a hierarchical way. A Spatial Hierarchy organizes the Geographic Objects into a hierarchy structure using a partial order $\leq_h$ where $S_i \leq_h S_j$ means that S_i is a less detailed level than S_j. Measures are aggregated according to the groups of spatial members defined by the tree $<_h$.

Field Hierarchy is defined as a hierarchy of field objects. A Field Hierarchy Structure, $\mathcal{H}_h$, is a tuple $\langle \mathcal{L}_h, \angle_h, \ulcorner_h, \leq_h \rangle$ where:

- $\angle_h$, $\ulcorner_h$, *are of Field Object Structures, and* $\mathcal{L}_h$ *is a set of Field Object Structures*
- $\leq_h$ *is a partial order defined on* $\mathcal{L}_h$, $\angle_h$, $\ulcorner_h$.

An Instance of a Field Hierarchy Structure $\mathcal{H}_h$ is two partial orders: $<_h$ and $<_f$ such that:

- $<_h$ *is defined on the instances of* $\mathcal{L}_h$, $\angle_h$, $\ulcorner_h$. *Noted as* $<_h$ *'geographic objects order'*

- $<_f$ *is defined on the field supports of the instances of* $\mathcal{L}_h$, $\angle_h$, Γ_h *such that:*

- *if* $cood_i <_f cood_j$ *then* $S_i \leq_h S_j$, *where* $cood_i$ *belongs to a field support of an instance of* S_i, *and* $cood_j$ *belongs to a field support of an instance of* S_j, *(*$cood_i$ *and* $cood_j$ *are geometric coordinates)*

- $\forall$ $cood_i$ *which does not belong to the field supports of the instances of* Γ_h, $\exists$ *one* $cood_j$ *belonging to the field support of an instance of* S_j *such that* $cood_i <_f cood_j$

- $\forall$ $cood_i$ *which does not belong to the field supports of the instances of* $\angle_h$, $\exists$ $cood_j$ *belonging to the field support of an instance of* S_j *such that* $cood_j <_f cood_i$.

$<_f$ *is 'field objects order'*

The set of leafs of the tree represented by $<_h$ *with root* t_i *are denoted as leafs(*$\mathcal{H}_h$, t_i*).*

The set of leafs of the tree represented by $<_f$ *with root* $cood_i$ *are denoted as leafsFieldSupport(*$\mathcal{H}_h$, $cood_i$*).*

Based on the definitions above, the model uses a concept of Field Cube Structure that represents the spatio-multidimensional model schema. The model supposes the existence of only one spatial dimension and one field measure.

b) Field Cube

A Field Cube Structure, $\mathcal{FC}_c$, *is a tuple (*$\mathcal{H}_1, \ldots \mathcal{H}_n$, $\mathcal{FieldObject}$*) where:*

- $\mathcal{H}_1$ *is a Field Hierarchy Structure (Spatial dimension)*
- $\forall i \in [2, \ldots n]$ $\mathcal{H}_i$ *is a Hierarchy Structure.*
- $\mathcal{FieldObject}$ *is Field Object Structure.*

An Instance of a Field Cube Structure $\mathcal{FC}_c$, $I(\mathcal{FC}_c)$, *is a set of tuples* $\{(t_{\mathcal{B}_1}, \ldots t_{\mathcal{B}_n}, t_{\mathcal{B}_f})\}$ *where:*

- $\forall i \in [1, \ldots n]$ $t_{\mathcal{B}_i}$ *is an instance of the bottom level of* $\mathcal{F}_i(\angle_i)$.
- $t_{\mathcal{B}_f}$ *is an instance of* $\mathcal{FieldObject}$.

The instance of the spatio-multidimensional model is a hypercube. A hypercube can be represented as a hierarchical lattice of cuboids.

Field measures are aggregated from fact table data (basic cuboid) to represent non-basic cuboids.

Aggregations from cuboids to higher levels are classified as in Figure 4.

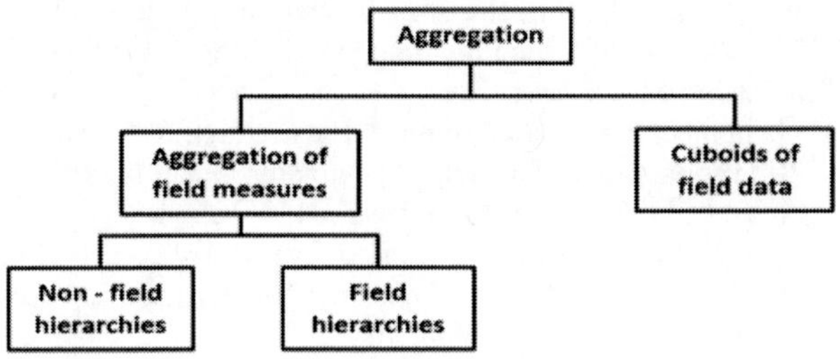

Figure 4. Types of aggregations

3) Aggregation of Field Measures

I. spatial aggregation

Let $\mathcal{G}$ *be the geometric attribute. Its aggregation is defined by means of a function* $O^{\mathcal{G}}$ *that has as input n geometries of the attribute* $\mathcal{G}$, *and that returns one geometry:*

$O_{\mathcal{G}}: dom(\mathcal{G}) \times \ldots \times dom(\mathcal{G}) \rightarrow 2^{\mathcal{G}}$ *where* $\mathcal{G}$ *is a subset of the Euclidian Space* R^2

II. alphanumeric aggregations

Let A be an alphanumeric attribute. Its aggregation is defined by means of a function O_A *that has in input n values of the attribute A, and that returns one value of the attribute A:*

$O_{\mathcal{A}}: dom(\mathcal{A}) \times \ldots \times dom(\mathcal{A}) \rightarrow dom(\mathcal{A})$

4) Gómez and Gómez, 2011, 2012

The model proposed in [23] is extended in [9][10]. The extension includes proposition of a closed generic map algebra over continuous fields. The algebra serves as basis for a language that allows analyzing continuous field data and OLAP cubes using traditional OLAP operations. For the sake of briefness, we will present cube operations for continuous data starting by basic definitions.

a) Spatial Dimension Schemas

A spatial schema is a tuple <*name*$\mathcal{DS}$, $\mathcal{L}$, →> where:

(a) name$\mathcal{DS}$ is a literal;

(b) $\mathcal{L}$ is a non-empty finite set of names called levels (e.g. province, country) which contains a distinguished level name *All;*

(c) Each level $l \in \mathcal{L}$ has a non-empty finite set of names, called level descriptions *LD*(*l*);

(d) Each level description is associated with a base type, called its domain;

(e) → is a partial order (*rollup*) relation on the levels in $\mathcal{L}$.

(f) The closure of rollup has a unique bottom level and a unique upper level called *all* such that *LD(all)={all}*

Based on this, a spatial dimension schema is a dimension schema <*name*$\mathcal{DS}$, $\mathcal{L}$, →> where at least one level $l \in \mathcal{L}$ has exactly one level description with domain of type geometry.

b) Cube Schema and Operations over Fields

A cube schema is a tuple <*nameCS, D, M*> where *nameCS* is a literal, *D* is a finite set of dimension schemas and *M* are also a finite set measures.

According to the definition of discretized fields, the value of the field at that point is the measure and the coordinates of the point are the dimension. The fact is represented by the field and its schema <*cubeName, D, M*>. Therefore, a field can be seen as an OLAP Cube. It is shown that DFields and traditional OLAP cubes can be easily integrated for data analysis.

They also define a set of aggregate functions $\mathcal{A}$ = {Max, Min, Avg, Sum}.

Dice operator. This operation selects values in dimensions or measures based on a Boolean condition σ which may introduce discontinuity. To avoid discontinuity, the operator is defined by setting the value of samples with ⊥ values where the σ operator is not satisfied.

ROLL-UP operator. It aggregates facts according to dimension hierarchy. In this model the spatial dimension is a single-level dimension which implies that rollup hierarchies must be introduced externally. Three roll-up operations are defined (spatial over spatial field, spatial over spatiotemporal field and temporal over spatiotemporal fields).

Drill-Down. This operations aggregates facts according to dimension hierarchy. In this model, the spatial dimension is a single-level dimension which implies that rollup hierarchies must be introduced externally. They define 3 roll-up operations (spatial over spatial field, spatial over spatiotemporal field and temporal over spatiotemporal fields).

Roll-Up. This operation reverses the effect of **Roll-Up** so it is just the inverse of the mentioned operator.

IV. Discussion

The approaches used in the above listed proposals (and in others) are diverse to say the least. Moreover, it seems that there is no build up on previous work or any attempts to criticize or enhance what has already been done which leads to a plethora of models without a clear attempt to define a mainstream model.

To compare the 4 models, one needs to define criteria and search which model meets the necessary requirements to become an applicable model. According to [6], true data models should have 3 components: A *structure* that defines how data are structured, *integrity rules* that define how data are kept correct and consistent and *operators* which define how data are manipulated. Therefore we will compare these models using the above mentioned conditions in addition to the requirements defined by [4] and additional requirements defined in [16][17]. The different models are evaluated against these six requirements (Table 2):

1) Structure

The common structure between all models is the hypercube. Each model proposes a different way of building its hypercube.

2) Integrity rules

Multidimensional structures are not concerned with integrity as much as they are concerned with fast response to analytical queries.

3) Operators

This complexity of SOLAP queries implies long query processing time. Therefore, most queries are run in advance and the results are stored as materialized views. Operators are either for navigation along the analysis dimensions or for returning previously computed results.

4) Continuous data as measures

Usually measures are numerical values that are analyzed according to axis of analysis (the dimensions). In the models we reviewed only one proposal imposes continuous data as measures constraint.

5) Explicit hierarchies in dimensions

The hierarchy should be explicit to allow the user to navigate with clear knowledge of the relationship between the different levels [15].

6) Symmetric treatment of dimensions and measures:

Since measures can be a level of a dimension, it is essential that measures can be transformed into attributes and vice versa [5]. This will provide an important functionality to any OLAP system.

TABLE II. Multidimensional Model Comparison Criteria

Criteria	Ahmed et al. [1]	Vaisman et al. [23]	Bimonte et al. [4]	Gómez et al. [9][10]
Structures	✓	✓	✓	✓
Integrity rules	x	x	x	x
Operators	✓	✓	✓	✓
Continuous data as measures	x	x	✓	x
Explicit hierarchies	✓	x	✓	x
Symmetric treatment of dimensions and measures	✓	x	x	x

To clarify some of the differences between the 4 models, we will present examples of how the aggregate *average* is handled by each model.

In [1], to find the average pollution for a specific region, the aggregation is done by applying interpolation functions to the basic cubes to obtain a continuous representation of the field. The sum of all values is calculated as in integral of the function representing the field. The average is then obtained by dividing the sum by the area of the field. In [23], the average monthly temperature for a land plot is calculated as follows :

{*l*.number, *m*.month, temp | LandPlot(*l*) ^ Month(*m*)^ first=min({*t*.date|Time(*t*) ^ *t*.month = *m*.id}^last= max({*t*.date|Time(t)^*t*.month=*m*.id}^ temp = avg ({atperiods (atregion(*t*.geometry,*l*.geometry), range(first, last)) | Temperature(*t*)})} Where *first* and *last* represent first and last day of the month.

In [4], the aggregation is performed by applying the average on the Field Hierarchy H_{regres}. $F_4(x;y)=AVG(leavesFieldSupport(H_{deptres}, (x_2;y_2))) = AVG(f_3(x;y), f_3(x_1;y_1))$.

For more details about the examples we refer the reader to [1][4][9][23].

From Table 2, none of the proposed models satisfies all criteria. Models proposed by Vaisman et al. [23] and Gómez et al. [9][10] satisfy only structure and operators constraints. The major weakness is the lack explicit hierarchies, which is essential for navigation in cubes. The model presented by Ahmed et al. [1] lacks treatment of continuous data as a measure which is supported in [4]. However, Bimonte et al. [4] does not treat dimensions and measures symmetrically.

V. Conclusion

Spatial data warehouses have been around for some time now. Most of the early work on this topic was oriented towards discrete spatial data. The combination of cartographic display and OLAP resulted in SOLAP. However it was also limited to discrete spatial representation. Attempts at integrating continuous or field based data in multidimensional structures began about 10 years ago. During this period, a number of models to represent spatial and/or spatiotemporal continuity were proposed. In this paper, we studied some of these models and compared them with respect to different criteria and conditions for multidimensional models. None of the different proposals covered all comparison criteria and hence there is still a considerable amount of work to be done on the subject. The other remark is that most of the work concentrated on the theoretical side without a mention of solid model that can be used in real life application. To the best of our knowledge, even though there is still an undiscovered wealth mine for research and development, there is a lack of recent work on this domain.

References

[1] T. O. Ahmed and M. Miquel. "Multidimensional Structures Dedicated to Continuous Spatiotemporal Phenomena". In proceedings of the 22nd British National Conference on Databases (BNCOD), (Sunderland, UK, July 5-7, 2005) 29-40.

[2] T. O. Ahmed. "Spatial On-line Analytical Processing (SOLAP): Overview and Current Trends". In proceedings of Internationa Conference on Advanced Computer Theory and Engineering (ICACTE), (Phuket, Thailand, December, 20-22, 2008) 1095-1099.

[3] Y. Bédard, T. Merrett and J. Han. "Fundamentals of Spatial Data Warehousing for Geographic Knowledge Discovery in Geographic Data Mining and Knowledge Discovery". Research Monographs in GIS Series. Edited by Peter Fisher and Jonathan Raper. 2001. 53-73.

[4] S. Bimonte and M. A. Kang. "Towards a Model for the Multidimensional Analysis of Field Data". In proceedings of the 14th East European Conference (ADBIS10) (Novi Sad, Serbia, Sep 20-24, 2010. 300-311.

[5] L. Cabibbo and R. Torlone. "From a procedural to a visual query language for OLAP". In proceedings of the 10th International Conference on Scientific and Statistical Database Management (SSDBM'98), IEEE Computer Society Press, Washington, DC, USA pp. 74–83, 1998.

[6] E. F. Codd. "Data Models in Database Management". ACM SIGMOD Record 11(2), 1981, pp. 112-114.

[7] R. Elmasri. and S. Navathe. Fundamentals of Database Systems. Pearson, 7th edition, 2015.

[8] C. Franklin. "An Introduction to geographic Information Systems: Linking Maps to databases". Database, 1992. pp. 13-21.

[9] L. Gómez, S. Gómez and A. Vaisman. "Analyzing Continuous Fields with OLAP Cubes". In proceedings of the 14th Workshop DOLAP (DOLAP'11), (Glasgow, Scotland, Oct 24-28, 2011). pp. 89-94

[10] L. Gómez, S. Gómez and A. Vaisman. "A Generic Data Model and Query Language for Spatiotemporal OLAP Cube Analysis". In proceedings of the 15th International Conference on Extending Database Technology (EDBT2012) (Berlin, Germany) Mar 27-30, 2012, pp. 300-311.

[11] J. Han, R. Altman, V. Kumar, H. Mannila and D. Pregibon. "Emerging Scientific Applications in Data Mining". Communication of the ACM, 45,8 (Aug 2002), pp. 54-58.

[12] E. Malinowski and E. Zimányi. "Advanced Data Warehouse Design: From Conventional to Spatial and Temporal Applications". Data-Centric Systems and Applications, Springer, 2008.

[13] P. Marchand, A. Brisebois, Y. Bedard and G. Edwards. "Implementation and Evaluation of a Hypercube-Based Method for Spatiotemporal Exploration and Analysis". ISPRS Journal of Photogrammetry and Remote Sensing. (Aug 2004) 59(1-2), pp. 6-20.

[14] F. Moreno, J. A. E. Arias and B. M. Losada. "A Conceptual Spatio-temporal Multidimensional Model". Revista Ingenierías Universidad de Medellín. (2011) 9(17), pp. 175-184.

[15] T. B. Pederson. "Managing complex multidimensional data". Business Intelligence: Lecture Notes in Business Information Processing. (2013) vol. 138. pp. 1-28.

[16] T. Pedersen and C. Jensen. "Multidimensional Data Modeling for Complex Data". In proceedings of the 15th International Conference on Data Engineering (ICDE99)(Sydney, Australia) March 23-26 1999, pp. 336-345.

[17] G. Pestana and M. Mira da Silva. "Multidimensional Modeling based on Spatial, Temporal and Spatio-Temporal Stereotypes". 5th ESRI International User Conference (ESRI) (San Diego, USA) Jul 25-29, 2005, pp. 5-15.

[18] E. Pourabbas and M. Rafanelli. "Characterization of Hierarchies and Some Operators in OLAP Environment." In proceedings of the 2nd ACM International Workshop on Data Warehousing and OLAP. (Kansas City, USA). Nov 2-6, 1999, pp. 54 - 59.

[19] S. Rivest, Y. Bedard and P. Marchand. "Towards better Support for Spatial Decision Making: Defining the Characteristics of Spatial On-Line Analytical Processing (SOLAP)". Journal of Canadian Institute of Geomatics, 55(4), 2001, pp. 539-555.

[20] S. Rivest, Y. Bedard, M. J. Proulx and M. Nadeau. "SOLAP: A New Type of User Interface to Support Spatiotemporal Multidimensional Data Exploration and Analysis". In proceedings of ISPRS workshop on Spatial, Temporal and Multi-Dimensional Data Modeling and Analysis, (Québec, Canada) Oct 2-3, 2003.

[21] M. Sampaio, A. Sousa and C. Baptista. "Towards a Logical Multidimensional Model for Spatial Data Warehousing and OLAP". In proceedings of 9th ACM International Workshop on Data Warehousing and OLAP (New York, USA) Nov 5-11, 2006, pp. 83-90.

[22] N. Stefanovic, J. Han and K. Koperski. "Object-based Selective Materialization for Efficient Implementation of Spatial Data Cubes". IEEE Transactions on Knowledge and Data Engineering, (Nov-Dec 2000) 12(6), pp. 938 – 957.

[23] A. A. Vaisman and E. Zimányi. "A Multidimensional Model Representing Continuous Fields in Spatial Data Warehouses". In proceedings of the International Conference on Advances in Geographic Information Systems (ACM SIGSPATIAL GIS 2009)(Seattle, USA) Nov 4-6, 2009, pp. 168-177.

[24] M. Zaamoune, S. Bimonte, F. Pinet and P. Beaune. "A New Relational Spatial OLAP Approach for Multi-resolution and Spatio-multidimensional Analysis of Incomplete Field Data". In proceedings of International Conference on Enterprise Information Systems (ICEIS 2013)(Angers, France) 4-7 Jul 2013, pp. 145 -152.

Some Heuristic Approaches for Reducing Energy Consumption on Database Systems

Miguel Guimarães
ALGORITMI R&D Center
University of Minho
Portugal
pg22800@alunos.uminho.pt

João Saraiva
HasLab R&D Center
INESC/University of Minho
Portugal
jas@di.uminho.pt

Orlando Belo
ALGORITMI R&D Center
University of Minho
Portugal
obelo@di.uminho.pt

***Abstract*—Today, one of the major concerns of administrators and managers of data centers is related with the cost of the energy that each database component consumes when involved in activities and processes they manage. In fact, it is not necessary to conduct a detailed assessment to realize that the cost of energy consumed in this type of systems is really great. So, it is not surprising the significant growing interest that researchers have in this domain. Various techniques have been developed to assess the energy consumption on database systems, demonstrating their utility in managing the power they use to consume. Basically, they come to confirm the paradigm shift on the issue of energy concern in database systems towards the reduction of its consumption. In this paper, we present and discuss a set of heuristics that we suggest to reduce, in particular, the energy consumption on the execution of a given query inside a relational database system. With this work, we intend to contribute to design and implement more efficient queries in terms of energy, i.e., green queries, based on the analysis of the various components that are used in their physical implementation, reducing as much as possible their energy consumption, taking into consideration the characteristics of the database operators used and the querying execution plans established for them.**

Keywords-data centers; database management systems; querying execution plans, database queries consumption, green queries; consumption heuristics.

I. Introduction

The assessment of energy consumption of any component is not an easy task. To carry out appropriately this kind of evaluation, it is necessary to study in detail how the component behaves and how it is used in practice. The same may be applied to the study of power consumption of a *DataBase Management System* (DBMS) or, in particular, of any query that can be performed in its environment [1]. Any process for the establishment of energy-efficient queries, usually recognized as green queries, and not its optimization in terms of processing time or usage of computing resources, requires a fairly deep knowledge of how queries are processed and optimized in the environment of a DBMS.

Database querying processing [2][3] is one of the most important activities of a DBMS, which involves a well-defined set of processes for supporting the way the system responds to users' queries. Optimizing querying processing is something that has been worked over the years by researchers in the databases field. See, for example, the work of Ceri and Gottlob [4] that presented a way to transform a SQL statement into relational algebra expressions representing equivalent SQL sub statements, a method revealed by Taniar [5] especially oriented to add additional instructions (e.g., optimizer hints, access method hints, or table joins hints) into SQL statements to instruct the SQL optimizer for executing the statement in an alternative better way, or how Li et al. [6] suggested a manner to improve querying performance with configuration options – e.g., table partitioning, materialized views, or storing plan outlines – increasing as well the efficiency of the code application.

However, as the number and capacity of data centers increases, beside the so usual issues of performance and querying processing abilities – always critical aspects for any DBMS –, the issue of power consumption is appearing very clear in their cost operational reports, year after year [7]. This caught the attention of data centers' managers all over the world up sharply their concerns related to energy consumption, not only because of the cost of electricity itself but also because of relevant environmental issues. In general, database servers are the biggest customers of computational resources of a conventional data center, which makes them also one of its biggest energy consumers [8]. Although these systems are very well equipped today, with powerful tools for querying optimization, quality of service, or overall performance, usually in terms of energy consumption DBMS do not have any means especially oriented to the management and control of consumption power. With the current trends and needs of the markets and DBMS users, this lack is considered quite serious. The non-availability of data about the energy consumption of a DBMS has been motivating a large diversity of research initiatives aiming to create means so that we can in addition to defining query optimization plans in DBMS environments also create energy consumption plans for executing queries.

In a previous work [9], we developed a study that allowed us to develop an energy consumption plan for a query that is usually executed in a conventional data center environment. At that time, the goal was reducing, as much as possible, the energy consumption of data centers queries without affecting their usual performance. We believed that such small reduction in the consumption of a simple query could be a great help in reducing the overall consumption of a data center – that was proved easily by multiplying these tiny savings by the huge number of queries (and transactions) that are executed per minute in a data center. Continuing this work, we studied a set of specific heuristics that we suggest to reduce, in particular, the energy consumption on the execution of a given query inside a relational DBMS, which we expect that contribute to design and implement more efficient queries in terms of energy – green queries.

In this paper, we present and discuss the referred energy consumption heuristics, giving particular attention to other related works (Section II), showing how we categorized the energy consumption of a SQL query, what kind of transformation rules were applied, and how the energy was consumed by each one of the transformation rules studied (Section III). Finally, we finish this paper with some brief conclusions and pointing out some future research lines (Section V).

II. RELATED WORK

Today, energy efficiency is a trend topic in terms of researching and development. Researchers of different fields of expertise work and discuss possible solutions to solve the energy crisis that we are facing today. On the one hand, saving energy allow us to reduce the energy billing costs; and on the other hand, by doing that, we are also preserving environment resources. Thus, saving energy and creating policies to develop green software is beneficial for everybody. Steps towards that direction have been already made. At software level, for instance, the works presented in [10] and [11] are some good examples of techniques and methods used to detect energy consumption. In [10], the authors adapted a technique known as Spectrum-based Fault Localization to identify parts of code responsible for a higher energetic consumption. The work done in [11] focused more on finding and detecting anomalous energy consumption in Android systems. Both works show us that reducing energy consumption has been tackled in a variety of systems by several researches, and its popularity in computer science domains has increased.

Database systems have also taken small steps towards green guidelines. The Claremont report was one of the first approaches concerning energy consumption in database systems [12]. The main goal of this report was to take into consideration, during the devise and implementation stages of a database system, the energy consumed by different tasks. Reinforcing such concerns, the work presented in [13] provided us a clear survey of how to control efficiently energy in data management operations. Later, other studies emerged approaching the same topic [14][15][16]. However, most of them have focus essentially on hardware questions. In terms of software, in [9] it was redesigned the execution plan of a DBMS in order to include, not only the default estimative values for query execution, but also an estimative of energy that will be consumed to run a specific query. Later, it was proposed a solution to redesign a DMBS kernel, in order to reduce energy consumption [15]. Afterward, in [17] other alternatives were suggested to reduce the high levels of energy consumption in DBMS, in general terms, while other works, were concerned about the prediction of the consumption of large join queries [18], or how to optimize queries to reduce global consumption of energy within a DBMS [19]. However, as far as we know, there are no works approaching the effect of regular querying optimization heuristics on the consumption of energy of a DBMS. Thus, we selected some of the most used heuristics on relational querying processing and studied their effect in terms of energy consumption.

III. ENERGY CONSUMPTION CATEGORIZATION

The energy consumption paradigm has been increasing its importance over the last few years, slowly replacing the performance paradigm, in terms of main concerns, to take into account when developing any kind of database querying task. Query processing is one of the most important activities performed by a DBMS. Today, it is possible to analyze and optimize the cost of a database query in terms of performance, establishing better execution plans and reducing querying processing time. Having access to these plans, we can also measure the energy that database operations consume in a similar way as we can measure their processing time. We only need appropriate tools.

A. Data and Test Configuration

In this work, we developed a tool with the ability to measure the energy consumption of SQL queries, categorizing which ones are green and which ones are not. We used the tool *gSQL*, shorten for *greenSQL*, to categorize the energy consumption of SQL queries. This tool uses as support the jRAPL framework, which allows for monitoring the energy consumption of different hardware levels for a certain code block [20]. In order to use jRAPL, there are certain conditions that must be fulfilled. The processor has to be from Intel architectures and support *Machine-Specific Registers* (MSR). The later are the registers used for storing the energy consumption information for code block that was monitored. Therefore, the role played by the jRAPL framework is exclusively dedicated to categorize and analyze the energy consumption of SQL queries. Regarding the *gSQL* tool, even though its use is simple, it gives us the required information to devise hypothesis and thus create heuristics to reduce the queries energy consumption. To run the tests it is necessary to specify three different parameters:

1) an input file, with all the queries that going to be tested;

2) the number of times each query will be repeated;

3) the number of times each test will be repeated.

In Figure 1, it is possible to see a brief description of the overall behavior of the *gSQL* tool, written in pseudo code. After all the tests have been executed, we obtain as result the energy and the time consumption for each query tested. The calculated aggregated values were maximum, minimum, average, and standard deviation. This set of aggregated values allows for us to find out if a certain test need to be executed again, by analyzing the standard deviation as well as the amplitude between maximum and minimum values. For the test environment, we choose the PostgreSQL DBMS, populated with data based on the TPC-H benchmark. Depending on the scaling factor, the database can assume different dimensions. In this case study, we used a scale factor of two, which means that we multiplied by two the cardinality of the tables that depends from the scale factor.

```
begin
resultsList ← initializeResults()
  for each query in queriesList do
    begin
      for each execution in executionsList do
      being
        for each repetition in repetitionList do
        begin
          initialEnergy ← getEnergy()
          initialTime   ← getTime ()
          executeQuery(query)
          finalEnergy ← getEnergy()
          finalTime ← getTime()
          energy ← initialEnergy - finalEnergy
          time ← finalTime - initialTime
          storeValues(resultsList, energy, time)
        end
      end
    end
    aggregate ← aggregateResults(results)
    writeFile(aggregate)
  end
```

Figure 1. A pseudo code excerpt describing the behavior of the gSQL tool

B. *Transformation Rules*

Often, we start a querying optimization process by analyzing the structure of the query, trying to see if it is well designed and use the most appropriated resources. In this kind of processes, it is common to see if some practical querying heuristics can be applied at a certain stage of the process, in order to improve the way the query is processed, having the goal to reduce its execution time. There are a set of heuristics well establish in the literature to improve querying processes [21]. In some particular application cases, such heuristics give us clear processing advantages, reducing the resources involved with and the response time of the query. The question now is: do those querying heuristics also help in reducing querying energy consumption?

The transformation rules used for the relational algebra operations suit well the requirements presented in [22] and posteriorly in [21]. The first six rules were tested using the *gSQL* tool. The results we got were analyzed in order to create the heuristics to optimize querying energy consumption. Each transformation rule (1-6) that was used will be explained and illustrated with a specific SQL query example. The SQL queries were devised specifically for each transformation rule. Due to the variety of tables in the TPC-H benchmark, there are plenty of options that could be used to design queries for each different transformation rule. However, TPC-H benchmark has a set of queries which, in this case study, were adapted to better represent transformation rules. Results can be consulted later in Table 1.

Transformation Rule 1 – this rule states that conjunctive selection operations can be separated into individual selection operations. To demonstrate this transformation rule, we create two SQL queries that are presented in Figure 2.

```
a)   select * from lineitem where l_quantity>40
         and l_discount>0.03;
b)   select * from ( select * from lineitem
        where l_discount>0.03) as sub
        where sub.l_quantity>40;
```

Figure 2. The SQL queries for testing rule 1.

The first query (Figure 2a) represents the conjunctive selection operations whereas the second one (Figure 2b) represents individual selections with the application of some filtering conditions.

Transformation Rule 2 – this second rule shows us how the selection operations have commutative proprieties. This means that doing the selection of a given predicate p followed by a predicate q have the same result as doing first the selection of the predicate q followed by the predicate p (Figure 3).

```
a)   select * from ( select * from lineitem
        where l_discount>0.03) as sub
        where sub.l_quantity>40;
b)   select * from ( select * from lineitem
        where l_quantity>40) as sub
        where sub.l_discount>0.03;
```

Figure 3. The SQL queries for testing rule 2.

Transformation Rule 3 – this rule denotes that in any sequence of projection operations, only the last one in the sequence is necessary. For instance, doing in first place the projection of the attributes a and b followed by b is equivalent of doing only the projection of the attribute b (Figure 4).

```
a) select sub.l_shipmode
     from ( select l_quantity, l_discount,
     l_shipmode from lineitem) as sub;
b) select l_shipmode
     from lineitem;
```

Figure 4. The SQL queries for testing rule 3.

Transformation Rule 4 – this rule states that between selection and projection operations there is a commutative propriety associated as long as the predicate belongs to the attributes in the projection list (Figure 5).

```
a) select sub.l_shipmode, sub.l_quantity
     from ( select * from lineitem
     where l_quantity>40) as sub;

b) select sub.*
     from ( select l_shipmode, l_quantity
            from lineitem) as sub
     where sub.l_quantity>40;
```

Figure 5. The SQL queries for testing rule 4.

Transformation Rule 5 – according to this rule, a cartesian product and theta join operations can be commuted. Therefore, doing a theta join between two relations, *R* and *S*, it is equivalent to do the theta join between the relation *S* and the relation *R*. The same principle can be applied to the cartesian product as well as to a natural join or an equijoin (Figure 6). For this example, we set a limit of five hundred thousand records to be selected, in order to have a faster query. Without the limit constraint, the difference between energy consumptions of both queries will be the same, but limiting the number of records to be selected, instead of the full length of the relation, allows us to save time when running tests.

```
a) select * from orders
     inner join customer
     on o_custkey = c_custkey limit 500000;

b) select * from customer
     inner join orders
     on o_custkey = c_custkey limit 500000;
```

Figure 6. The SQL queries for testing rule 5.

Transformation Rule 6 – Rule number six states that between selection and theta join operations there is a commutative propriety associated, if the selection predicate involves only attributes of one of the relations being joined (Figure 7).

```
a)   select sub.* from (select * from orders
     inner join customer
     on o_custkey = c_custkey) as sub
     where sub.c_mktsegment='BUILDING'
             and sub.o_orderpriority='2-HIGH';

b)   select * from
     (select * from customer
         where c_mktsegment='BUILDING') as t1
         inner join (select * from orders
         where o_orderpriority='2-HIGH') as t2
            on t1.c_custkey = t2.o_custkey;
```

Figure 7. The SQL queries for testing rule 5.

C. *Result Analyzes*

Through the data presented in Table 1 it is possible to analyze the average energy consumed for each transformation rule and take some conclusions regarding the heuristics for optimizing the energy consumption on SQL queries. If we observe rule 2, we can see that the second query (Figure 3b) consumes less energy than the first query (Figure 3a), because the second SQL query reduces the number of tuples that are processed by the DBMS. Thus, we can infer that doing first the selection operation that discards more tuples translates into an energy saving measure. Another conclusion that can be deduced based on the *gSQL* results, is that doing only the projection of necessary attributes consumes less energy than the projection of necessary and unnecessary attributes (transformation rule 3). An obvious conclusion, since there is less computational load required, a less execution time leads to a decrease in the energy consumption. Regarding the transformation rule 4, it is possible to conclude that reducing the cardinality of the relations it is a good green practice. Hence, eliminating unnecessary tuples before doing others relational algebra operations can be seen as a heuristic to optimize the energy consumption. With the data collected from *gSQL* tool, for cartesian products and theta joins operations, we can inferred the following: if the relation on the left side of the join operation have higher cardinality than the relation on the right side, then it consumes less energy (transformation rule 5).

TABLE I. AVERAGE ENERGY COMSUMPTION FOR EACH QUERY IN A TRANSFORMATION RULE

Query	Average Energy (Joules)	Average Time (seconds)
1 a)	251.3028	12.34
1 b)	256.1062	12.5102
2 a)	256.1062	12.5102
2 b)	249.4447	12.16
3 a)	196.2550	9.86
3 b)	195.3628	9.72
4 a)	78.74333	3.98
4 b)	80.18314	4.02
5 a)	77.5720	3.8
5 b)	78.17531	3.72
6 c)	21.04923	1.04
6 d)	21.92778	1.12

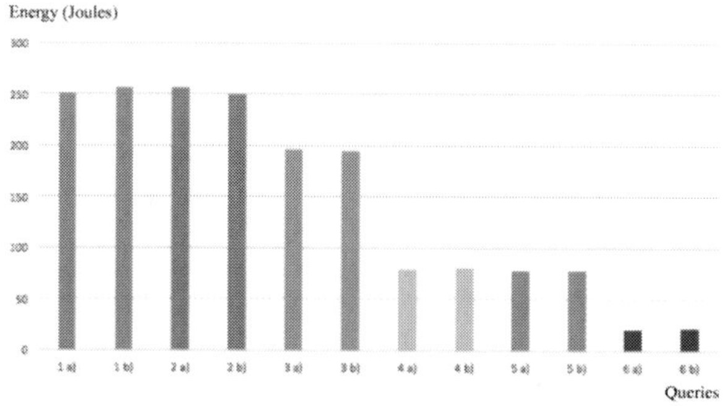

Figure 8. Energy consumed by each transformation rule version

Lastly, data from transformation rule 6 suggests that it is greener to do the selection operation before doing theta-join operations. As previously mentioned, cardinality reduction means less energy consumption. Finally, in Figure 8 we can see a chart showing the energy consumption of each one of the queries that were used and tested in each transformation rule.

IV. Conclusions and Future Work

In this paper, we presented some heuristics to optimize the energy consumption of relational database queries. The heuristics presented here were devised by analyzing the data from *gSQL* tool. This was a first approach towards the creation of a more refined set of energy consumption heuristics. As far as we know, nothing similar was done yet in this field of expertise. Saving energy on a query that is executed several times in a data center reduces the monthly energy bill and therefore, decreases the costs of a data center. It is interesting to notice different energy consumptions by doing simple tweaks and transformation rules. Although, we present some heuristics in this paper, some of them having a parallel that corresponds to performance optimization heuristics well defined in the area database systems. Hence, for systems with the same type of hardware optimizing a query to be greener is equivalent to optimizing a query to be faster.

In a near future, we intend to verify if the heuristics proposed here can be transposed to different DBMS. It is important to know how to rank the different DBMS, in order to offer to database administrators the possibility to adopt an eco-friendlier DBMS to support their operational systems. Another issue that we expect to explore is the impact of the established heuristics in DBMS performance structures, such as indexes, execution plans or materialized views, in order to prepare DBMS internal configuration structures regarding energy saving issues.

References

[1] G. Graefe, "Database servers tailored to improve energy efficiency," in Proceedings of the 2008 EDBT Workshop on Software Engineering for Tailor-made Data Management, 2008, pp. 24-28.

[2] M. Jarke, "Query optimization in database systems," in ACM Computing Surveys, Vol. 16, No. 2, 1984, pp 11-152.

[3] S. Chaudhuri, "An Overview of Query Optimization". In Proceedings of the seventeenth ACM SIGACT, 1998, pp. 34-43.

[4] S. Ceri and G. Gottlob, "Translating SQL Into Relational Algebra: Optimization, Semantics, and Equivalence of SQL Queries," in IEEE Transactions on Software Engineering, Vol. SE-11, No. 4, 1985, pp. 324-345.

[5] D. Taniar, H. Khaw, T. H. Cokrowijoyo, and E. Pardede, "The use of Hints in SQL-Nested query optimization," Information Sciences, Vol. 177, No 12, 2007, pp. 2493-2521.

[6] D. Li, L. Han, and Y. Ding, "YiSQL Query Optimization Methods of Relational Database System," in Second International Conference on Computer Engineering and Applications, 2010, pp. 557-560.

[7] S. Mittal, "Power Management Techniques for Data Centers: A Survey", 2014. [online] Available at: http://arxiv.org/abs/1404.6681 [Accessed 11 March 2016].

[8] M. Poess and R. O. Nambiar, "Energy cost, the key challenge of today's data centers: a power consumption analysis of TPC-C results," in Proceedings of the VLDB Endowment, vol. 1, 2008, pp. 1229-1240.

[9] R. Gonçalves, J. Saraiva, and O. Belo, "Defining Energy Consumption Plans for Data Querying Processes". In Proceedings of 2014 IEEE Fourth International Conference on Big Data and Cloud Computing (BdCloud 2014), IEEE computer Society, Sidney, Australia, 2014, pp. 641-647.

[10] T. Carção, "Measuring and visualizing energy consumption within software code". In: Visual Languages and Human-Centric Computing (VL/HCC), 2014 IEEE Symposium on, July, 2014, pp. 181– 182.

[11] M. Couto, T. Carção, J. Cunha, J. P. Fernandes, and J. Saraiva, "Detecting anomalous energy consumption in android applications". In Pereira, F.M.Q., ed.: Programming Languages - 18th Brazilian Symposium, SBLP 2014, Maceio, Brazil, October 2-3, 2014. Proceedings. Volume 8771 of Lecture Notes in Computer Science., Springer, 2014, pp. 77–91.

[12] R. Agrawal et al., "The claremont report on database research". SIGMOD Rec. 37(3), September, 2008, pp. 9–19.

[13] J. Wang, L. Feng, W. Xue, and Z. Song, "A Survey on Energy-efficient Data Management," in SIGMOD Rec. 40, 2, September, 2011, pp. 17-23.

[14] W. Lang, R. Kandhan, and J. M. Patel, "Rethinking query processing for energy efficiency: Slowing down to win the race". IEEE Data Eng. Bull. 34(1), 2011, pp. 12–23.

[15] W. Lang and J. M. Patel, "Towards eco-friendly database management systems". In CIDR 2009, Fourth Biennial Conference on Innovative Data Systems Research, Asilomar, CA, USA, January 4-7, 2009, Online Proceedings, www.cidrdb.org, 2009.

[16] Z. Xu, Y. Tu, and X. Wang, "Exploring power-performance tradeoffs in database systems". In Li, F., Moro, M.M., Ghandeharizadeh, S., Haritsa, J.R., Weikum, G., Carey, M.J., Casati, F., Chang, E.Y., Manolescu, I., Mehrotra, S., Dayal, U., Tsotras, V.J., eds.: Proceedings of the 26th International Conference on Data Engineering, ICDE 2010, March 1-6, 2010, Long Beach, California, USA, IEEE, 2010, pp. 485–496.

[17] M. Kunjir, P. K. Birwa, and J. R. Haritsa, "Peak power plays in database engines". In E. A. Rundensteiner, V. Markl, I. Manolescu, S. Amer-Yahia, F. Naumann, and I. Ari, eds.: 15th International Conference on Extending Database Technology, EDBT '12, Berlin, Germany, March 27-30, 2012, Proceedings, ACM, 2012, pp. 444–455.

[18] M. Rodriguez et al., "Analyzing power and energy consumption of large join queries in database systems," Industrial Electronics and Applications (ISIEA), 2013 IEEE Symposium on, Kuching, 2013, pp. 148-153.

[19] Z. Xu, Y. Tu, and X. Wang. "PET: reducing Database Energy Cost via Query Optimization," in Proc. VLDB Endow. 5, 12, August, 2012, pp. 1954-1957.

[20] K. Liu, G. Pinto, and D. Liu, "Data-oriented characterization of application-level energy optimization", in: Proceedings of the 18th International Conference on Fundamental Approaches to Software Engineering, FASE'15, 2015.

[21] T. Connoly and C. Begg, "Database Systems: A pratical Approach to Design, Implementation, and Management", 2005, Addison-Wesley Longman Publishing Co., Inc., Boston, USA

[22] A. V. Aho and J. D. Ullman, "Universality of Data Retrieval Languages", in Proceedings of the 6th ACM SIGACT-SIGPLAN Symposium on Principles of Programming Languages, POPL '79, (New York, NY, USA), ACM, 1979, pp. 110–119.

A Framework for Semantic Web of Patent Information

Yung Chang Chi[1]
Hei Chia Wang[2]
Department of Industrial and Information Management and
Institute of Information Management,
National Cheng Kung University,
Tainan City, Taiwan ROC
e-mail:charles.y.c.chi@gmail.com[1]
hcwang@mail.ncku.edu.tw[2]

Ying Maw Teng[3]
Department of International Business,
I-Shou University,
Kaohsiung City, Taiwan ROC
e-mail: morris@isu.edu.tw[3]

Abstract - **This paper aims to propose a framework for an ontology-based semantic web of patent information by employing PATExpert, which is based on the ontological approach of constructing knowledge and technique from patent documents. This method will analyze patent infringement issues from judicial judgments in the USA and Europe. Having examined relative patent documents and the analysis of patent infringement by comparison, one can identify particular kinds of products and technologies that are interrelated with the analysis of the two different databases while enhancing the feasible construction of the semantic web for patent information.**

Keywords-patent; PATExpert; patent infringement; content analysis; Ontology; semantic web.

I. INTRODUCTION

Patents are important sources of knowledge for industrial research and product development because of their innovation and practicability. In recent years, patent analyses have increased in importance for high-technology management as the process of innovation has become more complex, the cycle of innovation shorter, and the market demand more volatile [15].

An emerging research topic, patent mining consists of patent retrieval, patent categorization, and patent clustering [1]. So far, little research has been done on the topic.

The European project PATExpert, (Advanced Patent Document Processing Techniques), coordinated by Barcelona Media (BM), has successfully accomplished the objectives after the pre-established 30 months (from February 2006 to July 2008). Thus, it has been ratified by the representative and the two external supervisors designated by the European Commission, in the final review of the project celebrated on 21st October at the BM headquarters [19].

In the frame of the Sixth Framework Program of Research and Technological Development (2002-2006), PATExpert has a global objective to change the present textual processing of patents to semantic processing (treating the patents as multimedia knowledge objects) [19].

WordNet was created in the Cognitive Science Laboratory of Princeton University under the direction of psychology professor George Armitage Miller starting in 1985 [24].

WordNet superficially resembles a thesaurus, in that it groups words together based on their meanings. However, there are some important distinctions. First, WordNet interlinks not just word forms—strings of letters—but specific senses of words. As a result, words that are found in close proximity to one another in the network are semantically disambiguated. Second, WordNet labels the semantic relations among words, whereas the groupings of words in a thesaurus do not follow any explicit pattern other than meaning similarity [24].

The applications employ the Semantic Web to make useable sense out of large, distributed information found throughout the World Wide Web. A definition for the Semantic Web begins with defining semantic. Semantic simply means meaning. Meaning enables a more effective use of the underlying data. Meaning is often absent from most information sources, requiring users or complex programming instructions to supply it. For example, web pages are filled with information associated tags. Most of the tags represent formatting instructions, such as <H1> to indicate a major heading. Semantically, we know that words surrounded by <H1> tags are more important to readers than other texts because of the meaning of H1. Some web pages add basic semantics for search engines by using the <META> tag; however, they are merely isolating keywords and lack linkages to provide a more meaningful context. These semantics are weak and limit searches to find out the exact matches. Similarly, databases will render more accurate matches if tables and columns of database are well named and well organized. Semantics give a keyword symbol useful meaning through the establishment of relationships [4].

Relational databases depend on a schema for structure. A knowledge base depends on ontological statements to establish structure. Relational databases are limited to one kind of relationship – the foreign key. The Semantic Web offers multidimensional relationships such as inheritance, part of, associated with, and many other types, including logical relationships and constraints. One important note is that the language used to form structure and the instances themselves may be the same language in a knowledge base but actually quite different in relational databases [4].

Retrieving patent documents can be done through the cluster-based approach [10]. Distributed information retrieval for patents can be done by generating ranking lists for the query by CORI (The collection retrieval inference network) or KL (Kernighan–Lin) algorithms [13]. Categorizing patent documents can be done automatically by using the k-Nearest Neighbor classifiers and Bayesian classifiers [12][14], or a variety of machine learning algorithms [2], the k-Nearest Neighbor on the basis of patent's semantic structure [6], or the classifier built through back-propagation network [23]. Clustering algorithms can also be adopted to form a topic map for presenting patent analysis and summarization results [23], and to create a system interface for retrieving patent documents [5].

Content analysis is indigenous to communication research and is potentially one of the most important research techniques in social sciences. It seeks to analyze data within a specific context in view of the meaning someone – a group or a culture – attributes to them. Communications, messages, and symbols differ from observable events, things, properties, or people in that they inform about something other than themselves; they reveal some properties of their distant producers or carriers, and they have cognitive consequences for their senders, their receivers, and the institutions in which their exchange is embedded [7].

Content analysis is a research technique for making replicable and valid inferences from texts to the contexts of their use. As a technique, content analysis involves specialized procedures. It provides new insight, increases a researcher's understanding of particular phenomena, or informs practical actions. Content analysis is a scientific tool [8].

The judgements of patent infringement, unlike the patent documents, can be mined by using text mining techniques, since the judgments are legal documents. The judgments can be transformed into patterns by content analysis, and readers can easily access them the same way as reading newspapers to understand the key points and issues in dispute.

This study proposes to enhance a semantic web of patent information and patent infringement framework, and the rest of the paper is structured as follows. Section II presents the research background and states the objective. In Section III, we describe our proposed research method. The paper concludes with expected results and future work considerations.

II. Research Background and Objective

So far, patent analysis technologies include patent bibliometric data analysis [3], patent citation analysis [16], patent statistical analysis [22], and patent classification. Patent mining consists of patent retrieval, patent categorization and patent clustering [22]. However, patent infringement constitutes the biggest threat in patent use.

This framework proposes that through patent document mining and judgements of patent infringement analysis, one can discover newly developed products and their similarity with the claims of other patents, and foresee where potential patent threats are and the likelihood of patent infringement. While constructing the patent Semantic Web, the ontology and rules engines must include it.

This framework of patent database is based on the databases of United States Patent and Trademark Office (USPTO) and the European Patent Office (EPO). The patent infringement judgements are based on the judicial judgments in United States and European Union.

The purposes of this study is to construct the Semantic Web of patent information, and reference regarding patent infringement, technology trends for new product designers and technology research engineers at the stage before and after developing a new product or technology. With the analyzed information, managerial team can make sound strategic decisions.

It is difficult for laymen or ordinary readers who are short of legal background to fully grasp the gist of judicial judgments rendered by judges. With the implementation of content analysis and the big data concept, ordinary people can use content analysis technology to analyze patent infringements with the help of a semantic web.

III. Research Method

Patent documents can be collected from United States Patent and Trademark Office (USPTO) patent database and the European Patent Office (EPO) patent database. The patent infringement content can be collected from the "West Law" database.

A. *Patent documents analysis*

Based on the collected patent documents and the subject-action-object (SAO) structures extracted by using Natural Language Processing (NLP), the study uses a content analysis approach to generate the concepts and relationships of related patent documents.

NLP is a text mining technique that can conduct syntactic analysis of natural language; NLP tools include the Stanford parser (Stanford 2013) [21], Minipar (Lin 2003) [17], and Knowledgist TM2.5 [11].

NLP tools will be used for building a set of SAO structures from the collected patents.

Multidimensional scaling (MDS) is a statistical technique used to visualize similarities in data [9][20]. Patent documents in different fields have different key issues that trigger different multidimensional scaling, so the paper will design a new algorithm to identify which particular patent field shall correspond to what extent of scaling.

The analysis patent documents for specified keywords and returns a list of the documents where the keywords were found. Then, the framework will use data and text mining technology to design a specified algorithm (still in progress) in order to analyze the legal documents and try to find out the most similar patents or patent group.

B. *Patent infringement content analysis*

The most obvious source of data appropriate for content analysis is the text to which meanings are conventionally attributed: verbal discourse, written documents, and visual representations. The text in the patent infringement judgements is important because that is where the meanings are. For this reason, it is essential for the content analysis technology to analyze the patent infringement text in order to develop strategies and preventive measures in patent litigation.

The judgements of patent infringement, unlike the patent documents, can be mined using text mining techniques, since the judgements are legal documents. The judgements can be transformed into patterns by content analysis, and readers can easily access them the same way as reading newspapers to understand the key points and issues in dispute.

Content analyses commonly contain six steps that define the technique procedurally, as follows:

Design. Design is a conceptual phase during which analysts (i) define their context, what they wish to know and are unable to observe directly; (ii)explore the source of relevant data that either are or may become available; and (iii)adopt an analytical construct that formalizes the knowledge available about the data-context relationship thereby justifying the inferential step involved in going from one to the other.

Unitizing. Unitizing is the phase of defining and ultimately identifying units of analysis in the volume of available data. Sampling units make possible the drawing of a statistically representative sample from a population of potentially available data, such as issues of a newspaper, whole books, television episodes, fictional characters, essays, advertisements.

Sampling. While the process of drawing representative samples is not indigenous to content analysis, there is the need to (1) undo the statistical biases inherent in much of the symbolic material analyzed and (2) ensure that the often conditional hierarchy of chosen sampling units become representative of the organization of the symbolic phenomena under investigation.

Coding. Coding is the step of describing the recording units or classifying them in terms of the categories of the analytical constructs chosen. This step replicates an elementary notion of meaning and can be accomplished either by explicit instructions to trained human coders or by computer coding. The two evaluative criteria, reliability as measured by inter coder agreement and relevance or meaningfulness, are often at odds.

Drawing inferences. Drawing inferences is the most important phase in a content analysis. It applies the stable knowledge about how the variable accounts of coded data are related to the phenomena the researcher wants to know about.

Validation. Validation is the desideratum of any research effort. However, validation of content analysis results is limited by the intention of the technique to infer what cannot be observed directly and for which validation evidence is not readily available.

The patent infringement content analysis searches the patent infringement judgements for specific keywords and returns a list of the documents as above patent documents by introducing the content analysis technology into specified design algorithm (still in progress) in order to analyze the infringement cases/precedents. It also finds the nearest infringement judgements/precedents.

C. *Constructing Semantic Web*

Our proposed semantic web, which has a structure based on Figure 4, is a program that has the following parts:

(1) The first part searches patent documents for specified keywords and returns a list of the documents where the keywords were found. Then, the program will use data and text mining technology to design a specified algorithm in order to analyze the legal documents and try to find out the most similar patents or patent group concepts and relationships. The results from part (1) constructing the knowledge repository for the Reasoners are shown in Figure 1.

(2) Next, it searches the patent infringement judgments for specific keywords and returns a list of the documents as above patent documents by introducing the content analysis technology into a specified design algorithm in order to analyze the infringement cases/precedents. It also finds the nearest infringement judgements/precedents and description logic. The results from part (2) constructing the knowledge repository for the Rules engines are shown in Figure 3.

(3) Reasoners: Reasoners add inference to the Semantic Web. Inference creates logical additions that offer classification and realization. Classification populates the class structure, allowing concepts and relationships to relate properly to others, such as a person is a living thing, father is a parent, married is a type of relationship, or married is a symmetric relationship. Realization offers the same, for example, John H is the same as JH, for instance. There are several types of reasoners offering various levels of reasoning. Reasoners often plug in other tools and frameworks. Reasoners leverage asserted statements to create logically valid ancillary statements [4].

(4)The semantic web components of Rules engines support inference typically beyond what can be deduced from description logic. The engines add a powerful dimension to the knowledge constructs. Rules enable the merging of ontologies and other larger logical tasks, including programming methods such as count and string searches [4].

So far, the whole approach is purely theoretical at the moment. But in the patent document analysis, we have successful employed WordNet by the word similarity matrix clustering of words and merged with the similar semantic terms from a lower term dimensional approach. In the related data-mining fields, the semantic web system as WordNet can be employed to identify keywords, connect similar words, features, and sparse matrix to prevent the miscarriage of patent retrievals, waste of time and risks of patent infringement as well. The WordNet can also save storage memory while advancing the accuracy of text-mining in regards to ordinary, literal, and professional meaning of keywords and promoting the retrieval speed of patent research.

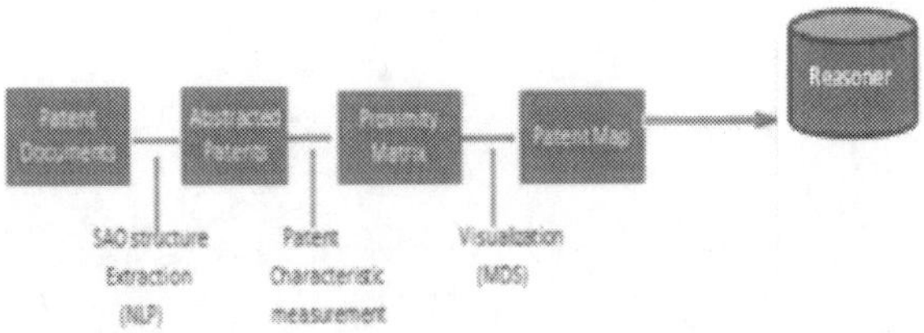

Figure 1. Part (1) the patent map result construct knowledge repository for the Reasoners modul

D. *The framework for semantic web of patent information*

The top part of framework in Figure 2 is the PATExpert, Ontology Modules and use of the W3C standard RDF. We implement the patent information in this process. The framework will construct the ontology base for Semantic Web shown in Figure 3.

As Reasoners module, the patent documents analysis process includes SAO structure extraction (NLP) and patent characteristic measurement and visualization (MDS). Here, we attempt to generate the patent concepts and relationships. In this phase, the study has generated some results based on the past research.

The other part in Figure 3 is the Rules engine modules that represent the content analysis research process [7]. The process is to implement the patent infringement judgments. The framework of the process is designed as an algorithm. Then, the study will construct the knowledge and technology logic in order to support the semantic web.

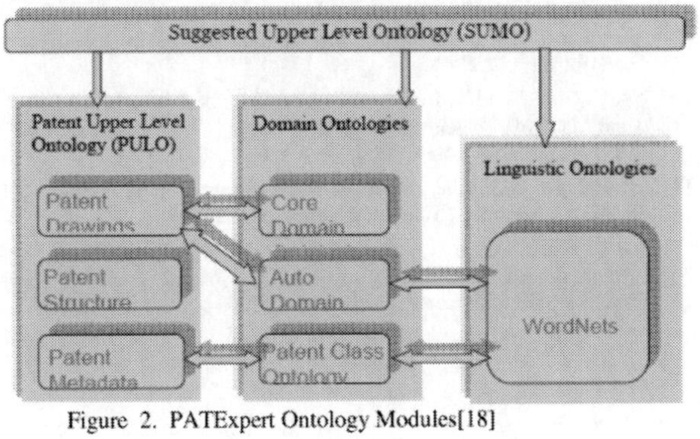

Figure 2. PATExpert Ontology Modules[18]

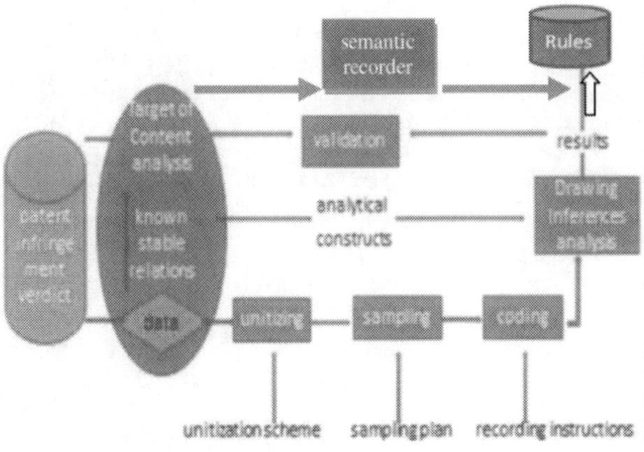

Figure 3. Part (2)content analysis result construct knowledge repository for the Rules engines

IV. Expected Result and Future Work

This study proposes to enhance a semantic web of patent information and patent infringement. When the user enters a keyword, the semantic web will automatically analyze the text or phrases in correspondence to related patents and potential patent threats. It can also provide the knowledge, technology, knowhow trend, and analysis. The challenge is in developing a semantic web that has the AI function.

So far the study experiment has explored WordNet to enhance the accuracy of patent searches. The evaluation index for this experiment is "Precision", "Recall" and "F-measure", and "Precision" implies that how much documents are retrieved by the system and how much are necessarily retrieved. "Recall" means how many documents need to be retrieved and how many need to be retrieved by the system. "F-measure" is compared to the harmonic mean of Precision and Recall.

A patent engineer will mark a most familiar patent document from the experiment in comparison with ten other similar articles of different patents, as the first row shows in Table I. Given the similarity threshold of hypothesis, the mark over "High" refers to Doca, Docb, Docc and Docd which is shown by implementing WordNet.

Given the same similarity threshold of hypothesis above, failure to use the similarity WordNet shown in the second row in Table I, Doca、Docb、Docf will be indicated as retrieved files. Without the implementation of WordNet, the value of "precision" appears to be "High", "Recall" is "Mid", and "F-measure" is "High".

By incorporating the similarity of the WordNet as the third row shows in Table I, given the similarity threshold is "High" or equivalent to "High", Doca、Docb、Docc、Docf and Docg are indicated as the retrieved files. Thus, by incorporating WordNet, the value of "Precision" tends to be is "High", "Recall" is becoming "More High", and "F-measure" also indicates "More High". Finally, the value of "F-measure" with WordNet is higher than the value of "F-measure" without WordNet. Thus, the integration of WordNet is more likely to generate more precise meanings for patent searches.

The finding of the experiment is that WordNet can generate more wording accuracy of text-mining as to ordinary, literal and professional meanings of keywords, while promoting the retrieval speed of patent research and mitigating waste of time.

TABLE I. WORDNET SIMILARITY COMPARISON TABLE

	Patent Engineer marked similarity	No include WordNet income of similarity	Include WordNet income of similarity
Similarity(Doc_x,Doc_a)	**Most High**	**High**	**More High**
Similarity(Docx,Doc_b)	**More High**	**More High**	**More High**
Similarity(Docx,Doc_c)	**More High**	Mid	**High**
Similarity(Docx,Doc_d)	**High**	Low	Mid
Similarity(Docx,Doc_e)	Mid	Low	Mid
Similarity(Docx,Doc_f)	Low	**High**	**More High**
Similarity(Docx,Doc_g)	More Low	Mid	**High**
Similarity(Docx,Doc_h)	More Low	Low	Mid
Similarity(Docx,Doc_i)	Most Low	Most Low	More Low
Similarity(Docx,Doc_j)	None	Most Low	More Low

The study difficulties are in employing different analysis methods to analyze different databases and further, integrating these analysis results with the semantic web. An accurate algorithm in different fields must be constructed and achieved with the semantic web.

The obstacles are in integrating much more research math and different databases. Results need to be standardized and communicated, compared, and exchanged with each other.

Furthermore, the study aims to employ different analysis methods to analyze various databases with the analysis results in Semantic Web. An accurate algorithm in different fields can be feasibly constructed and achieved in the analysis of patent information and patent infringement.

The next steps will be to employ the Semantic Web impacts functions to increase the new data automatically. Figure 4 indicates major Semantic Web components: the right side is Rules engine, the left side is the Reasoner, over the center side is base ontology from the PATExpert ontology modules, and under the center side is language. The next steps of Semantic Web will be developed to use different languages, construct a multi-language Semantic Web, in order to retrieve from different country's patent databases.

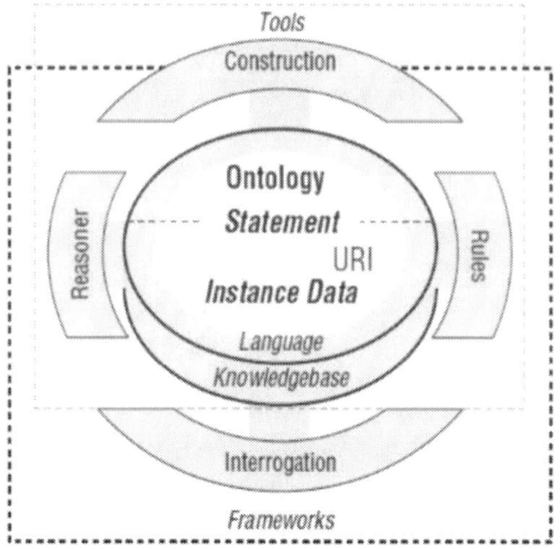

Figure 4. Major Semantic Web components [4]

The Semantic Web can employ the image recognition functions to identify drawings and pictures. If the Semantic Web has the capability of analyzing drawings and pictures, the accuracy of the results will be increased in the future.

References

[1] Y. L. Chen, and Y. T. Chiu, "An IPC-based vector space model for patent retrieval" Information Processing and Management, pp.309-322.47, 2011.

[2] C. J. Fall, A. Torcsrari, K. Benzineb, and G. Karetka, "SIGIR Forum" Automated categorization in the international patent classification, pp.10-25. 37(1), 2003.

[3] V. K. Gupta, and N. B. Pangannaya, Carbon nanotubes; "Bibliometric analysis of patents", World Patent Information, pp.185-189.Vol.22,issue 3, Sep. 2000.

[4] J. Hebeler, M. Fisher, R. Blace and A. Perez-Lopez, "Semantic Web Programming "Wiley Publishing, Inc.2009.

[5] S. H. Huang, C. C. Liu, C. W. Wang, H. R. Ke, and W. P. Yang, "International Computer Symposium" Knowledge annotation and discovery for patent analysis, pp.15-20, 2004.

[6] J.H. Kim, and K.S. Choi, Patent document categorization based on semantic structural information, "Information processing & Management", pp.1200-1215.43(5), 2007.

[7] K. Krippendorff, Content analysis In E. Barnouw, G. Gerbner, W. Schramm, T. L. Worth, and L. Gross (Eds.), International encyclopedia of communication New York, NY: Oxford University Press, pp.403-407.Vol. 1, 1989.

[8] K. Krippendorff, "Content Analysis An Introduction to Its Methodology" second Edition, Sage Publications, Inc. 2004.

[9] J. B. Kruskal, Multidimensional scaling by optimizing goodness of fit to a nonmetric hypothesis. Psychometrika, pp.1-27.29(1), 1964.

[10] I. S. Kang, S. H. Na, J. Kim, and J. H. Lee, "Information Processing & Management"Cluster-based patent retrieval, pp.1173-1182.43(5), 2007.

[11] Knowledgist retrieves, analyzes, and organizes information. https://invention-machine.com/ , retrieved: Apr., 2016

[12] L. S Larkey., Some issues in the automatic classification of U.S. patents. In: Working notes for the AAAI-98 workshop on learning for text categorization, pp.87-90, 1998.

[13] L. S. Larkey, Connell, M. E., and Callan, J. Collection selection and results merging with topically organized US patents and TREC data.

In Proceedings of ninth international conference on informaiton knowledge and management, pp.282-289, 2000.

[14] L. S. Larkey, A patent search and classification system. In: Proceedings of the fourth ACM conference on digital libraries, pp.79-87, 1999.

[15] Y. Liang, R. Tan, and J. Ma, "Patent Analysis with Text Mining for TRIZ" IEEE ICMIT, pp.1147-1151, 2008.

[16] J. Michel, and B. Bettels, "Patent citation analysis: a closer look at the basic input data from patent search reports", Scientometrics, pp.185-201. Vol.51. no. 1, 2001.

[17] MINIPAR http://webdocs.cs.ualberta.ca/~lindek/minipar.htm , retrieved:Dec., 2015

[18] PATExpert http://cordis.europa.eu/ist/kct/patexpert_synopsis.htm , retrieved: Feb., 2016

[19] PATExpet http://www.barcelonamedia.org/report/the-european-project-patexpert-coordinated-by-bm-finishes-with-fulfilled-objectives-and-success , retrieved: Feb., 2016

[20] U. Schmoch, "International Journal of Technology Management" Evaluation of technological strategies of companies by means of MDS maps., pp.4-5.10(4-5), 1995.

[21] The Stanford Natural Language Processing Group, The Stanford Parser: A statistical parser, http://nlp.stanford.edu/software/lex-parser.shtml

[22] Y. H. Tseng, C. J. Lin, and Y. I. Lin, "Text mining for patent mapanalysis", Information Processing & Mangement, pp.1216-1247. vol.43, issue 5, Sep. 2007.

[23] A. J.C. Trappey, F. C. Hsu, C V. Trappy,and C. I. Lin," Development of a patent document classification and search platform using a back-propagation network", Expert Systems with Applications, pp.755-765.31(4), 2006.

[24] WordNet https://wordnet.princeton.edu/, retrieved: May, 2016

A Comparison of Two MLEM2 Rule Induction Algorithms Applied to Data with Many Missing Attribute Values

Patrick G. Clark and Cheng Gao

Department of Electrical Engineering
and Computer Science,
University of Kansas
Lawrence, KS, USA
Email: patrick.g.clark@gmail.com
cheng.gao@ku.edu

Jerzy W. Grzymala-Busse

Department of Electrical Engineering
and Computer Science,
University of Kansas,
Lawrence, KS, USA
Department of Expert Systems
and Artificial Intelligence,
University of Information
Technology and Management,
Rzeszow, Poland
Email: jerzy@ku.edu

***Abstract*—We present results of novel experiments, conducted on 18 data sets with many missing attribute values, interpreted as lost values, attribute-concept values and "do not care" conditions. The main objective was to compare two versions of the Modified Learning from Examples, version 2 (MLEM2) rule induction algorithm, emulated and true, using concept probabilistic approximations. Our secondary objective was to check which interpretation of missing attribute values provides the smallest error rate, computed as a result of ten-fold cross validation. Results of our experiments show that both versions of the MLEM2 rule induction algorithms do not differ much. On the other hand, there is some evidence that the lost value interpretation of missing attribute values is the best: in seven cases this interpretation was significantly better (with 5% of significance level, two-tailed test) than attribute-concept values, and in eight cases it was better than "do not care" conditions. Additionally, attribute-concept values and "do not care" conditions were never significantly better than lost values.**

Keywords–Probabilistic approximations; generalization of probabilistic approximations; concept probabilistic approximations; true MLEM2 algorithm; emulated MLEM2 algorithm.

I. Introduction

Lower and upper approximations are basic ideas of rough set theory. Probabilistic approximations, associated with a probability α, are a generalization of that idea. If $\alpha = 1$, the probabilistic approximation is identical with the lower approximation, if α is a very small positive number, the probabilistic approximation is identical with the upper approximation. Probabilistic approximations, for completely specified data sets, were studied, e.g., in [1]–[9]. Probabilistic approximations were additionally generalized to describe incomplete data sets in [10]. Experimental research associated with such probabilistic approximations was initiated in [11][12].

In this paper, missing attribute values are interpreted as *lost values*, *attribute-concept values*, and *"do not care" conditions*. A lost value is denoted by "?", an attribute-concept value is denoted by "−", and a "do not care" condition is denoted by "*". With lost values we assume that the original attribute value was erased, and that we should induce rules from existing, specified attribute values. With attribute-concept value we assume that such missing attribute values may be replaced by any actual attribute value restricted to the concept to which the case belongs. For example, if our concept is a specific disease, an attribute is a diastolic pressure, and all patients affected by the disease have high or very high diastolic pressure, a missing attribute value of the diastolic pressure for a sick patient will be high or very-high. With the third interpretation of missing attribute values, the "do not care" condition, we assume that it does not matter what is the attribute value. Such value may be replaced by any value from the set of all possible attribute values.

For any concept X and probability α, its probabilistic approximations may be computed directly from corresponding definitions and implemented as a new program. The output of this program may be used as an input to an implementation of the MLEM2 algorithm. The respective MLEM2 rule induction algorithm will be called a *true* MLEM2 algorithm.

Another possibility is to use the existing data mining system Learning from Examples using Rough Set theory (LERS). LERS computes standard lower and upper approximations for any concept. In LERS there exists a component that implements the MLEM2 rule induction algorithm. This component may be used to compute possible rules from the probabilistic approximation of X. Some modification of the strength of induced rules is required. This approach will be called an *emulated* MLEM2 algorithm. It is easier to implement since all what we need to do is to compute the probabilistic approximation of X and to modify strengths. The main part, the MLEM2 rule induction algorithm, does not need to be separately implemented. The idea of the emulated MLEM2 algorithm was introduced in [13] and further developed in [14][15].

Experiments conducted on eight incomplete data sets with 35% of missing attribute values to compare true version of the MLEM2 rule induction algorithm with the emulated one were reported in [16]. All three interpretations of missing attribute values were used in experiments, so experiments were conducted on 24 data sets. In these experiments true and emulated versions of the MLEM2 algorithm were compared using the resulting classification error rate of the induced rules against the ten-fold cross validated data set as the quality criterion. Results were inconclusive. For six data sets, for all values of the parameter α, results were identical; for other 14 data sets results did not differ significantly (we used the Wilcoxon matched-pairs signed rank test, 5% significance level, two-tailed test). For three other data sets, the true MLEM2 algorithm was better than emulated, for remaining one data set the emulated MLEM2 algorithm was better than the true one.

Usually, experiments conducted on data sets with many missing attribute values provide for more conclusive results. As a result our first objective in this paper was to conduct new experiments with data sets that contain more than 35% missing attribute values. We used three interpretations of missing attribute values, resulting in 18 combinations. Results of the same comparison of error rate of the induced rules are measurably more conclusive: in five combinations (out of 18) the emulated approach to MLEM2 algorithm was better, in one case the true approach was better (5% significance level, two-tailed test).

Our second objective was to check which interpretation of missing attribute values should be used to accomplish a lower error rate. There is some evidence that the lost value interpretation of missing attribute values is the best: in seven cases this interpretation was significantly better (with 5% of significance level, two-tailed test) than attribute-concept values, and in eight cases it was better than "do not care" conditions. Additionally, attribute-concept values and "do not care" conditions were never significantly better than lost values.

In Sections II and III background information on incomplete data sets and probabilistic approximations is covered. Section IV describes the two algorithms used in our rule induction experiments and Section V explains the experimental setup with our results. Finally we provide concluding remarks in Section VI.

II. Incomplete Data Sets

An example of incomplete data set is presented in Table I. In Table I, the set A of all attributes consists of three variables *Wind*, *Humidity* and *Temperature*. A *concept* is a set of all cases with the same decision value. There are two concepts in Table I, the first one contains cases 1, 2, 3 and 4 and is characterized by the decision value *yes* of decision *Trip*. The other concept contains cases 5, 6, 7 and 8 and is characterized by the decision value *no*.

The fact that an attribute a has the value v for the case x will be denoted by $a(x) = v$. The set of all cases will be denoted by U. In Table I, $U = \{1, 2, 3, 4, 5, 6, 7, 8\}$.

For complete data sets, an attribute-value pair $(a,\ v) = t$, a *block* of t, denoted by $[t]$, is a set of all cases from U such that attribute a has a value v. An *indiscernibility relation* R on U is defined for all $x, y \in U$ by

$$xRy \text{ if and only if } a(x) = a(y) \text{ for all } a \in A.$$

For incomplete decision tables the definition of a block of an attribute-value pair must be modified in the following way [17][18]:

- If for an attribute a there exists a case x such that $a(x) =?$, i.e., the corresponding value is lost, then the case x should not be included in any blocks $[(a, v)]$ for all values v of attribute a,
- If for an attribute a there exists a case x such that the corresponding value is an attribute-concept value, i.e., $a(x) = -$, then the corresponding case x should be included in blocks $[(a, v)]$ for all specified values $v \in V(x, a)$ of attribute a, where

$$V(x,a) = \{a(y) \mid a(y) \ is\ specified,\ y \in U,\ d(y) = d(x)\}, \quad (1)$$

  and d is the decision.
- If for an attribute a there exists a case x such that the corresponding value is a "do not care" condition, i.e., $a(x) = *$, then the case x should be included in blocks $[(a, v)]$ for all specified values v of attribute a.

TABLE I. AN INCOMPLETE DATA SET

	Attributes			Decision
Case	Wind	Humidity	Temperature	Trip
1	low	*	low	yes
2	*	low	–	yes
3	high	low	low	yes
4	low	*	*	yes
5	high	high	high	no
6	?	–	high	no
7	low	low	*	no
8	high	?	low	no

For a case $x \in U$ the *characteristic set* $K_B(x)$ is defined as the intersection of the sets $K(x, a)$, for all $a \in B$, where B is a subset of the set A of all attributes and the set $K(x, a)$ is defined in the following way:

- If $a(x)$ is specified, then $K(x, a)$ is the block $[(a, a(x))]$ of attribute a and its value $a(x)$,
- If $a(x) =?$ or $a(x) = *$ then the set $K(x, a) = U$,
- If $a(x) = -$, then the corresponding set $K(x, a)$ is equal to the union of all blocks of attribute-value pairs (a, v), where $v \in V(x, a)$ if $V(x, a)$ is nonempty. If $V(x, a)$ is empty, $K(x, a) = U$.

The characteristic set $K_B(x)$ may be interpreted as the set of cases that are indistinguishable from x using all attributes from B and using a given interpretation of missing attribute values.

For the data set from Table I, the set of blocks of attribute-value pairs is

$[(Wind, low)] = \{1, 2, 4, 7\}$,
$[(Wind, high)] = \{2, 3, 5, 8\}$,
$[(Humidity, low)] = \{1, 2, 3, 4, 6, 7\}$,
$[(Humidity, high)] = \{1, 4, 5, 6\}$,
$[(Temperature, low)] = \{1, 2, 3, 4, 7, 8\}$,
$[(Temperature, high)] = \{4, 5, 6, 7\}$.

For Table I, $V(2, Temperature) = \{low\}$ and $V(6, Humidity) = \{low, high\}$.

The corresponding characteristic sets are

TABLE II. CONDITIONAL PROBABILITIES

Case x	Characteristic set $K_A(x)$	$Pr(\{1,2,3,4\} \mid K_A(x))$
1	{1, 2, 4, 7}	0.75
2	{1, 2, 3, 4, 7}	0.8
3	{2, 3}	1
4	{1, 2, 4, 7 }	0.75
5	{5}	0
6	{4, 5, 6, 7}	0.25
7	{1, 2, 4, 7}	0.75
8	{2, 3, 8}	0.667

$$\begin{aligned} K_A(1) &= [(Wind, low)] \cap [(Humidity, *)] \cap [(Temp, low)] \\ &= \{1,2,4,7\} \cap U \cap \{1,2,3,4,7,8\} \\ &= \{1,2,4,7\}, \end{aligned}$$

$K_A(2) = \{1,2,3,4,7\}$,
$K_A(3) = \{2,3\}$,
$K_A(4) = \{1,2,4,7\}$,
$K_A(5) = \{5\}$,
$K_A(6) = \{4,5,6,7\}$,
$K_A(7) = \{1,2,4,7\}$,
$K_A(8) = \{2,3,8\}$.

III. Probabilistic Approximations

For incomplete data sets there exist a number of different definitions of approximations, in this paper we will use only *concept* approximations, we will skip the word *concept*.

The B-*lower approximation* of X, denoted by $\underline{appr}(X)$, is defined as follows

$$\cup \{K_B(x) \mid x \in X, K_B(x) \subseteq X\}. \tag{2}$$

Such lower approximations were introduced in [17][19].

The B-*upper approximation* of X, denoted by $\overline{appr}(X)$, is defined as follows

$$\begin{aligned} &\cup \{K_B(x) \mid x \in X, K_B(x) \cap X \neq \emptyset\} \\ &= \cup \{K_B(x) \mid x \in X\}. \end{aligned} \tag{3}$$

These approximations were studied in [17][19][20].

For incomplete data sets there exist a few definitions of probabilistic approximations, we will use only *concept* probabilistic approximations, again, we will skip the word *concept*.

A B-probabilistic approximation of the set X with the threshold α, $0 < \alpha \leq 1$, denoted by B-$appr_\alpha(X)$, is defined as follows

$$\cup\{K_B(x) \mid x \in X,\ Pr(X|K_B(x)) \geq \alpha\}, \tag{4}$$

where $Pr(X|K_B(x)) = \frac{|X \cap K_B(x)|}{|K_B(x)|}$ is the conditional probability of X given $K_B(x)$. A-probabilistic approximations of X with the threshold α will be denoted by $appr_\alpha(X)$.

For Table I and the concept X = [(*Trip*, *yes*)] = {1, 2, 3, 4}, for any characteristic set $K_A(x)$, $x \in U$, all conditional probabilities $P(X|K_A(x))$ are presented in Table II.

There are five distinct conditional probabilities $Pr(\{1,2,3,4\} \mid K_A(x))$, $x \in U$: 0.25, 0.667, 0.75, 0.8 and 1. Therefore, there exist at most five distinct probabilistic approximations of {1, 2, 3, 4} (in our example, there are only two distinct probabilistic approximations of {1, 2, 3, 4}). A probabilistic approximation $appr_\beta(\{1,2,3,4\})$, with $\beta > 0$ and not listed below, is equal to the closest probabilistic approximation $appr_\alpha(\{1,2,3,4\})$ with α larger than or equal to β. For example, $appr_{0.7}(\{1,2,3,4\}) = appr_{0.8}(\{1,2,3,4\})$. For Table I, all distinct probabilistic approximations are

$$\begin{aligned} appr_{0.8}(\{1,2,3,4\}) &= K_B(2) \cup K_B(3) \\ &= \{1,2,3,4,7\} \cup \{2,3\} \\ &= \{1,2,3,4,7\}, \\ appr_1(\{1,2,3,4\}) &= K_B(3) = \{2,3\}, \\ appr_{0.25}(\{5,6,7,8\}) &= \{1,2,3,4,5,6,7,8\}, \\ appr_{0.333}(\{5,6,7,8\}) &= \{2,3,4,5,6,7,8\}, \\ appr_{0.75}(\{5,6,7,8\}) &= \{4,5,6,7\}, \\ appr_1(\{5,6,7,8\}) &= \{5\}. \end{aligned}$$

IV. Rule Induction

In this section we will discuss two different ways to induce rule sets using probabilistic approximations: true MLEM2 and emulated MLEM2.

A. *True MLEM2*

In the true MLEM2 approach, for a given concept X and parameter α, first we compute the probabilistic approximation $appr_\alpha(X)$. The set $appr_\alpha(X)$ is a union of characteristic sets, so it is globally definable [21]. Thus, we may use the MLEM2 strategy to induce rule sets [22][23] by inducing rules directly from the set $appr_\alpha(X)$. For example, for Table I, for the concept [(*Trip*, *no*)] = {5, 6, 7, 8} and for the probabilistic approximation $appr_{0.75}(\{5,6,7,8\}) = \{4,5,6,7\}$, using the true MLEM2 approach, the following single rule is induced

1, 3, 4

(Temperature, high) -> (Trip, no).

Rules are presented in the LERS format, every rule is associated with three numbers: the total number of attribute-value pairs on the left-hand side of the rule, the total number of cases correctly classified by the rule during training, and the total number of training cases matching the left-hand side of the rule, i.e., the rule domain size.

B. *Emulated MLEM2*

We will discuss how the existing rough set based data mining systems, such as LERS, may be used to induce rules using probabilistic approximations. All what we need to do, for every concept, is to modify the input data set, run LERS, and then edit the induced rule set [14]. We will illustrate this procedure by inducing a rule set for Table I and the concept [(*Trip*, *no*)] = {5, 6, 7, 8} using the probabilistic approximation $appr_{0.75}(\{5,6,7,8\}) = \{4,5,6,7\}$. First, a new data set should be created in which for all cases that are members of the set $appr_{0.75}(\{5,6,7,8\})$ the decision values are copied from the original data set (Table I). For all remaining cases, those not being in the set $appr_{0.75}(\{5,6,7,8\})$, a new decision value

TABLE III. A PRELIMINARY MODIFIED DATA SET

	Attributes			Decision
Case	Wind	Humidity	Temperature	Trip
1	low	*	low	SPECIAL
2	*	low	—	SPECIAL
3	high	low	low	SPECIAL
4	low	*	*	yes
5	high	high	high	no
6	?	—	high	no
7	low	low	*	no
8	high	?	low	SPECIAL

is introduced. In our experiments the new decision value was named SPECIAL. Thus a new data set is created, see Table III.

This data set is input into the LERS data mining system. The concept [(*Trip*, *no*)], computed from Table III, is {5, 6, 7}. The LERS system computes the concept upper concept approximation of the set {5, 6, 7} to be {1, 2, 4, 5, 6, 7}, and using this approximation, computes the corresponding final modified data set. The MLEM2 algorithm induces the following preliminary rule set from the final modified data sets

1, 4, 6
(Temperature, low) -> (Trip, SPECIAL)
1, 1, 4
(Wind, low) -> (Trip, yes)
1, 1, 4
(Wind, low) -> (Trip, no)
1, 2, 4
(Humidity, high) -> (Trip, no)

where the three numbers that precede every rule are computed from Table III. Because we are inducing rules for the approximation from (Trip, no) ({5, 6, 7}), only the last two rules

1, 1, 4
(Wind, low) -> (Trip, no)
1, 2, 4
(Humidity, high) -> (Trip, no)

should be saved and the remaining two rules should be deleted in computing the final rule set.

In the preliminary rule set, the three numbers that precede every rule are adjusted taking into account the preliminary modified data set. Thus during classification of unseen cases by the LERS classification system rules describe the original concept probabilistic approximation of the concept X.

V. Experiments

In our experiments, we used six real-life data sets taken from the University of California at Irvine *Machine Learning Repository*, see Table IV. For every data set a set of templates was created. Templates were formed by replacing incrementally (with 5% increment) existing specified attribute values by *lost* values. Thus, we started each series of experiments with no *lost* values, then we added 5% of *lost* values, then we added additional 5% of *lost* values, etc., until at least one entire row of the data sets was full of *lost* values. Then, three attempts were made to change the configuration of new *lost* values and either a new data set with extra 5% of *lost* values was created or the process was terminated. Additionally, the same

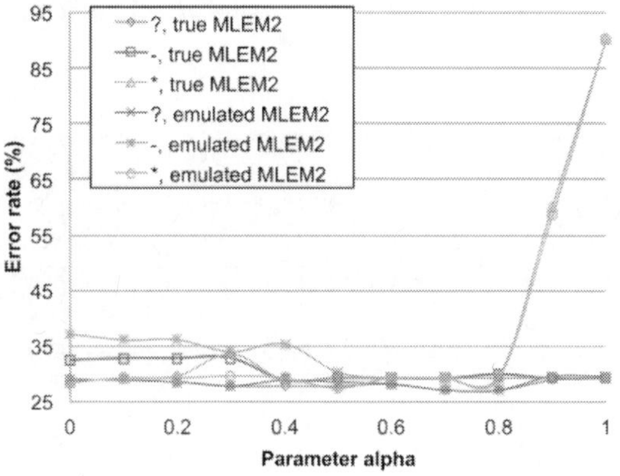

Figure 1. *Breast cancer* data set

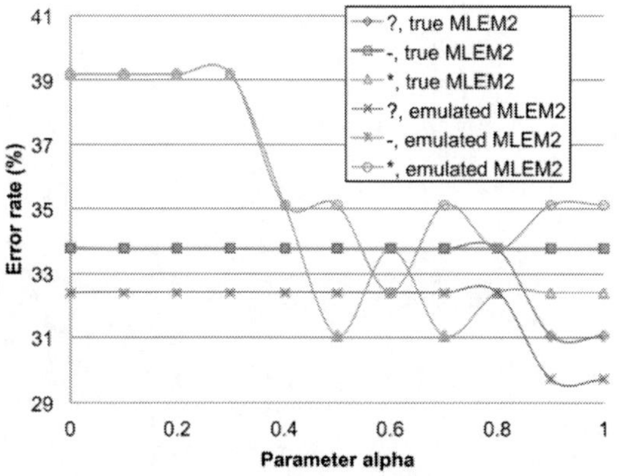

Figure 2. *Echocardiogram* data set

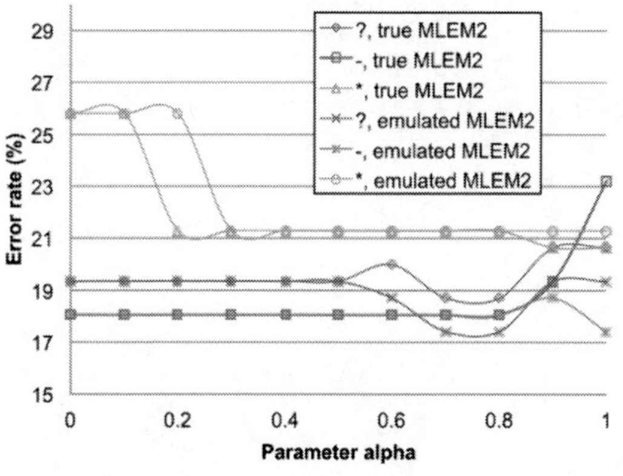

Figure 3. *Hepatitis* data set

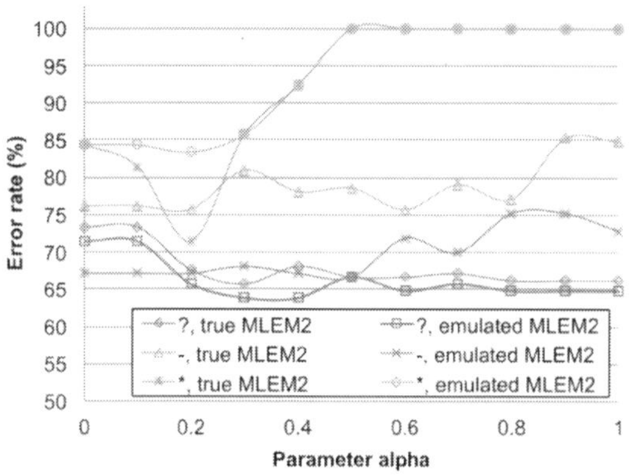

Figure 4. *Image segmentation* data set

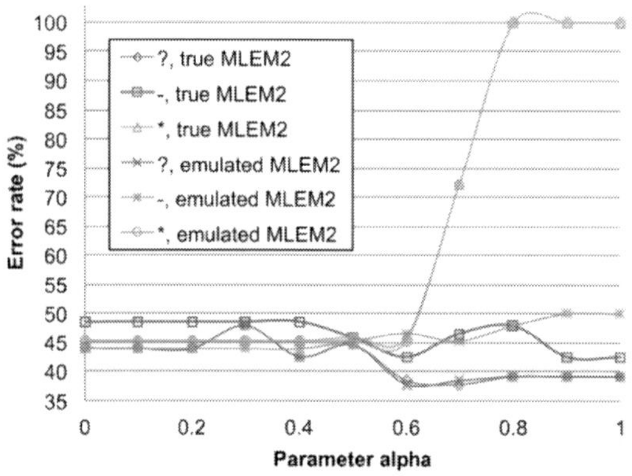

Figure 5. *Lymphography* data set

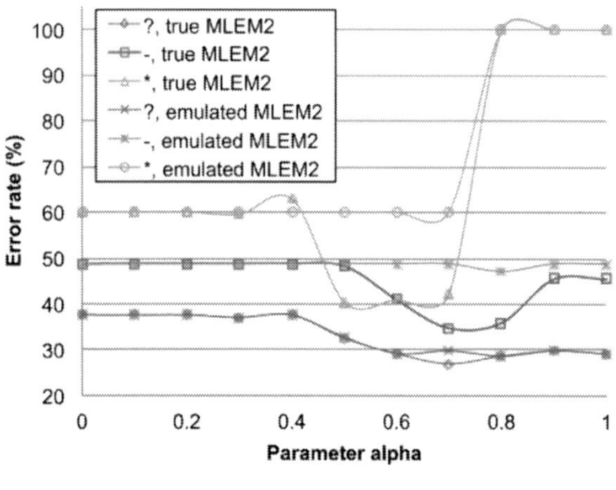

Figure 6. *Wine recognition* data set

templates were edited for further experiments by replacing question marks, representing *lost* values by "−"s, representing *attribute-concept* values, and then by "*"s, representing "do not care" conditions.

For any data set, there was some maximum for the percentage of missing attribute values. For example, for the *Breast cancer* data set, it was 44.81%. In our experiments we used only such incomplete data sets, with as many missing attribute values as possible. Note that for some data sets the maximum of the number of missing attribute values was less than 40%, we have not used such data for our experiments. Thus, for any data set from Table IV, three data sets were used for experiments, so the total number of data sets was 18.

Our first objective was to compare both approaches to rule induction, true MLEM2 and emulated MLEM2, in terms of the classification error rate of the induced rules. Results of our experiments are presented in Figures 1–6, with lost values denoted by "?", attribute-concept values denoted by "−", and "do not care" conditions denoted by "*".

For five combinations of data set and interpretation of missing attribute values the error rate was significantly smaller for the emulated version of MLEM2. The five combinations included *Breast cancer* and *Image segmentation* with "?" and "−", and *Echocardiogram* with "?". For *Wine recognition* with "−", the error rate was significantly smaller for the true version of MLEM2. In the remaining 12 combinations the difference in error rate was not significant (5% significance level, two-tailed test) and for the *Breast cancer* with "−" combination, the error rate for both versions of the MLEM2 algorithm was identical for all 11 values of α.

Our second objective was to check which interpretation of missing attribute value provides the smallest error rate, computed as a result of ten-fold cross validation. In eight combinations the error rate was significantly smaller for "?" than for "*". The eight combinations included both true and emulated MLEM2 with the *Image segmentation*, *Lymphography* and *Wine recognition* data sets, and emulated MLEM2 with the *Echocardiogram* and *Hepatitis* data sets.

For the following seven combinations the error rate was significantly smaller for "?" than for "−". The seven combinations included both true and emulated MLEM2 with the *Breast cancer* and *Wine recognition* data sets, true MLEM2 with *Image segmentation* and *Lymphography*, and emulated MLEM2 with the *Echocardiogram* data set.

In four combinations the error rate was measurably smaller for "−" than "?". The four combinations included both true and emulated MLEM2 with the *Hepatitis* data set and emulated MLEM2 with the *Image segmentation* and *Wine recognition* data sets.

For one combination the error rate was smaller for "*" than for "−", true MLEM2 and the *Breast cancer* data set. However, for the remaining combinations the difference in error rate was not significant. In addition, "−" and "*" values were never significantly better than "?".

VI. CONCLUSIONS

In our experiments we compared true and emulated versions of the MLEM2 algorithm using the error rate of the induced rule set, a result of ten-fold cross validation, as the quality criterion. Results of the same comparison of error rate of the induced rules are measurably more conclusive than previous experiments: in five combinations (out of 18) the emulated approach to MLEM2 algorithm was better, in one

TABLE IV. DATA SETS USED FOR EXPERIMENTS

Data set	Number of			% of
	cases	attributes	concepts	missing values
Breast cancer	277	9	2	44.81
Echocardiogram	74	7	2	40.15
Hepatitis	155	19	2	60.27
Image segmentation	210	19	7	69.85
Lymphography	148	18	4	69.89
Wine recognition	178	13	3	64.65

case the true approach was better (5% significance level, two-tailed test). In addition, there is some evidence that the lost value interpretation of missing attribute values is the best: in seven cases this interpretation was significantly better than attribute-concept values, and in eight cases it was better than "do not care" conditions. Additionally, attribute-concept values and "do not care" conditions were never significantly better than lost values.

REFERENCES

[1] J. W. Grzymala-Busse and W. Ziarko, "Data mining based on rough sets," in Data Mining: Opportunities and Challenges, J. Wang, Ed. Hershey, PA: Idea Group Publ., 2003, pp. 142–173.

[2] Z. Pawlak and A. Skowron, "Rough sets: Some extensions," Information Sciences, vol. 177, 2007, pp. 28–40.

[3] Z. Pawlak, S. K. M. Wong, and W. Ziarko, "Rough sets: probabilistic versus deterministic approach," International Journal of Man-Machine Studies, vol. 29, 1988, pp. 81–95.

[4] D. Ślęzak and W. Ziarko, "The investigation of the bayesian rough set model," International Journal of Approximate Reasoning, vol. 40, 2005, pp. 81–91.

[5] S. K. M. Wong and W. Ziarko, "INFER—an adaptive decision support system based on the probabilistic approximate classification," in Proceedings of the 6-th International Workshop on Expert Systems and their Applications, 1986, pp. 713–726.

[6] Y. Y. Yao, "Probabilistic rough set approximations," International Journal of Approximate Reasoning, vol. 49, 2008, pp. 255–271.

[7] Y. Y. Yao and S. K. M. Wong, "A decision theoretic framework for approximate concepts," International Journal of Man-Machine Studies, vol. 37, 1992, pp. 793–809.

[8] W. Ziarko, "Variable precision rough set model," Journal of Computer and System Sciences, vol. 46, no. 1, 1993, pp. 39–59.

[9] ——, "Probabilistic approach to rough sets," International Journal of Approximate Reasoning, vol. 49, 2008, pp. 272–284.

[10] J. W. Grzymala-Busse, "Generalized parameterized approximations," in Proceedings of the 6-th International Conference on Rough Sets and Knowledge Technology, 2011, pp. 136–145.

[11] P. G. Clark and J. W. Grzymala-Busse, "Experiments on probabilistic approximations," in Proceedings of the 2011 IEEE International Conference on Granular Computing, 2011, pp. 144–149.

[12] ——, "Rule induction using probabilistic approximations and data with missing attribute values," in Proceedings of the 15-th IASTED International Conference on Artificial Intelligence and Soft Computing ASC 2012, 2012, pp. 235–242.

[13] J. W. Grzymala-Busse, S. R. Marepally, and Y. Yao, "A comparison of positive, boundary, and possible rules using the MLEM2 rule induction algorithm," in Proceedings of the 10-th International Conference on Hybrid Intelligent Systems, 2010, pp. 7–12.

[14] J. W. Grzymala-Busse, "Generalized probabilistic approximations," Transactions on Rough Sets, vol. 16, 2013, pp. 1–16.

[15] J. W. Grzymala-Busse, S. R. Marepally, and Y. Yao, "An empirical comparison of rule sets induced by LERS and probabilistic rough classification," in Proceedings of the 7-th International Conference on Rough Sets and Current Trends in Computing, 2010, pp. 590–599.

[16] P. G. Clark and J. W. Grzymala-Busse, "A comparison of two versions of the MLEM2 rule induction algorithm extended to probabilistic approximations," in Proceedings of the 9-th International Conference on Rough Sets and Current Trends in Computing, 2014, pp. 109–119.

[17] J. W. Grzymala-Busse, "Rough set strategies to data with missing attribute values," in Notes of the Workshop on Foundations and New Directions of Data Mining, in conjunction with the Third International Conference on Data Mining, 2003, pp. 56–63.

[18] ——, "Three approaches to missing attribute values—a rough set perspective," in Proceedings of the Workshop on Foundation of Data Mining, in conjunction with the Fourth IEEE International Conference on Data Mining, 2004, pp. 55–62.

[19] ——, "Data with missing attribute values: Generalization of indiscernibility relation and rule induction," Transactions on Rough Sets, vol. 1, 2004, pp. 78–95.

[20] T. Y. Lin, "Topological and fuzzy rough sets," in Intelligent Decision Support. Handbook of Applications and Advances of the Rough Sets Theory, R. Slowinski, Ed. Dordrecht, Boston, London: Kluwer Academic Publishers, 1992, pp. 287–304.

[21] J. W. Grzymala-Busse and W. Rzasa, "Local and global approximations for incomplete data," in Proceedings of the Fifth International Conference on Rough Sets and Current Trends in Computing, 2006, pp. 244–253.

[22] J. W. Grzymala-Busse, "A new version of the rule induction system LERS," Fundamenta Informaticae, vol. 31, 1997, pp. 27–39.

[23] ——, "MLEM2: A new algorithm for rule induction from imperfect data," in Proceedings of the 9th International Conference on Information Processing and Management of Uncertainty in Knowledge-Based Systems, 2002, pp. 243–250.

A Distributed Algorithm for Graph Edit Distance

Zeina Abu-Aisheh, Romain Raveaux, Jean-Yves Ramel and Patrick Martineau

Laboratoire d'Informatique (LI), Université François Rabelais
37200, Tours, France
Email: f_author,s_author@univ-tours.fr

***Abstract*—Graph edit distance is an error-tolerant matching paradigm that can be used efficiently to address different tasks in pattern recognition, machine learning, and data mining. The literature is rich of many fast heuristics with unbounded errors but few works are devoted to exact graph edit distance computation. Exact graph edit distance methods suffer from high time and memory consumption. In the meantime, heavy computation tasks have moved from desktop applications to servers in order to spread the computation load on many machines. This paradigm leads to re-design methods in terms of scalability and performance. In this paper, a distributed and optimized branch-and-bound algorithm for exact graph edit distance computation is proposed. The search tree is cleverly pruned thanks to a lower and upper bounds' strategy. In addition, tree branches are explored in a completely distributed manner to speed up the tree traversal. Meaningful performance evaluation metrics are presented. Experiments were conducted on two publicly available datasets. Results demonstrate that under time constraints the most precise solutions were obtained by our method against five methods from the literature.**

Keywords–Pattern Recognition; Graph Matching; Graph Edit Distance; Branch-and-Bound; Distribution; Hadoop; MPI.

I. Introduction

Graph is an efficient data structure for object representation in structural pattern recognition (PR). Graphs can be divided into two main categories. First, graphs that are only based on their topological structures. Second, graphs with attributes on edges, vertices or both of them. Such attributes efficiently describe objects in terms of shape, color, coordinate, size, etc. and their relations [1]. The latter type of graphs is referred to as attributed graphs.

Representing objects by graphs turns the problem of object comparison into a graph matching (GM) one where evaluation of topological and/or statistical similarity of two graphs has to be found [2]. Researchers often shed light on error-tolerant GM, where an error model can be easily integrated into the GM process. The complexity of error-tolerant GM is NP-complete [3]. Consequently, the Graduated Assignment algorithm [4] has been employed to solve suboptimally error-tolerant GM. However, its complexity is $o(n^6)$ where n is number of vertices of both graphs. Several methods have a reduced complexity. However, they are not flexible as they do not cope with all the types of vertices and edges. For instance, the spectral methods [5], [6] deal with unlabeled graphs or only allow severely constrained label alphabets. Other methods are restricted to specific types of graphs [7]–[9], to name just a few.

Among error-tolerant problems for matching arbitrarily structured and arbitrarily attributed graphs, Graph Edit Distance (GED) is of great interest. GED is a discrete optimization problem. The search space of possible matching is represented as an ordered tree where a tree node is partial matching between two graphs. GED is NP-complete where its complexity is exponential in the number of vertices of the involved graphs [10]. GED can be applied to any type of graphs, including hypergraphs [11]. Many fast heuristic methods with unbounded errors have been proposed in the literature (e.g., [10]–[15]). On the other hand, few exact approaches have been proposed [16]–[18].

Recently, an exact Depth-First GED algorithm, referred to as *DF*, has been proposed in [18]. *DF* outperforms a well-known Best-First algorithm [16], referred to as A^*, in terms of memory consumption and run time. *DF* works well on relatively small graphs. To solve bigger matching problems, in this paper, we propose to extend *DF* to a distributed version which aims at spreading the workload over a cluster of machines. The distribution scheme is based on tree-decomposition and notification techniques. Instead of simply proposing a distributed *DF* algorithm using Message Passing Interface [19], we propose a master-slave distributed *DF* on top of Hadoop [20] with one synchronized variable achieved via ZooKeeper [21]. Roughly speaking, our algorithm consists of three main steps: First, a decomposition step where the master process divides the big matching problem into sub-problems. Second, a distribution stage where the master dispatches the sub problems among slave processes or so-called workers (i.e., processes to which a portion of work is associated). Third, a search-tree exploration step where each worker starts to explore its assigned problem by performing a partial *DF*. A notification step occurs when a worker succeeds in finding a better solution. In this case, the master informs the other workers and all of them update their upper bound. When a worker finishes the exploration of its assigned sub-problem, it asks the master for another one. Finally, the execution of the algorithm finishes when all the sub-problems generated in the decomposition stage are explored. The proposed algorithm is supported by novel evaluation performance metrics [22]. These metrics aim at comparing our algorithm with a set of GED approaches based on several significant criteria.

The rest of the paper is organized as follows. In Section II, the notations used in the paper are introduced. Moreover, the state of the art of GED approaches and distributed branch-and-bound techniques is presented. In Section III, the proposed distributed model is demonstrated. In Section IV, the datasets and the experimental protocols used to point out the performance of the proposed approaches are determined. Section V presents the obtained results and raises a discussion afterwards. Finally, conclusions are drawn and future perspectives are discussed in Section VI.

II. Related Works

In this section, we first define our basic notations and introduce GED and its computation.

A. Notations

1) Graph Based Notations: An attributed Graph (AG) is represented by a four-tuple, AG = (V, E, μ, ζ), where V and E are sets of vertices and edges such as $E \subseteq V \times V$. Both $\mu : V \to L_V$ and $\zeta : E \to L_E$ are vertex and edge labeling functions which associate an attribute or a label to each vertex v_i and edge e_i. L_V and L_E are unconstrained vertex and edge attributes sets, respectively. L_V and L_E can be given by a set of floats $L = \{1, 2, 3\}$, a vector space $L = \mathbb{R}^N$ and/or a finite set of symbolic attributes $L = \{x, y, b\}$.

GED is a graph matching method whose concept was first reported in [3], [23]. Its basic idea is to find the best set of transformations that can transform graph g_1 into graph g_2 by means of edit operations on graph g_2.

Let $g_1 = (V_1, E_1, \mu_1, \zeta_1)$ and $g_2 = (V_2, E_2, \mu_2, \zeta_2)$ be two graphs, GED between g_1 and g_2 is defined by:

$$GED(g_1, g_2) = \min_{ed_1, \cdots, ed_k \in \gamma(g_1, g_2)} \sum_{i=1}^{k} c(ed_i) \qquad (1)$$

where c denotes the cost function measuring the strength $c(ed_i)$ of an edit operation ed_i and $\gamma(g_1, g_2)$ denotes the set of edit paths transforming g_1 into g_2. The penalty, or cost, is dependent on the strength of the difference between the actual attributes information. Structure violations are also subject to a cost which is usually dependent on the magnitude of the structure violation [24]. And so, the penalty costs of each of deletion, insertion and substitution affect the matching process.

A standard set of edit operations is given by insertions, deletions and substitutions of both vertices and edges. We denote the substitution of two vertices u and v by $(u \to v)$, the deletion of vertex u by $(u \to \epsilon)$ and the insertion of vertex v by $(\epsilon \to v)$. For edges (*e.g.* e and z), we use the same notations used for vertices. A complete edit path (EP) refers to an edit path that fully transforms g_1 into g_2 (i.e., complete solution). Mathematically, $EP = \{ed_i\}_{i=1}^{k}$.

2) Distribution Based Notations:

Definition II.1. Master-Slave Architecture
Master-Slave refers to an architecture in which one device (the master) controls one or more other devices (the slaves).

Definition II.2. Job
A job is a distributed procedure which has one or more *workers* (i.e., processes that are assigned to tasks). Each worker takes a task or a bunch of tasks to be solved.

B. Graph Edit Distance Computation

The methods of the literature can be divided into two categories depending on whether they can ensure the optimal matching to be found or not.

1) Exact Graph Edit Distance Approaches: A widely used method for edit distance computation is based on the A^* algorithm [25]. This algorithm is considered as a foundation work for solving GED. A^* is a Best-First algorithm where the enumeration of all possible solutions is achieved by means of an ordered tree that is constructed dynamically at run time by iteratively creating successor nodes. At each time, the node or so called partial edit path p that has the least $g(p) + h(p)$ is chosen. $g(p)$ represents the cost of the partial edit path accumulated so far while $h(p)$ denotes the estimated cost from p to a leaf node representing a complete edit path. The sum $g(p) + h(p)$ is referred to as a lower bound $lb(p)$. Given that the estimation of the future costs $h(p)$ is lower than, or equal to, the real costs, an optimal path from the root node to a leaf node is guaranteed to be found [26]. Leaf nodes correspond to feasible solutions and so complete edit paths. In the worst case, the space complexity can be expressed as $O(|\gamma|)$ [27] where $|\gamma|$ is the cardinality of the set of all possible edit paths. Since $|\gamma|$ is exponentional in the number of vertices involved in the graphs, the memory usage is still an issue.

To overcome the memory consumption problem of A^*, a recent Depth-First GED algorithm, referred to as *DF*, has been proposed in [18]. This algorithm speeds up the computations of GED thanks to its upper and lower bounds pruning strategy and its some associated preprocessing steps. Moreover, *DF* does not exhaust memory as the number of pending edit paths that are stored in the set, called *OPEN*, is relatively small thanks to the Depth-First search where the number of pending nodes is $|V_1|.|V_2|$ in the worst case.

2) Approximate Graph Edit Distance Approaches: Variants of approximate GED algorithms are proposed to make GED computation substantially faster. A modification of A^*, called Beam-Search (*BS*), has been proposed in [28]. Instead of exploring all edit paths in the search tree, only x most promising partial edit paths are kept in the set of promising candidates.

In [26], the problem of graph matching is reduced to finding an optimal matching in a complete bipartite GM, this algorithm is referred to as *BP*. In the worst case, the maximum number of operations needed by *BP* is $O(n^3)$. Since *BP* considers local structures rather than global ones, an overestimation of the exact GED cannot be neglected. A recent algorithm [29], named *FBP*, reduced the size of *BP*'s matrices. Recently, researchers have observed that *BP*'s overestimation is very often due to a few incorrectly assigned vertices. That is, only few vertex substitutions from the next step are responsible for additional (unnecessary) edge operations in the step after and thus resulting in the overestimation of the exact edit distance. Thus, recent works have been proposed to swap the misleading mappings [30], [31]. These improvements increase run times. However, they improve the accuracy of *BP*.

C. Distributed Branch-and-Bound Algorithms

Our interest in this paper is to propose a distributed extension of *DF* to be able to match large graphs. The best computing design that suits *DF* is SPMD [32] where a portion of the data (i.e., sub-search tree) is given to each process and all processes execute the proposed method on their associated sub-search trees. Since *DF* is a Branch-and-Bound (BnB) algorithm, we survey the state of art of distributed BnB approaches. However, before surveying the literature, some challenging questions should be listed:

- What is(are) the sub-task(s) associated to each process?
- What is the estimated time/needed memory per sub-task?

- What is the number of needed processes?
- How many sub-tasks one may generate before the distribution starts?
- How to efficiently distribute the search tree nodes of the irregular search tree among a large set of processes? Note that the decomposition, or distribution, can be irregular due to the bounding, or pruning with the help of $g(p)+h(p)$. Such a thing cannot be known except at run time.

These raised questions will be answered after exploring the state-of-art's methods dedicated to distributed BnB.

In [33], a one-iteration MPI approach was proposed. This approach is dedicated to solving three-phase electrical distribution networks. In the beginning, a specific number of nodes are generated by the master process. When this number is reached, no more nodes could be generated. The master then gives, or sends, a node to each slave. Then, each slave starts the exploration of the search tree in a Depth-First way. Once a slave finds a better upper bound, it sends to the master that updates all slaves. Once a slave finishes its the exploration of its assigned node, it sends a message to the master asking for a new node and the process continues. The drawback of such an approach is that once all the nodes, generated by the master, are given to all processes, some processes might become idle because they finished their associated nodes. Such a fact does not allow this approach to use all its resources at each time. In [34], a MPI BnB approach was proposed to solve the knapsack problem. This work is similar to [33]. However, the way of exploring the tree is left to the user so one can choose either Depth-First, a Best-First or a Breadth-First.

To the best of our knowledge, in the literature there is no distributed BnB method dedicated to solving GED. Both [33] and [34] are based on MPI which has no fault-tolerance. That is, if one slave process fails, one needs to re-execute all the processes. In this paper, instead of proposing an approach bases on MPI, we build MPI upon Hadoop [20]. Hadoop is tolerant to faults, thus, if one process fails, a master program selects another a free process to do its task. Roughly speaking, only the upper bound *UB* has to be shared with all processes. However, Hadoop is a model with restricted communication patterns. In order to allow processes to send messages and notify the other processes when finding a better *UB*, a message passing tool is adopted [21].

The search tree of GED contains nodes that represent partial edit paths. When thinking of a distributed approach of *DF*, these edit paths can be given to processes as tasks to be solved. Such a step divides the GED problem into smaller problems. The GED problem is irregular in the sense of having an irregular search tree where the number of nodes differs, depending on the ability of $lb(p)$ to prune the search tree. Based on that, it becomes hard to estimate the time needed by processes to explore a branch.

In [33] and [34], the authors did not mention the method they followed in order to generate nodes before the distribution starts. In our GED problem, one may think of A^* since it starts exploring nodes that lead to the optimal solution, if $lb(p)$ is carefully chosen. But, there are two key issues: First, how many nodes shall be generated by A^* before a *DF* procedure starts? Second, how to divide the nodes between processes?.

Input: Non-empty attributed graphs $g_1 = (V_1, E_1, \mu_1, v_1)$ and $g_2 = (V_2, E_2, \mu_2, v_2)$ where $V_1 = \{u_1, ..., u_{|v_1|}\}$ and $V_2 = \{v_1, ..., v_{|v_2|}\}$. A parameter N which is the number of the first generated partial edit paths.
Output: A minimum distance $UBCOST_{shared}$ and a minimum cost edit path (*UB*) from g_1 to g_2 e.g., *UB*= $\{u_1 \rightarrow v_3, u_2 \rightarrow \epsilon, \epsilon \rightarrow v_2\}$

1: (*UB* , *UBCOST*) $\leftarrow$ BP(g_1, g_2)
2: $OPEN \leftarrow \{\phi\}$
3: $Q \leftarrow A^*(N)$
4: $Q \leftarrow$ SortAscending(Q)
5: **for** $q \in Q$ **do**
6:     $OPEN$.AddFirst(q);
7: **end for**
8: $UBCOST_{shared} \leftarrow UBCOST$ {put *UBCOST* in an accessible place to all workers}
9: $UB_{shared} \leftarrow UB$ {put *UB* in an accessible place to all workers}
10: $File_{OPENshared} \leftarrow OPEN$
11: **parallel for** $w \in W$ **do**
12:     Get-Next-Task: $p \leftarrow File_{OPENshared}$.popFirst()
13:     Call PartialDF(p,W,$UBCOST_{shared}$, UB_{shared})
14:     **if** $File_{OPENshared}$ is not empty **then**
15:         Repeat Get-Next-Task
16:     **end if**
17: **end parallel for**
18: Return (UB_{shared}, $UBCOST_{shared}$).

Figure 1. Distributed *DF* (*D-DF*).

III. Distributed Depth-First GED Approach

Our distributed approach, referred to as *D-DF*, consists of a single *job*. Figure 1 represents the three main steps of *D-DF*. First, the master matches g_1 and g_2 using *BP* and outputs both the matching sequence *UB* and its edit distance *UBCOST* (line 1). Second, A^* is executed and stopped once N partial edit paths are generated (line 3). Afterwards, these partial edit paths (Q) are sorted in ascending order and inserted to *OPEN* (lines 4 to 7). The master also saves *UB* and its *UBCOST* in a place/space accessible by all workers W (lines 8 and 9). Finally, the master distributes the work (i.e., Q) among workers, each worker takes one edit path from the master at a time (line 12). This step adapts the dynamic scheduling where tasks are associated to processes at run time. Thus, each process takes one and only one edit path at a time t instead of having a predefined list of edit paths. Workers start the exploration of their associated partial edit paths (line 13). If a worker finishes its assigned partial edit path, it sends a message to the master asking for a new edit path (lines 14 to 16). When finishing all the partial edit paths, saved in $File_{OPENshared}$, the program outputs UB_{shared} and $UBCOST_{shared}$ as an optimal solution of matching g_1 and g_2 (line 18).

Figure 2 demonstrates the function *PartialDF* that each worker w executes on its assigned partial edit path p. Note that each p is given to an available worker by the master. The procedures of this algorithm are similar to *DF*, the only difference is that *UBCOST* and *UB* are saved in a shared space that is accessible by all workers W. These shared variables are

Input: An edit path p, the set of workers W, $UBCOST_{shared}$ and UB_{shared}

```
1: OPEN ← {φ}, p_min ← φ
2: OPEN.addFirst(p)
3: r ← parent(u_1), r_tmp ← r
4: UBCOST ← read(UBCOST_shared)
5: Set watch on UBCOST_shared
6: while OPEN != {φ} do
7:     p ← OPEN.popFirst()          ▷ Take first element and remove it from OPEN
8:     Listp ← GenerateChildren(p)
9:     if Listp = {φ} then
10:        for v_i ∈ pendingV_2(p) do
11:            q ← insertion(ε , v_i)          ▷ i.e., {ε → v_i}
12:            p.AddFirst(q)
13:        end for
14:        if g(p) < UB then
15:            UB ← g(p), Bestedit path ← p
16:            UBCOST_shared ← g(p) + h(p)
17:            UB_shared ← p
18:            MASTER: notify-all-workers w ∈ W
19:            for w ∈ W do
20:                UBCOST ← read(UBCOST_shared)
21:                Reset watch on UBCOST_shared
22:            end for
23:        end if
24:    else
25:        Listp ← SortAscending(Listp)          ▷ according to g(p)+h(p)
26:        for q ∈ Listp do
27:            if g(q) + h(q) < UB then
28:                OPEN.AddFirst(q)
29:            end if
30:        end for
31:    end if
32: end while
```

Figure 2. Function PartialDF.

referred to as $UBCOST_{shared}$ and UB_{shared}. All the workers read the value stored in $UBCOST_{shared}$ through *read* message (line 4). They also put a watch on $UBCOST_{shared}$ via *Set-Watch* message so as to be awaken when any change happens to its value (line 5). All the workers solve their associated partial edit path. Whenever worker w succeeds in finding a better value of its *UBCOST*, it updates both $UBCOST_{shared}$ and UB_{shared} through *update* messages (lines 15 and 17), the master then sends a notification via *notify-Worker* message to all the other workers (line 18). Workers read the new value, update their local *UB* and continue solving their problems. Moreover, workers re-establish, or reset, the watch for data changes through *Reset-Watch* message (lines 19 to 22). The update of $UBCOST_{shared}$ is done carefully as only one worker can change $UBCOST_{shared}$ at any time t. That is, if two workers want to change $UBCOST_{shared}$ at the same time, one of them is delayed by the master for some milliseconds before entering the critical point. The final answers (i.e., the optimal matching and its distance) are found in UB_{shared} and $UBCOST_{shared}$ respectively when all workers finish their associated tasks.

A. *Advantages and Drawbacks*

D-DF is a fully distributed approach where each worker accomplishes its task without waiting for each other. Moreover, the search tree is cleverly pruned. As soon as any worker finds a better $UBCOST_{shared}$, it sends the new value to the master. Then, the notification to all the other workers is achieved by the master. Finally, all the workers receive the new value. Such operations help at pruning the workers' search trees as fast as possible. *D-DF* is a single-job approach and thus the drawback behind such an approach is that some workers might become idle because there is no more edit path in $File_{OPENshared}$ while the other ones are still working as they have not finished their assigned edit paths. To overcome such a problem, in future work, this algorithm can be transformed into a multi-jobs, or multi-iteration, algorithm.

IV. EXPERIMENTS

A. *Environment*

D-DF is built on top of Hadoop [20] with a notification tool called *ZooKeeper* [21] used to share $UBCOST_{shared}$ and UB_{shared} with all workers. Synchronizing these variables does not break the scalability. On the contrary, it helps in pruning the search tree as fast as possible. The evaluation of *D-DF* is conducted on 5 machines running Hadoop MapReduce version 1.0.4. Each node contains a 4-core Intel i7 processor 3.07GHz, 8GB memory and one hard drive with 380GB capacity. Hadoop was allocated 20 workers (4 workers per machine), each with a maximum JVM memory size of 1GB. Hadoop Distributed File System is used for dispatching edit paths with a replication factor that is equal to 3. For sequential algorithms, evaluations are conducted on one machine.

B. *Studied Methods*

We compare *D-DF* with five GED algorithms from the literature. From the related work, we chose two exact methods and three approximate ones. On the exact methods' side, we have chosen, A* and *DF*. In both algorithms *h(p)* is calculated by applying *BP* on vertices and edges in a separated manner [18]. On the approximate methods' side, we include *BS-1*, *BS-10*, *BS-100*, *BP* and *FBP*, see Section II-B.

C. *Datasets*

Recently, a new repository has been put forward to test the scalability of graphs [22]. Databases are divided into subsets each of which represents graphs with the same number of vertices. In this work, we use two PR datasets (GREC and Mutagenicity (MUTA)) taken from the repository. However, we eliminate the easy graph matching problems from both datasets since we are interested in difficult problems for distribution issues. To filter these databases, we run *DF* on each pair of graphs and stop it after 5 minutes. If there is no optimal solution found within 5 minutes, then the matching problem is considered as difficult. This results in 627 problems on MUTA and 92 problems on GREC. For more details about these datasets, please visit the GDR4GED repository [35].

D. *Protocol*

First, the effect the variable N (number of initial edit paths) is tested on several values. Five values of N are chosen: 20, 100, 250, 500 and 1000, where N=20 represents the least distributed case (i.e., one edit path per worker), N= 100 and

250 moderately amortize the communication between master and slaves whereas N=500 and 1000 is the more complete case where workers have to cross the network many times in order to ask for a new edit path once they finish solving an already assigned one. We also study the effect of increasing the number of machines, from 2 to 5 machines, on run time. Both tests are evaluated on GREC-20 (i.e., graphs of GREC whose number of vertices is twenty) [22].

The deviation was chosen as a metric to compare all the included methods [22]. We compute the error committed by each method m over the reference distances. For each pair of graphs matched by method m, we provide the following deviation measure:

$$dev(g_i, g_j)^m = \frac{|d(g_i, g_j)^m - R_{g_i, g_j}|}{R_{g_i, g_j}}, \ \forall (i,j) \in [\![1, G]\!]^2, \ \forall m \in \mathcal{M} \tag{2}$$

where G is the number of graphs. $d(g_i, g_j)^m$ is the distance obtained when matching g_i and g_j using method m while R_{g_i, g_j} corresponds to the best known solution among all the included methods. We also measure the overall time in milliseconds (ms), for each GED computation, including all the inherits costs computations. The mean run time is calculated per subset s and for each method m. Due to the high complexity of GED methods, we propose to evaluate them under a time constraint C_T that is equal to 300 seconds and a memory constraint C_M that is equal to 1GB. Note that the only algorithm that violates memory is A^*.

V. Results and Discussions

Figure 3 depicts the parameters study. One can see that increasing the number of machines decreases the run time. For some instances, the runtime was not reduced due to the difficulty of matching problems. As for N, the best case was when it equals 250, owing to moderately performing tasks-dispatch. These values were used for the rest of experiments.

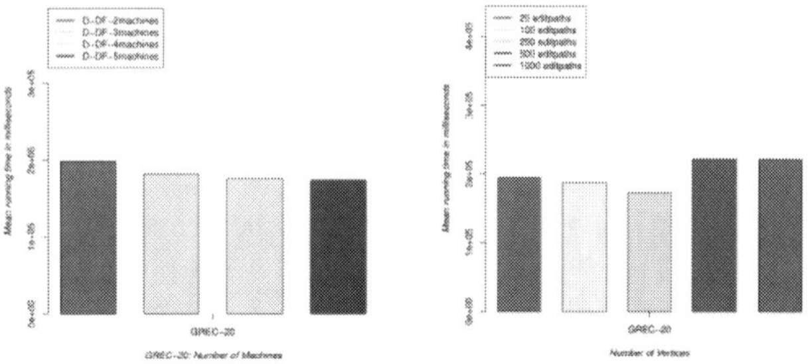

Figure 3. Parameters: Left (Number of Machines), Right (Variable N). The objective of this study is to choose the values that minimize *D-DF*'s run time.

Figure 4 illustrates the deviation of the included methods on GREC and MUTA. Figure 4(a) shows that *D-DF* has the least deviation (0%) on all subsets, followed by *DF*. However, that was not the case on MUTA, see Figure 4(b). *BS100* outperformed *D-DF* in terms of number of best found solutions. The major differences between these algorithms are a) The search space exploration manner and b) the Vertices-Sorting strategy which is adapted in *DF* [18] and not in *BS*. In fact, *BP* is integrated in the preprocessing step of *DF* to sort vertices of g_1. Since *BP* did not give a good estimation on MUTA, it was also irrelevant when sorting the vertices of g_1 resulting in the exploration of misleading nodes in the search tree. Since the graphs of MUTA are relatively large, backtracking nodes took time. MUTA contains symbolic attributes while *DF* and *D-DF* are designed for rich attributed graphs where the use of *BP* in the vertices sort is meaningful. However, the deviation of *BS* and *D-DF* was relatively similar. Both *D-DF* and *DF* succeeded in finding upper bounds that are better than *BP*. *D-DF*, however, has always outperformed *DF* in terms of deviation. This can be remarkably seen on MUTA where, in average, the deviation of *DF* was 18% while the deviation of *D-DF* was 6.5%.

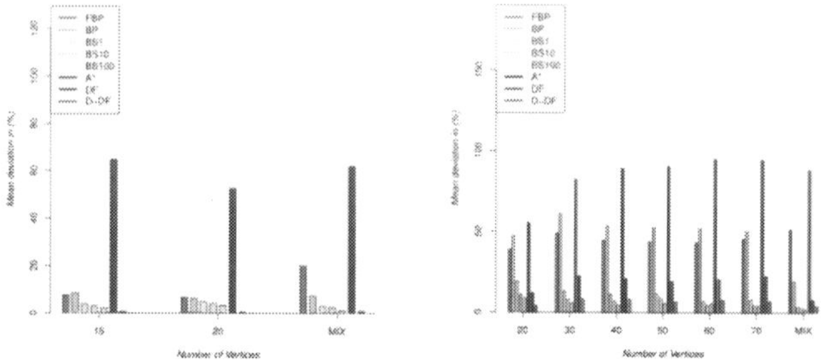

Figure 4. Deviation: Left (GREC), Right (MUTA). Note that the lower the deviation the better the algorithm.

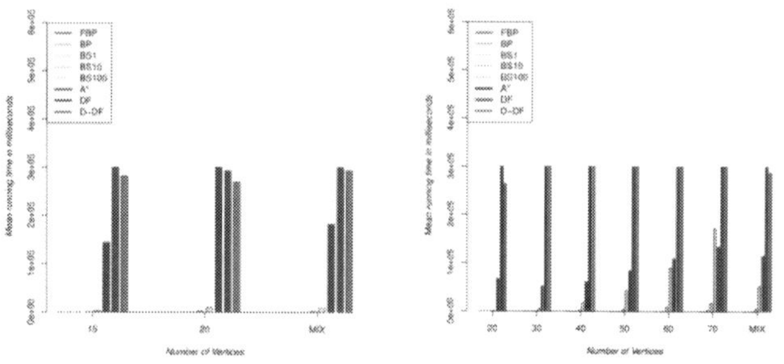

Figure 5. Run time: Left (GREC), Right (MUTA). Note that the lower the run time the better the algorithm.

D-DF was always faster or equal to *DF*, see Figure 5. At a first glance, one can think that A^* was faster than both *DF* and *D-DF*. However, that was not the case. In fact, A^* was unable to output feasible solutions and was stopped because of its memory bottleneck. *BP* was the fastest algorithm (12.3 milliseconds on GREC and 11 milliseconds on MUTA).

VI. Conclusion and Perspectives

In the present paper, we have considered the problem of GED computation for PR. GED is a powerful and flexible paradigm that has been used in different applications in PR. In the literature, few exact GED algorithms have been proposed. Recently, a Depth-First GED algorithm (*DF*) has shown to be effective. *DF*, thanks to its Depth-First exploration, upper and lower bounds pruning strategies, overcomes the high memory consumption from which a well-known A^* algorithm suffers. However, *DF* can match relatively small graphs. In this paper, we have proposed to extend it to a distributed version called *D-DF*. We build a master-slave architecture over Hadoop in order to take advantage of the fault-tolerance of Hadoop. Each worker gets one partial edit path and all workers solve their assigned edit paths in a fully distributed manner. In addition, a notification process is integrated. When any worker finds a better upper bound, it notifies the master to share the new upper bound with all workers.

In the experiments part, we have proposed to evaluate both exact and approximate GED approaches, using novel performance evaluation metrics under time and memory constraints, on two different datasets (GREC and MUTA). Experiments have pointed out that *D-DF* has the minimum deviation. *BS* is slightly superior to *D-DF* in terms of deviation on the MUTA dataset. In fact, one weakness of *DF* and so *D-DF* is that their sorting strategy is *BP*-dependent. One solution could be to better learn the upper bound and so the sorting strategy in function of dataset type/nature. Experiments have also demonstrated that *D-DF* always outperforms *DF* in terms of deviation and run time. Indeed, *D-DF* is flexible as one can add more machines and thus decrease the running time. Results have also indicated that there is always a trade-off between deviation and running time. In other words, approximate methods are fast, however, they are not as accurate as exact ones. On the other hand, *DF* and *D-DF* take longer time but lead to better results.

The main drawback behind *D-DF* is that it is a single-job algorithm. When there is no time constraint, some workers work while others may become idle after finishing the exploration of their assigned partial edit paths. To overcome this drawback and as future work, we aim at transforming *D-DF* into a multi-iteration method where all workers work without becoming idle. Moreover, two ideas can be applied for both *DF* and *D-DF*. First, coming up with a better lower bound and thus making the calculations faster. Second, learning to sort the vertices of each dataset in a way that minimizes its deviation. Such an extension of *DF* and *D-DF* can beat the approximate approaches when matching graphs of MUTA.

References

[1] K. Riesen and H. Bunke, "Iam graph database repository for graph based pattern recognition and machine learning," 2008, pp. 287–297.

[2] M. Vento, "A long trip in the charming world of graphs for pattern recognition," Pattern Recognition, vol. 48, no. 2, 2015, pp. 291–301.

[3] H. Bunke, "Inexact graph matching for structural pattern recognition," Pattern Recognition Letters, vol. 1, no. 4, 1983, pp. 245–253.

[4] S. Gold and A. Rangarajan, "A graduated assignment algorithm for graph matching," Pattern Analysis and Machine Intelligence, IEEE Transactions on, vol. 18, 1996, pp. 377–388.

[5] S. Umeyama, "An eigendecomposition approach to weighted graph matching problems," Pattern Analysis and Machine Intelligence, IEEE Transactions on, vol. 10, 1988, pp. 695–703.

[6] R. Wilson, E. Hancock, and B. Luo, "Pattern vectors from algebraic graph theory," Pattern Analysis and Machine Intelligence, IEEE Transactions on, vol. 27, 2005, pp. 1112–1124.

[7] X. Jiang and H. Bunke, "Optimal quadratic-time isomorphism of ordered graphs," Pattern Recognition, vol. 32, no. 7, 1999, pp. 1273 – 1283.

[8] J. E. Hopcroft and J. K. Wong, "Linear time algorithm for isomorphism of planar graphs (preliminary report)," in Proceedings of the Sixth Annual ACM Symposium on Theory of Computing. New York, NY, USA: ACM, 1974, pp. 172–184.

[9] M. Neuhaus and H. Bunke, "An error-tolerant approximate matching algorithm for attributed planar graphs and its application to fingerprint classification," in SSPR WORKSHOP. LNCS 3138. Springer, 2004, pp. 180–189.

[10] Z. Zeng, A. K. H. Tung, J. Wang, J. Feng, and L. Zhou, "Comparing stars: On approximating graph edit distance," vol. 2, 2009, pp. 25–36.

[11] W.-H. Tsai and K.-S. Fu, "Error-correcting isomorphisms of attributed relational graphs for pattern analysis," Systems, Man and Cybernetics, IEEE Transactions on, vol. 9, no. 12, 1979, pp. 757–768.

[12] J. K. W. Christmas and M. Petrou., "Structural matching in computer vision using probabilistic relaxation." IEEE Trans. PAMI,, vol. 2, 1995, pp. 749–764.

[13] A. D. J. Cross and E. R. Hancock, "Graph matching with a dual-step em algorithm," IEEE Trans. Pattern Anal. Mach. Intell., vol. 20, 1998, pp. 1236–1253.

[14] e. a. Finch, Wilson, "An energy function and continuous edit process for graph matching," Neural Computat, vol. 10, 1998, pp. 1873–1894.

[15] P. Kuner and B. Ueberreiter, "Pattern recognition by graph matching: Combinatorial versus continuous optimization," International journal in Pattern Recognition and Artificial Intelligence, vol. 2, 1988, pp. 527—-542.

[16] P. Hart, N. Nilsson, and B. Raphael., "A formal basis for the heuristic determination of minimum cost paths," IEEE Transactions of Systems, Science, and Cybernetics., vol. 28, 2004, pp. 100–107.

[17] D. Justice and A. Hero, "A binary linear programming formulation of the graph edit distance," IEEE Transactions on Pattern Analysis and Machine Intelligence, vol. 28, 2006, pp. 1200–1214.

[18] Z. Abu-Aisheh, R. Raveaux, J.-Y. Ramel, and P. Martineau, "An exact graph edit distance algorithm for solving pattern recognition problems," Proceedings of ICPRAM, 2015, pp. 271–278.

[19] M. Snir, S. Otto, S. Huss-Lederman, D. Walker, and J. Dongarra, MPI-The Complete Reference, volume 1: The MPI Core, 2nd ed. Cambridge, MA, USA: MIT Press, 1998.

[20] T. White and D. Cutting, Hadoop : the definitive guide. O'Reilly, 2009.

[21] F. Junqueira and B. Reed, Zookeeper: Distributed Process Coordination, 2013.

[22] Z. Abu-Aisheh, R. Raveaux, and J.-Y. Ramel, "A graph database repository and performance evaluation metrics for graph edit distance," in Graph-Based Representations in Pattern Recognition - GbRPR 2015., 2015, pp. 138–147.

[23] A. Sanfeliu and K. Fu, "A distance measure between attributed relational graphs for pattern recognition," IEEE Transactions on Systems, Man, and Cybernetics, vol. 13, 1983, pp. 353–362.

[24] K. Riesen and H. Bunke, Graph Classification and Clustering Based on Vector Space Embedding. River Edge, NJ, USA: World Scientific Publishing Co., Inc., 2010.

[25] S. Fankhauser, K. Riesen, and H. Bunke, "Speeding up graph edit distance computation with a bipartite heuristic," no. 6658, 2011, pp. 102–111.

[26] B. H. Riesen, K., "Approximate graph edit distance computation by means of bipartite graph matching." Image and Vision Computing., vol. 28, 2009, pp. 950–959.

[27] T. H. Cormen, C. E. Leiserson, R. L. Rivest, and C. Stein, Introduction to Algorithms, Third Edition, 3rd ed. The MIT Press, 2009.

[28] H. B. M. Neuhaus, K. Riesen, "Fast suboptimal algorithms for the computation of graph edit distance," Proceedings of SSPR., 2006, pp. 163–172.

[29] F. Serratosa, "Computation of graph edit distance: Reasoning about optimality and speed-up," Image and Vision Computing, vol. 40, 2015, pp. 38–48.

[30] K. Riesen and H. Bunke, "Improving Approximate Graph Edit Distance by Means of a Greedy Swap Strategy," vol. 8509, 2014, pp. 314–321.

[31] K. Riesen, A. Fischer, and H. Bunke, "Improving approximate graph edit distance using genetic algorithms," 2014, pp. 63–72.

[32] M. J. Atallah and S. Fox, Eds., Algorithms and Theory of Computation Handbook, 1st ed. Boca Raton, FL, USA: CRC Press, Inc., 1998.

[33] L. Barreto and M. Bauer, "Parallel branch and bound algorithm - a comparison between serial, openmp and mpi implementations," journal of Physics: Conference Series, vol. 256, no. 5, 2010, pp. 012–018.

[34] I. Dorta, C. León, and C. Rodríguez, "A comparison between mpi and openmp branch-and-bound skeletons." in IPDPS, 2003.

[35] "Gdr4ged," http://www.rfai.li.univ-tours.fr/PublicData/GDR4GED/home.html., 2015.

Discovering the Most Dominant Nodes in Frequent Subgraphs

Farah Chanchary
School of Computer Science
Carleton University
Ottawa, Canada K1S 5B6
Email: farah.chanchary@carleton.ca

Herna Viktor
School of Elec Eng. and Comp Sc.
University of Ottawa
Ottawa, Canada K1N 6N5
Email: hviktor@uottawa.ca

Anil Maheshwari
School of Computer Science
Carleton University
Ottawa, Canada K1S 5B6
Email: anil@scs.carleton.ca

***Abstract*—Recently, there is a growing trend to utilize data mining algorithms to explore datasets being modeled using graphs. In most cases, these graphs evolve over time, thus exhibiting more complex patterns and relationships among nodes. In particular, social networks are believed to manifest the preferential attachment property which assumes that new graph nodes have a higher probability of forming links with high-degree nodes. Often, these high-degree nodes have the tendency to become the articulation points in frequent subgraphs (also known as the most dominant nodes). Thus, their identification is important, because their disappearance may have greater influence on their peer nodes. Also, exploring their properties is essential when aiming to predict future frequent patterns. In this paper, we introduce a binary classification model *DetectMDN* to correctly classify the most dominant nodes in frequently occurring subgraphs. A set of experimental results confirms the feasibility and accuracy of our approach.**

Keywords–Frequent subgraphs; Graph mining; Most dominant nodes; Time evolving graph.

I. Introduction

In recent years, there has been considerable interest in graph structures arising in technological, sociological, and scientific settings. These domains include computer networks (routers or autonomous systems connected together); networks of users exchanging e-mails or instant messages; citation networks and hyperlink networks and social networks [25]. Frequent pattern mining provides a way to extract significant and interesting patterns from large datasets that otherwise commonly remain unexplored. This idea was first proposed by Agrawal and Srikant [1] in their work on proposing faster association rules mining. At present, frequent pattern mining is used in numerous scientific, business and legal application domains where the datasets are generally large, multidimensional and dynamic, and traditional approaches of exploratory data analysis yield limited success [14].

Other than association rule mining, frequent pattern mining is also used in many standard knowledge discovery tasks such as classification and clustering to achieve better outcomes from these patterns. At the same time the applications have expanded extensively in domains where objects of various datasets are modeled using graphs [21] [22], trees [19], sequences [16] or time evolving networks [7] [24]. Following the trend, research has been carried out on graph and tree pattern mining to discover complex associations that are frequent according to some predefined concept.

Interesting frequent patterns can further be used as a source of features in a supervised learning task when the database events are labeled. In many networks, e.g., communication, social networks, citation and co-authorship networks, this idea can play a significant role in solving problems like hidden group identification and link prediction. In cases when similar patterns of groups or links occur very frequently within large networks, they can provide important information for predicting future patterns. This leads to the problem of efficiently identifying most dominant nodes (MDNs) in these frequent sub-groups. It follows that MDNs tend to dominate the interests and activities of their peer nodes. Thus, knowing their attachment patterns is valuable to many entities, including marketers, employers, credit rating agencies, insurers, spammers, phishers, police, and intelligence agencies [8].

The main contributions of this study are three-fold. Our paper describes and presents the performance of *DetectMDN* algorithm designed to find, and subsequently correctly label MDNs in hidden frequent subgraphs of any large network. We further analyze the impact of different types of networks on the prediction results. Thirdly, we identify the most relevant attributes to accurately define frequent subgraphs.

The paper is organized as follows. Section 2 describes the problem domain and highlights related work. This is followed, in Section 3, with a description of our *DetectMDN* algorithms. Section 4 details our experimental setup and evaluation, while Section 5 concludes the paper.

II. Description of the Problem Domain and Related Work

There are generally two distinct settings for subgraph mining. The first one is the *graph-transactional* setting, where a set of graphs $\{G_1, ..., G_n\}$ and a threshold t are given, and our goal is to find patterns that occur in at least t graphs in the set. The second graph mining setting is called the *single network* setting, where a single graph G and a threshold t are given, and we aim to find patterns that have a support of at least t in G according to some appropriate support measure. We use both settings as inputs to evaluate our classification model.

Formally, the problem definitions are as follows:

1) In a graph-transactional setting, a graph dataset $D_1 = \{G_1, ..., G_n\}$ and a threshold t are given.

2) In the single network setting, a dataset D_2 consisting of a large graph G and a threshold t are given.

In this setting, our task is thus to correctly identify all MDNs in D_1 and D_2.

All graph datasets used in this study are undirected. We revisit relevant definitions below.

Definition 1: A graph $G = (V, E)$ has a set of nodes denoted by V and the edge set denoted by E. A graph G' is a subgraph of another graph G if there exists a subgraph isomorphism from G' to G, denoted by $G' \subseteq G$.

Definition 2: A subgraph is frequent if its support (occurrence frequency) in a given dataset is no less than a minimum support threshold t, where $t > 0$.

Hence, the frequent subgraph is a relative concept, whether or not a subgraph is frequent depends on the value of t [28].

Definition 3: A subgraph isomorphism is an injective function $f : V(G) \rightarrow V(G')$, such that, (1) $\forall u \in V(G)$, $l(u) = l'(f(u))$, and (2) $\forall (u, v) \in E(G), (f(u), f(v)) \in E(G')$ and $l(u, v) = l'(f(u), f(v))$ where l and l' are the label function of G and G', respectively.

These labels represent some properties of the nodes (or edges) from the same domain, e.g., location or gender, and for simplicity it is assumed that they do not change with time. We also assume that labels do not represent any combinations of properties (i.e., both location and gender). Each node (or edge) of the graph is not required to have a unique label and the same label can be assigned to many nodes (or edges) in the same graph. Here, f is called an embedding of G in G'.

Figure 1 presents an example of frequency counts of subgraphs X and Y in a source graph G. Subgraph X on top has a frequency count of 2 and the subgraph Y on bottom has frequency counts of 4 in the source graph on the left.

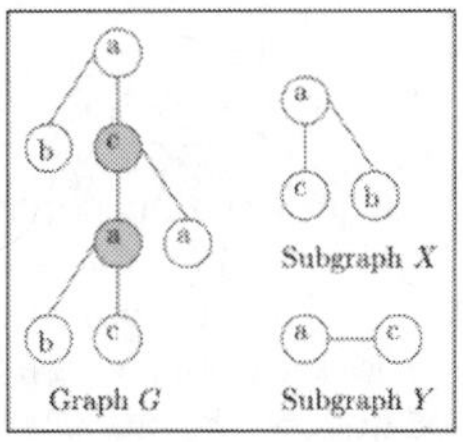

Figure 1. Frequency counts of subgraphs.

Definition 4: A most dominant node $u \in V$ in an undirected graph G is an articulation point having maximum degree in a frequent subgraph of G.

Definition 5: A node $x \in V$ in an undirected graph G is an articulation point if removing x disconnects the graph into two or more connected components. In other words, node $x \in V$ is an articulation point if there exists distinct nodes v and w, such that every path between v and w goes through x.

Figure 1 has three articulation points but only two of these are MDNs (shaded nodes). Note that more than one articulation point may have the same maximum degree, and these are all considered as MDNs.

Definition 6: A time evolving graph is a conceptual representation of a series of undirected graphs $G_0, \cdots, G_T$, so that $G_t = (V_t, E_t)$ represents the graph at time t over time 0 to T. Thus, $\{G_0, G_1, \cdots, G_T\}$ is combined as one undirected graph $G = (V, E)$ with $V = \cup_{t=0}^{T} V_t = V_T$ and $E = \cup_{t=0}^{T} E_t = E_T$. To each edge $e = (u, v)$ a time-stamp $t(e) = \min_j \{E_j | e \in E_j\}$ is assigned. So, formally a time evolving graph is defined as $G = (V, E, t, \lambda)$ with t assigning time-stamps to E and a labeling function $\lambda : V \cup E \rightarrow \Sigma$, assigning labels to nodes and edges from an alphabet Σ [24].

The edge labels of the graph shown in Figure 2 represent collaboration time between pairs of authors. Label 0 represents the starting time (e.g., month, day or year) and it increases by 1 after every time unit.

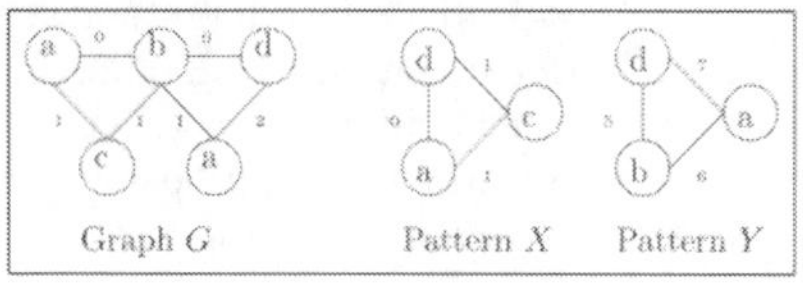

Figure 2. Time evolving graph.

Time evolving graphs support relative-time pattern matching.

Definition 7: Let $G = (V, E, t, \lambda)$ be a time evolving graph and $P = (V_P, E_P, t_P, \lambda_P)$ is a pattern subgraph. Let us assume that P is connected. P occurs in G at relative time if there exists a $\Delta \in R$ and a function $\psi : V_P \rightarrow V$ mapping the nodes of P to the nodes in G such that, $\forall u, v \in V_P$:

1) $(u, v) \in E_P$ implies $(\psi(u), \psi(v)) \in E$
2) $(u, v) \in E_P$ implies $t((\psi(u), \psi(v))) = t(u, v) + \Delta$
3) $\lambda_P(u, v) = \lambda(\psi(v))\lambda_P(u, v) = \lambda((\psi(u), \psi(v)))$

Figure 2 shows an example of how relative-time pattern matches subgraphs with the source graph. Here, pattern X is not a valid subgraph of G since node labels do not match properly. On the other hand, pattern Y is valid according to property 2 of Definition 7.

Definition 8: Minimum Image Based Support is based on the number of unique nodes in the graph $G = (V, E)$ that a node of the pattern $P = (V', E')$ is mapped to, and defined as $\delta(P, G) = min_{v \in V'} |\{\psi_i(v) : \psi_i \text{ is an occurance of } P \text{ in } G\}|$.

Figure 3 shows the host graph (a) and a pattern (b). According to minimum image based support measure the frequency of the given pattern in the host graph will be 1, though in general the pattern can be matched with multiple embeddings of the host graph.

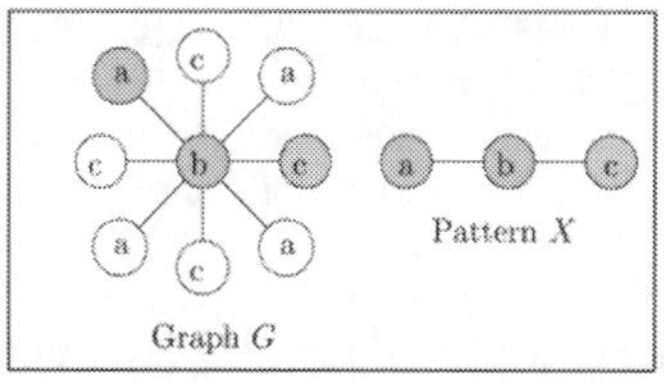

Figure 3. A graph with possible different occurrences of a pattern.

A. Related Work

A number of research has been carried out on the separate themes of the effect of node removal from large graphs and discovering influential or important nodes from large graphs based on different measurement and characteristics of graph elements, such as a model based on semi-local centrality measure [5], another model based on bio-inspired centrality measure [6], stochastic diffusion models [20], and the information transfer probability between any pair of nodes and the k-medoid clustering algorithm [33]. In [3], Albert et al. showed that a class of inhomogenously wired networks (such as the World Wide Web, social networks and communication networks) are extremely vulnerable to the selection and removal of a few nodes that play a vital role in maintaining the network connectivity. Shetty et al. [27] worked on an entropy model to identify the most interesting nodes in a graph. Here, the concept of importance depends on the amount of commands/messages forwarded through the network. A different measure using principal component centrality has been used in [15] to identify social hubs, nodes at the center of influential neighborhoods. Further, the problem of identifying influential spreaders in complex networks has also been studied in [34]. As far as we are aware, this paper presents the first work in which a classifier is used to find the MDN in frequent subgraphs.

III. DetectMDN Algorithm

This section describes main components of our DetectMDN algorithm.

Step 1. Extract frequent patterns: From input graph datasets $D_1 = \{G_1, ..., G_n\}$ and D_2, all frequent subgraphs are extracted where frequency occurs more than a given threshold t. By applying a graph mining algorithm (gSpan [32]) on D_1, we construct a set of frequent subgraphs $D'_1 = \{F_1, ...F_n\}$. Another graph mining algorithm (GERM [24]) is applied on D_2 to obtain another set of frequent subgraphs $D'_2 = \{F_1, ...F_m\}$.

We describe these algorithms here briefly. The *gSpan* algorithm uses a pattern growth approach to discover frequent subgraphs from large graphs, as depicted in Figure 4 and 5. The gSpan method builds a new lexicographic order among graphs, and maps each graph to a unique minimum depth first search (DFS) code as its canonical label. Based on this lexicographic order, gSpan adopts the DFS strategy to mine frequent connected subgraphs efficiently. This algorithm uses the DFS lexicographic order and rely on the minimum DFS concept, which forms a novel canonical labeling system to support the DFS search [32].

Data: Graph set $\mathcal{GS}$
Result: Set of frequent subgraphs $\mathcal{S}$
sort labels in $\mathcal{GS}$ by their frequency;
remove infrequent nodes and edges and relabel remaining nodes and edges;
$S' \leftarrow$ all frequent 1-edge graphs in $\mathcal{GS}$;
sort S' in DFS lexicographic order;
$S \leftarrow S'$;
for *each edge* $e \in S'$ **do**
  initialize s with e, set $s.\mathcal{GS}$ by graphs which contains e;
  SubgraphMining($\mathcal{GS}, \mathcal{S}$,s);
  $\mathcal{GS} \leftarrow \mathcal{GS} - e$;
  if $|\mathcal{GS}| < minSupp$ **then**
    break;
  end
end

Figure 4. GraphSet_Projection Algorithm

On the other hand, *GERM* mines patterns from a single large graph. The GERM algorithm is adapted from gSpan where the support calculation is replaced by the minimum image based support (see Definition 8). GERM has made another modification in gSpan's use of minimum DFS code by modifying the canonical form used in DFS code. This is done so that the first edge in the canonical form is always the one with the lowest time-stamp, as compared to gSpan where the highest label is used as a starting node [22].

Data: Graph set $\mathcal{GS}$, DFS code s
Result: Set of frequent subgraphs $\mathcal{S}$
if $s \neq min(s)$ **then**
  return;
end
$S \leftarrow S \cup s$;
enumerate s in each graph in D and count its children;
for *all* c, c *is* s' *child* **do**
  if $support(c) \geq minSupp$ **then**
    $s \leftarrow c$;
    $SubgraphMining(\mathcal{D}, \mathcal{S}, s)$;
  end
end

Figure 5. SubgraphMining Algorithm

Step 2. Apply LabelMDN algorithm: The algorithm works as follows (see Figure 7).

For each frequent pattern F_i of every datasets D'_1 and D'_2, it identifies the set of articulation points A. If $|A| = p > 1$, we identify the total number of nodes $V(F_i)$ and edges $E(F_i)$, and number of connected components $BC(F_i)$. We also calculate the degree $deg(a_j)$ and associated time stamps $ts(a_j)$ of each articulation point $a_j \in A$, where $1 \leq j \leq p$. An articulation point can be associated with multiple time stamps as it evolves with time.

To compute the articulation points, we implement the standard linear time DFS approach proposed by Hopcroft and Tarjan [18]. All articulation points satisfy the following conditions: Any node x is an articulation point if and only if either (a) x is the root of the DFS tree and x has more than one child, or (b) x is not the root and for some child w of x there is no back-edge between any descendent of w (including w) and a proper ancestor of x. (For further reading, we refer the interested reader to [4].)

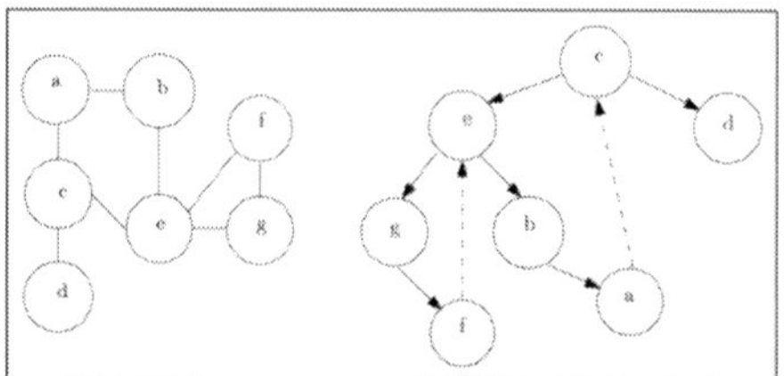

Figure 6. Labelling articulation points using DFS tree.

Figure 6 gives an example of a given subgraph F in (a) and its DFS tree starting at c in (b). Backedges are shown with dotted lines. It is clear that F has two articulation points c and e, but only e will be labeled as MDN since it has the maximum degree in F.

The next step is to correctly label each a_j whenever it is a MDN in F_i. This is done by verifying whether $deg(a_j)$ of each articulation point a_j is maximum within it's corresponding F_i.

Thus, each a_i is labeled with a class label C_1 if it is a MDN, with C_0 otherwise. Now, we have a training dataset T having records for each a_j with the expectation to train a classifier for correctly predicting the labels of unclassified test datasets. *Step 3. Classify MDNs:* A number of classification algorithms

Data: Set of frequent subgraphs D'_1, D'_2
Result: Training dataset T
for *all frequent subgraphs* $F_i \in D'_1$ *(or* D'_2*)* **do**
    find set of articulation points $A \in F_i$. [use the standard DFS based algorithm];
    if $|A| \geq 1$ **then**
        find $V(F_i)$, $E(F_i)$, and $BC(F_i)$;
        for *each* $a_j \in A$ *from* $j = 1$ *to* p **do**
            find $deg(a_j)$ and $ts(a_j)$;
            if $deg(a_j) = \max\{deg(u) : u \in V(F_i)\}$ **then**
                label a_j with class C_1. [a_j is a MDN];
            else
                label a_j with class C_0. [a_j is not a MDN];
            end
            store information of each a_j as a record in T;
        end
    end
end

Figure 7. LabelMDN Algorithm

was used from the WEKA environment [31]. The baseline model is constructed using ZeroR, where the classifier assigns all items to the largest class. We also utilized a number of other classifiers, including the Naive Bayes probabilistic approach, Support Vector Machines (SMO), a rule based method (JRip) and a decision tree based classifier (J48). We also built models using the Boosting and Bagging meta-learning techniques, both using J48 decision trees as base learner.

IV. Experimental Setup and Evaluation

This section describes our experimental setup and evaluation. We have used the implementations of gSpan and GERM that are available in [13] and [24] respectively. We made use of the previously mentioned WEKA classifiers, as noted earlier. All other algorithms have been implemented in Java programming language.

A. Datasets

Five datasets have been used for evaluating *DetectMDN* algorithm. Brief descriptions of these datasets are given below, and their summary information is shown in Table I.

(a) Co-authorship network data, DBLP [11]: Three sample datasets from the same DBLP network span over three periods, namely 1992-2002, 2003-2005 and 2005-2007. In this dataset, authors are represented by nodes with a connecting edge if they are co-authors. The assigned time-stamp on an edge represents the year of the first co-authorship. The three different samples each contains the edges created in the corresponding years. We also aggregate all datasets into one large DBLP dataset with information from the year 1992 to 2007. This is done for analyzing both long and short term trends.

(b) Social network dataset, Facebook [12]: This network describes friendship relations between users of Facebook. It was collected in April of 2009 through data scraping from Facebook. Each node represents a user and an edge represents friendship between two users. The graph is undirected and unweighted thus all nodes are labeled with the same default value.

(c) Citation network [10]: The format for the Citation dataset is similar to the Facebook dataset. It contains a sorted 2 column vector where the left column is the *arxiv id* of the paper cited from and the right column is the *arxiv id* of the paper being cited.

TABLE I. Dataset Properties.

Dataset	*Date*	*Node*	*Edge*	*Avg Degree*	*Time Stamp*
dblp92-02	92-02	129073	277081	2.15	0-10
dblp02-05	02-05	109044	233961	2.15	0-3
dblp05-07	05-07	135116	290363	2.15	0-2
facebook	2009	4039	88234	21.85	NA
citation	92-03	27718	352806	12.73	NA

B. Experimental Results

This section generalizes the results we obtained against the above-mentioned datasets. Firstly, the GERM algorithm has been applied to all the DBLP datasets to extract frequent subgraphs. These files are compatible with GERM and need no further modification. In the DBLP datasets the timestamps vary from 0 to 10. To normalize this range, each timestamp has been categorized as *initial, middle* and *final* and a three-digit bit string is generated which later is converted into a numeric value. Note that, since the Facebook and Citation datasets do not have timestamps, the ts attribute in Algorithm 7 is not relevant for these datasets. Subsequently, the original gSpan algorithm has been used for these two datasets. Table II gives brief explanations of the set of attributes generated by LabelMDN from all frequent patterns. Table III gives a summary of the results found in this level. The numbers under *Nodes, Edges, Degrees* and *BC* columns come with the format min-max-average. The *ts* column shows only min-max numbers. Although there is no significant differences in the average numbers of nodes and edges in frequent subgraphs of all five datasets, articulation points in Facebook and Citation datasets have higher degrees than that in the DBLP datasets.

TABLE II. Attributes extracted from given datasets.

Attributes	*Description*	*Type*
$V(F_i)$	Total number of nodes in frequent subgraph F_i	Numeric
$E(F_i)$	Total number of edges in frequent subgraph F_i	Numeric
$BC(F_i)$	Total number of biconnected components in F_i	Numeric
$deg(a_j)$	Total degrees of articulation point a_j	Numeric
$ts(a_j)$	Time stamps associated with a_j	Numeric
C_k	Class of a_j, where $k \in \{0, 1\}$	Binary

TABLE III. Summary of extracted attributes.

Datasets	*Inst*	*Nodes*	*Edges*	*Degrees*	*BC*	*ts*
dblp92-02	2471	3-10-5.8	2-9-4.9	2-5-2.4	2-9-4.7	1-5
dblp03-05	1971	3-11-5.7	2-10-4.9	2-6-2.5	2-10 4.6	1-7
dblp05-07	2923	3-12-5.7	2-11-4.9	2-7-2.5	2-11-4.6	1-7
Facebook	65	3-14-6.3	2-13-5.5	2-13-4.2	2-13-5.2	—
Citation	80	3-13-6.0	2-12-5.1	2-12-3.8	2-12-4.9	—

C. Research Questions

In this study, experiments are conducted to answer the following research questions:

Q1. Do our *DetectMDN* algorithm result in accurate models of the studied networks? (See Section C.1)

Q2. Do different types of networks (co-authorship and social) influence the prediction results? (See Section C.2)

Q3. What type of frequent pattern attributes are more effective than others? (See Section C.3)

C1. Performance of DetectMDN Algorithm

Table IV shows the accuracies achieved by each of the classifiers against all the datasets. In this table the names *DBLP1, DBLP2, DBLP3, FB* and *Cita* are used to represent *dblp92-02, dblp03-05, dblp05-07, Facebook* and *Citation* datasets respectively. All WEKA classification algorithms are used with 10-fold cross validation for each of the datasets. Compared with the baseline all other classifiers performed significantly better, and for all datasets, the best performances are shown by JRip and AdaBoost (with J48) both are ranked as 1. It should be noted that the differences among these top ranked classifiers' performances are not significant. Our algorithm successfully classifies MDNs in both full-term and short-term time-evolving DBLP datasets, while the classifier performs equally well for the static graph datasets, namely Facebook and Citation. These results show that our classifiers are able to encompass both the duration and the variation of the relationship patterns among all MDNs.

TABLE IV. ACCURACY OF CLASSIFICATION MODELS (%).

Classifiers	*DBLP1*	*DBLP2*	*DBLP3*	*DBLP*	*FB*	*Cita*	*Rank*
Base	67.5	65.7	66.8	66.7	81.8	82.5	4
JRip	74.3	74.4	74.2	73.8	90.8	85.0	1
NaiveBayes	71.6	72.0	71.8	72.0	80.0	78.8	4
J48	74.1	74.4	74.2	73.6	88.0	86.3	2
SMO	73.3	74.0	74.3	74.0	81.5	82.5	3
Boosting	73.5	74.5	74.3	73.6	90.8	85.0	1
Bagging	73.7	74.4	74.2	73.8	87.7	81.3	2

C2. Influence of Network Types on Prediction Results

Since a classifier's performance does not only depend on the percentage of accuracy value, we present another set of analysis in Table V. We consider two classifiers, namely Boosting (AdaBoostM1) with a J48 base learner, as well as J48 on its own, for this analysis. These two classifiers were chosen based on their high rankings during our earlier experiments.

ROC analysis and AUC: For all datasets, the high percentage of Area Under Curve (AUC) value demonstrates the efficiency of our model since it depicts the relative trade-offs between true positives and false positives across a range of thresholds of a classification model. Figure 8 shows the comparison between the ROC graphs of the AdaBoostM1 (J48) and J48 algorithms for the Citation, Facebook and DBLP datasets.

F-measure represents a harmonic mean between recall and precision.

$$F-measure = \frac{2 \times Recall \times Precision}{Recall + Precision}$$

A lower recall value (69%) for DBLP results a comparatively lower F-measure (75%). For the static datasets, the accuracy rates are more than 90% for Facebook dataset and 85% for Citation dataset. Figure 9 plots the Precision-Recall (PR) graph demonstrating performance of the classifier for all datasets. From these results it can be said that static networks are more predictable than time evolving graphs.

TABLE V. AUC AND F-MEASURE VALUES USING ADABOOST WITH J48.

Dataset	*AUC*	*Precision*	*Recall*	*F-measure*
DBLP	0.82	0.78	0.69	0.75
Facebook	0.96	0.90	0.91	0.91
Citation	0.93	0.85	0.85	0.85

Figure 8. Comparisons between ROC Graphs of AdaBoostM1 and J48 for (a) Citation, (b) Facebook and (c) DBLP. The x-axis represents the false positive (FP) rates and y-axis represents the true posotive (TP) rates.

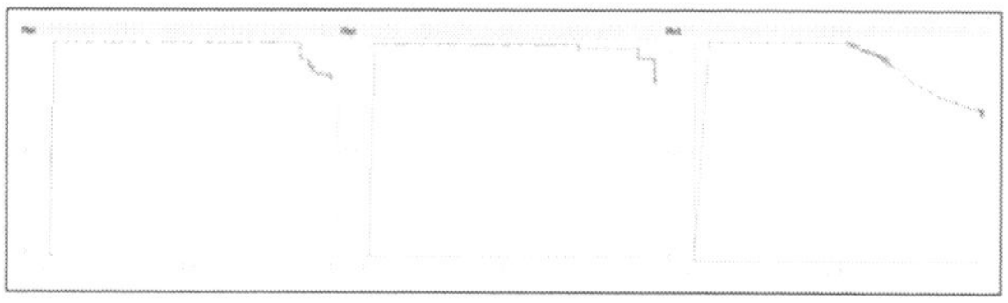

Figure 9. Precision and Recall graph for (a) Citation, (b) Facebook and (c) DBLP. Here, x-axis represents Recall and y-axis represents Precision.

C3. Effective Attributes for Classification

The aim of this section is to evaluate the contribution of a subset of attributes by considering the individual predictive ability of each feature along with the degree of redundancy between them. We employed the *CfsSubsetEval* function for this task, which has been successfully applied previously in many studies including [9] [17] [26] to improve the accuracy. For all datasets, the *degrees* attribute has been identified as the most important attribute to aid the classifier, while DBLP dataset utilizes a second attribute, namely *nodes*. Both the Facebook and Citation datasets have comparatively higher average degrees than the DBLP dataset (see Table I). Recall that the first two datasets represent a static view of the network where the communication with peer nodes are not labeled with time. Therefore, the total number of peer nodes (i.e., degrees) associated with each articulation point mostly governs the classification rules. In the case of the DBLP datasets, our classifier performs the labeling task based on the total number of authors (*nodes*) and consider when they are connected with peer nodes (*degrees*). It should be noted that dependency on different attribute sets do not degrade the overall performance of our classifier.

D. Discussions

In this study, we are interested to correctly classify all most dominant nodes in frequent subgraphs of large networks. Based on the results reported above it can be concluded that our model can successfully classify both static and time-evolving graphs with reasonable accuracy. However, the large number of frequent subgraphs that are often present in network settings constitutes some challenges [28]. The first one is *redundancy*, in that most frequent subgraphs only differ slightly in structure and repeat in many subgraphs. The second is the *statistical significance* of subgraphs. Since both frequent and infrequent subgraphs may be uniformly distributed over all classes, only frequent subgraphs whose presence is statistically significantly correlated with class membership are promising contributors for classification.

In our research, MDNs are defined irrespective of their direction of communications with peer nodes. Although it has little impact in co-authorship networks, we may expect a conceptual change in social and communication networks where a MDN either communicates with (both-way) or only broadcasts to (one-way) their peer nodes in a frequent subgraph. For example, a fan page of Facebook may have many responses from a group of members for each post. On the other hand, an online marketing page may post news to many of its clients, but typically does not receive responses equally.

V. Conclusion and Future Work

We presented an algorithm to classify the most dominant nodes in frequent subgraphs of large networks. We considered both static and time-evolving graphs. We evaluated the performance of our algorithm with percentage of accuracy, precision and recall. We also identified the attributes (i.e., *degrees* in general, and a second attribute *nodes* in DBLP dataset) that are the most effective for successful classification. Our experimental results showed that our method achieved good performance in terms of accuracy and other statistical measurements. Our future work will center on finding scalable solutions to effectively deal with numerous frequent subgraphs that are similar in structure and scope. We are also interested in studying the effects of changes in properties, in order to extend our work to deal with concept drift in a graph setting.

References

[1] R. Agrawal and R. Srikant, "Fast Algorithms for Mining Association Rules in Large Databases," *In Proc. of ACM SIGKDD Conference on KDDM*, pp. 12-19, 1994.

[2] A. L. Barabasi and R. Albert, "Emergence of scaling in random networks," *Science* 286, no. 5439, pp. 509-512, 1999.

[3] R. Albert, H. Jeong, and A. L. Barabasi, "Error and attack tolerance of complex networks," *Nature*, 406(6794), pp. 509-512, 2000.

[4] Biconnected Component, (2016, Mar.) [Online]. Available: https://en.wikipedia.org/wiki/Biconnected_component

[5] D. Chen, L. Lu, M. S. Shang, Y. C. Zhang, and T. Zhou, "Identifying influential nodes in complex networks," *Physica a: Statistical mechanics and its applications*, 391(4), 2012.

[6] C. Gao, X. Lan, X. Zhang, and Y. Deng, "A bio-inspired methodology of identifying influential nodes in complex networks," *PloS one*, 8(6), 2013.

[7] B. Bringmann and S. Nijssen, "What is frequent in a single graph?," *In Advances in Knowledge Discovery and Data Mining*, Springer Berlin Heidelberg, pp. 858-863, 2008.

[8] J. Bonneau, J. Anderson, R. Anderson, and F. Stajano, "Eight friends are enough: social graph approximation via public listings," *In Proc. of the 2nd ACM EuroSys Workshop on Social Network Systems*, ACM, pp. 13-18, 2009.

[9] P. Chanda, Y. R. Cho, A. Zhang, and M. Ramanathan, "Mining of attribute interactions using information theoretic metrics," *IEEE International Conference on Data Mining Workshops*, 2009.

[10] Citation network, (2016, Jan.) [Online]. Available: http://www.cs.cornell.edu/projects/kddcup/datasets.html

[11] Co-authorship Network, (2016, Mar.) [Online]. Available: http://www-kdd.isti.cnr.it/GERM/

[12] Facebook Dataset, (2016, Mar.) [Online]. Available: http://snap.stanford.edu/data/egonets-Facebook.html

[13] gSpan: Frequent Graph Mining Package, (2016, Mar.) [Online]. Available: http://www.cs.ucsb.edu/~xyan/software/gSpan.htm

[14] M. A. Hasan, "Mining Interesting Subgraphs by Output Space Sampling," PhD Thesis, Rensselaer Polytechnic Institute, New York, 2009.

[15] M. U. Ilyas and H. Radha, "Identifying influential nodes in online social networks using principal component centrality," *IEEE International Conference on ICC*, IEEE, pp. 1-5, 2011.

[16] J. Pei, J. Han, B. Mortazavi-Asl, H. Pinto, Q. Chen, U. Dayal, and M. C. Hsu, "Prefixspan: Mining sequential patterns efficiently by prefix-projected pattern growth," *In Proc. on ICCCN*, IEEE, pp. 2-15, 2001.

[17] J. Hancke and D. Meurers, "Exploring CEFR classification for German based on rich linguistic modeling," *In Learner Corpus Research Conference*, 2013.

[18] J. Hopcroft and R. Tarjan, "Algorithm 447: efficient algorithms for graph manipulation," *Communications of the ACM* 16 (6), pp. 372-378, 1973.

[19] A. M. Kibriya and J. Ramon, "Nearly exact mining of frequent trees in large networks," *Machine Learning and Knowledge Discovery in Databases*, Springer Berlin Heidelberg, pp. 426-441, 2012.

[20] M. Kimura, S. Kazumi, N. Ryohei, and H. Motoda, "Extracting influential nodes on a social network for information diffusion," *Data Mining and Knowledge Discovery* 20, no. 1, pp. 70-97, 2010.

[21] M. Kuramochi and G. Karypis, "Frequent Subgraph Discovery," *In Proc. IEEE International Conference on Data Mining, ICDM*, pp. 313-320, 2001.

[22] M. Kuramochi and G. Karypis, "An efficient algorithm for discovering frequent subgraphs," *IEEE Transactions on Knowledge and Data Engineering*, 16.9, pp. 1038-1051, 2004.

[23] KDD cup 2003 Datasets, (2016, Mar.) [Online]. Available: http://www.cs.cornell.edu/projects/kddcup/datasets.html

[24] B. Michele, F. Bonchi, B. Bringmann, and A. Gionis, "Mining graph evolution rules," *In Machine learning and knowledge discovery in databases*, Springer Berlin Heidelberg, pp. 115-130, 2009.

[25] M. E. J. Newman, "The structure and function of complex networks," *SIAM Review* 45, no. 2, pp. 167-256, 2003.

[26] K. Selvakuberan, M. Indradevi, and R. Rajaram, "Combined feature selection and classification - A novel approach for categorization of web pages," *Journal of Information and Computing Science*, 3 (2), 2008.

[27] J. Shetty and J. Adibi, "Discovering important nodes through graph entropy the case of enron email database," *In Proc. of the 3rd international workshop on Link discovery*, ACM, pp. 74-81, 2005.

[28] M. Thoma, H. Cheng, A. Gretton, J. Han, H. Kriegel, A. Smola, L. Song, P. S. Yu, X. Yan, and K. M. Borgwardt, "Discriminative frequent subgraph mining with optimality guarantees," *Statistical Analysis and Data Mining* 3, no. 5, pp. 302-318, 2010.

[29] The Graph Evolution Rule Miner, (2016, Mar.) [Online]. Available: http://www-kdd.isti.cnr.it/GERM/

[30] S. Wasserman and K. Faust, *Social Network Analysis: Methods and Applications*, Cambridge, ENG and New York: Cambridge University Press, Vol.8, 1994.

[31] Weka 3: Data Mining Software in Java, Machine Learning Group at the University of Waikato, (2016, Mar.) [Online]. Available: http://www.cs.waikato.ac.nz/~ml/weka/

[32] X. Yan and J. Han, "gspan: Graph-based substructure pattern mining," *IEEE International Conference on Data Mining*, pp. 721-724, 2003.

[33] X. Zhang, J. Zhu, Q. Wang, and H. Zhao, "Identifying influential nodes in complex networks with community structure," *Knowledge-Based Systems*, 42, 2013.

[34] Z. Zhao, X. Wang, W. Zhang, and Z. Zhu, "A Community-Based Approach to Identifying Influential Spreaders," *Entropy*, 17(4), 2015.

Managing 3D Simulation Models with the Graph Database Neo4j

Martin Hoppen, Juergen Rossmann, Sebastian Hiester

Institute for Man-Machine Interaction
RWTH Aachen University
Aachen, Germany
Email: {hoppen,rossmann}@mmi.rwth-aachen.de, sebastian.hiester@rwth-aachen.de

***Abstract*—Every simulation is based on an appropriate model. Particularly in 3D simulation, models are often large and complex recommending the usage of database technology for an efficient data management. However, the predominant and well-known relational databases are less suitable for the hierarchical structure of 3D models. In contrast, graph databases from the NoSQL field store their contents in the nodes and edges of a mathematical graph. The open source Neo4j is such a graph database. In this paper, we introduce an approach to use Neo4j as persistent storage for 3D simulation models. For that purpose, a runtime in-memory simulation database is synchronized with the graph database back end.**

Keywords–3D Simulation; 3D Models; Simulation Database; Graph Database; Database Synchronization

I. Introduction

Before a technical system can get into mass production and is ready for execution it has to pass certain stages of development. Besides the new component's design, an intense test phase is compulsory in order to confirm its operability, increase its prospects and if necessary to initiate some steps of optimization. For such tests, engineers utilize simulation tools like block-oriented simulation or 3D simulation to analyze their target system in a virtual environment. In particular, 3D simulation systems allow to analyze the spatial properties and behavior of the intended system and its interaction with its surroundings in an expressive visual way.

Every simulation is based on an appropriate model describing properties and behavior of the system under development. This model data needs to be managed conveniently. The usage of database technology has established for such requirements. In contrast to flat files, they offer high performance data evaluation and simplify data management with regard to security, reliability, recovery, replication and concurrency control. Currently, relational databases are dominating the market. Due to different problems with scalability and effective processing of big data with relational databases the field of NoSQL ("Not only SQL") databases has emerged [1]. In this context, the approach of graph databases (GDBs) has become popular. GDBs save their data in the nodes and edges of a mathematical graph, in particular, to manage highly linked information. As such, they are ideally suited for 3D simulation models. Like in Computer-aided Design (CAD), such 3D data usually comprises a huge number of parts of many different types (mostly, each with only few instances), structured hierarchically with interdependencies. This recommends a graph-like data structure. For the same reason, the scene graph is a common approach to manage 3D data at runtime.

In this paper, we present a concept for a synchronization interface between a GDB and a 3D simulation database, i.e., the runtime database of a 3D simulation system. The applied data mapping strategy is bidirectional and in part incremental. The approach was developed in the context of a student project and is based on our previous work [2]. Its feasibility is shown with a prototypical implementation using the GDB Neo4j and the 3D simulation system VEROSIM and its Versatile Simulation Database (VSD) (Figure 1).

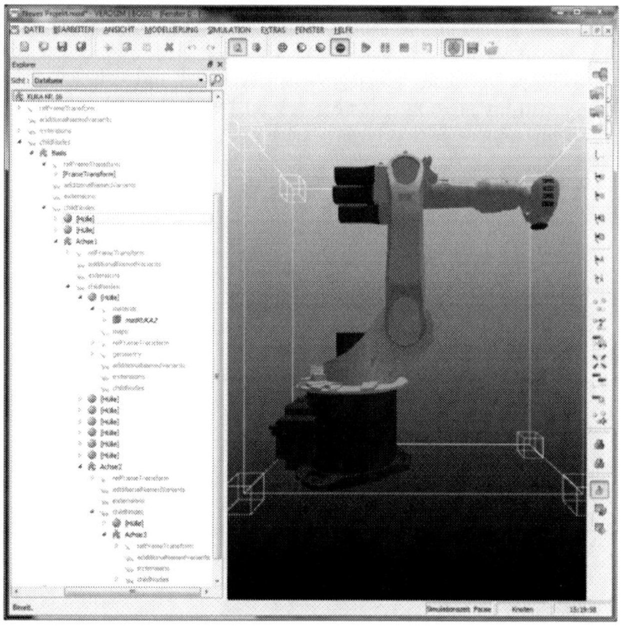

Figure 1. Robot model (from Figure 9) loaded from Neo4j into the in-memory simulation database VSD.

In Section II, we start with the basics of GDBs and a short introduction to Neo4j and VEROSIM including VSD. Section III gives an overview of different GDBs and motivates the decision for Neo4j. In Section IV, the prototype's general requirements are itemized and Section V describes the specific implementation of the interface with Neo4j and the VSD. Subsequently, Section VI presents an evaluation of the interface and Section VII recaps our work with a concluding statement.

II. State of the Art

In this section, the necessary basics for our work are presented.

A. Graph Databases

The idea of a GDB relies on the mathematical graph theory. Information is saved in the nodes (or vertices) and edges (or relationships) of a graph as shown in Figure 9. A graph is a tuple $G = (V, E)$, where V describes the set of nodes and E the set of edges, i.e., $v_i \in V$ and $e_{i,j} = (v_i, v_j) \in E$ [3]. To specify records, properties of nodes and (depending on the GDB) even relationships can be described by key-value pairs [4]. An important aspect of GDBs is the fact that all relationships are directly stored with the nodes so that there is no need to infer them as in relational databases using foreign keys and joins. Hence, read operations on highly connected data can be performed very fast. During a read access, the graph is traversed along paths so that the individual data records (nodes and edges) can be read in situ and do not have to be searched globally. Therefore, the execution time depends only on the traversal's depth [1].

GDBs also provide standard database features like security, recovery from hard- or software failures, concurrency control for parallel access, or methods for data integrity and reliability.

In contrast to flat files, using a (graph) database, data can be modified with a query language. Such languages are a powerful tool to manipulate the database content so that the data is not only stored persistently and securely but can also be handled simply.

B. Neo4j

Neo4j is a GDB implemented in Java. It can be run in server or embedded mode. Figure 2 shows its data model. Central elements are nodes and relationships containing the stored records. These records are described by an arbitrary number of properties (key-value pairs). Neo4j offers the concept of *labels* and *types* to divide the graph in logical substructures. A node is extendible with several labels characterizing the node's classification. Similarly, a relationship is identified by a type (exactly one). Besides the classification of the data, this also improves reading performance as just a part of the graph must be traversed to find the desired record [4][5]. Apart from that, Neo4j is schemaless, i.e., it does not require any metadata definition before inserting actual user data.

All Neo4j accesses are processed in ACID (Atomicity, Consistency, Isolation, Durability) compliant transactions guaranteeing the reliability, consistency and durability of the database content [1]. Accesses are either performed with Neo4j's own query language called Cypher or using its Java API.

C. VEROSIM and VSD

VEROSIM is a 3D simulation system rooted in the field of robotics [6]. In recent years, it evolved to a versatile framework for simulation in various fields of application (in particular: environment, space, industry). During runtime, simulation models are managed by its VSD. This in-memory database not only stores the passive structure and properties of a 3D simulation model but also its active behavior, i.e., the simulation algorithms themselves. VSD is an object-orientated GDB.

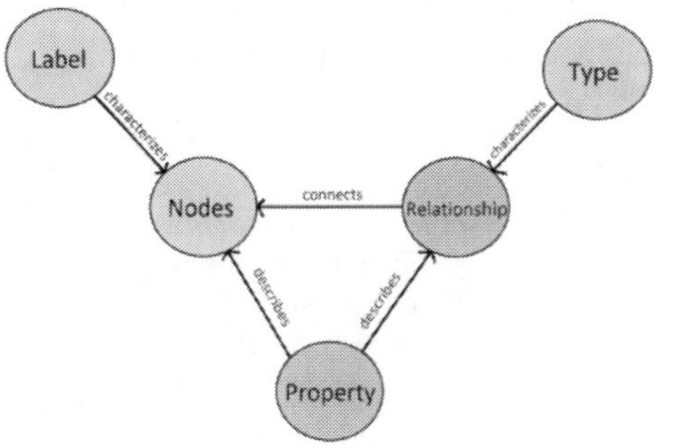

Figure 2. Neo4j data model.

Objects are called instances and are characterized by properties. Such properties can either be value properties (Val-Properties) with basic or complex data types or reference properties. The latter model $1:1$ (Ref-Properties) or $1:n$ (RefList-Properties) directed relationships between instances. Furthermore, these relationships can be marked to *contain* target instances using an *autodelete* flag allowing to model UML composite aggregations.

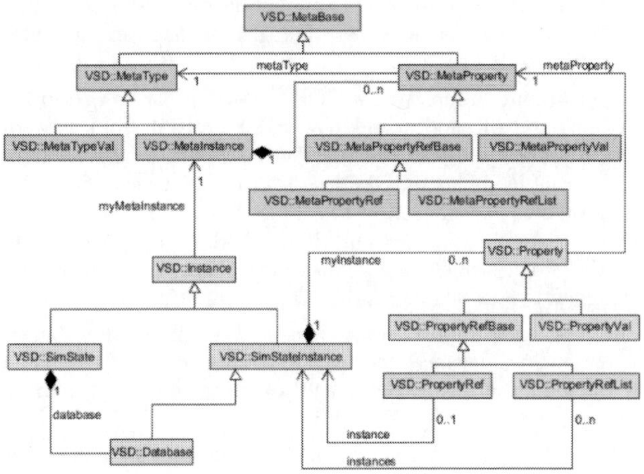

Figure 3. VSD data model (top: metadata, bottom: instance data).

VSD comprises a meta information system providing access to its schema and also to specify its schema. So-called meta instances describe an instance's class (name, inheritance, etc.) and so-called meta properties its properties (name, type, etc.). Figure 3 shows VSD's data model.

III. Related Work

Besides Neo4j, there are many other GDBs in the market. They differ in their conceptual structure and application area.

DEX is a GDB based on the labeled and directed attributed multigraph model. All nodes and edges are classified (labeled), edges are directed, nodes can be extended with properties (attributes), and edges can be connected with more than two nodes (multigraph) [7]. The graph is represented by bitmaps and other secondary structures. DEX has been designed for high performance and scalable graph scenarios. The good performance is achieved by the bitmap-based structure and the indexing of all attributes, which are efficiently processed by the C++ kernel [8].

Trinity [9][10] is a memory-based graph store with many database features like concurrency or ACID-conform transactions. The graph storage is distributed among multiple well connected machines in a globally addressable memory address space yielding big data support. A unified declarative language provides data manipulation and message passing between the different machines. The great advantage of Trinity is the fast access to large data records. It is based on a multigraph model, which can exceed one billion nodes. Since there is no strict database schema, Trinity can flexibly be adapted to many data sets.

HypergraphDB stores its data in a directed multigraph, whose implementation is based on BerkeleyDB. All graph elements are called atoms. Every atom is characterized by its atom arity indicating the number of linked atoms. The arity determines an atom's type: An arity larger than zero yields an edge atom, or else, a node atom. Each atom has a typed value containing the user data [11].

InfoGrid is a framework specialized in the development of REpresentational State Transfer (REST)-full web applications. One part of this framework is a proprietary GDB used for data management. The graph's nodes are called MeshObjects, which are classified by one or more so-called EntityTypes, properties, and their linked relationships. MeshObjects not only contain the user data but also manage events relevant to the node [12].

Infinite Graph is a GDB based on an object-oriented concept. All nodes and edges are derived from two basic Java classes. Thus, the database schema is represented by user-defined classes. Besides data management, Infinite Graph provides a visualization tool [13]. Since the database can be distributed on multiple machines working in parallel, Infinite Graph can achieve a high data throughput. To manage concurrency, a lock server handles the different lock requests [8].

AllegroGraph [14] provides a REST protocol architecture. With this interface, the user has full control of the database including indexing, query and session management. All transactions satisfy ACID conditions.

Despite this wide range of GDBs, for the following reasons, we decide to use Neo4j in our approach:

- In many tests it proves to process data fast and efficiently,
- it can handle more than one billion nodes – even enough for extremely large 3D simulation models – which could be useful in coming stages of extension,
- Neo4j is a full native GDB so that traversal and other graph operations can be performed efficiently,
- Neo4j provides a comprehensive and powerful query language (e.g., for efficient partial loading strategies in future versions of the presented prototype),
- directed edges allow to model object interdependencies more accurately, however, without disadvantages in traversal performance,
- properties on relationships allow for a more flexible modeling (e.g., to distinguish between shared and composite aggregation relationships),
- finally, Neo4j is currently the most prevalent GDB in the market indicating it to be especially well explored and developed. Hence, it provides the best prospects of success.

Note that while we choose Neo4j for the reasons given above, the presented concepts are mostly independent of the choice of the particular GDB.

IV. Concept

In this section, we describe the fundamental concept and the required features of our synchronization component's prototype. Its implementation using Neo4j and VSD is described in Section V.

A. *Structure Mapping*

An essential question when synchronizing two databases is: How do we map the different data structures? Depending on the database paradigm, entities with attributes and relationships (connecting two or more entities) are represented differently. For example, a relational database uses relations, attributes and foreign keys while a GDB uses nodes, relationships and properties.

1) **Schema Mapping:** Before synchronizing user data, a generic schema mapping is performed mapping the metadata of one database to the other as described in [15]. This is performed once on system startup. For example, when performed between a relational and an object-oriented database, each table of the former might be mapped to a corresponding class of the latter (columns and class attributes accordingly).
2) **Schemaless Approach:** When a schemaless database is involved, a different approach has to be applied. Here, metadata from a non-schemaless database must be mapped onto the user data of the schemaless one. For example, class names from an object-oriented database are mapped onto node labels of a schemaless GDB.

For the schemaless Neo4j, in our prototype, we chose the second approach.

B. *Object Mapper*

Another key aspect of the concept is the object mapper. It maps objects from one database to an equivalent counterpart in the other database. For example, an object from an object-oriented database is mapped to a corresponding node in the GDB. The mapping is based on the counterparts' identities and includes a transfer of all property (or attribute) values in between. Based on these mappings, individual object or property changes can be tracked and resynchronized. Summarized the mapping is bidirectional and in part incremental.

C. *Transactions*

Any changes (insert, update, delete) to the data are tracked and stored in transactions, which can be processed independently. By executing these transactions, data is (re)synchronized on object level. During the accumulation (and before the execution) of such transactions, the operations stored within can be filtered for redundancies. For example, a transaction for creating a new object followed by a transaction for deleting the very same object can both be discarded.

V. Prototype

This section gives an insight into the prototypical implementation of the interface between VSD and Neo4j. The prototype should have the ability to save simulation data from VSD in Neo4j and to load it back into VSD. Initially, when storing a simulation model in Neo4j, VSD's contents are archived once. Subsequently, changes in VSD are tracked and updated to Neo4j individually. That is, when a VSD instance has been changed just the changes are transferred as mentioned above. In the current version of the interface, only changes within VSD are tracked for resynchronization. Thus, Neo4j serves as database back end, which can store simulation models persistently.

The prototype is realized in a C++ based VEROSIM plugin, which uses Neo4j's Java API in embedded mode in order to communicate with Neo4j.

A. Data Mapping

In the context of this work, synchronization represents data transfer from one database to another. However, the structure of one database's data elements often differs from the other's. Thus, it becomes necessary to map these different structures on each other. Figure 4 shows our intuitive approach.

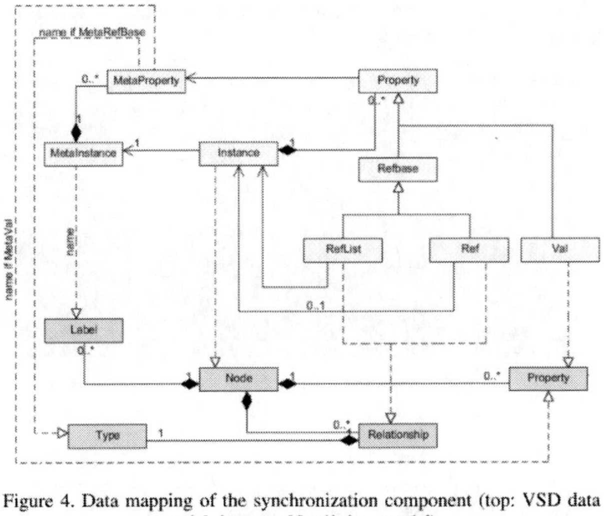

Figure 4. Data mapping of the synchronization component (top: VSD data model, bottom: Neo4j data model).

Single VSD instances are mapped to single Neo4j nodes and references (Ref/List-Properties) from one instance to another are represented by relationships between the corresponding nodes. The relationship is orientated to the referenced node's direction. Furthermore, we transfer the Val-Properties of a VSD instance to Neo4j node properties.

As mentioned above, a basic difference between VSD and Neo4j is that the former comprises metadata describing (and prescribing) a schema while the latter is schemaless. VSD metadata contains important information for the simulation and is indispensable for a correct data mapping. Thus, it is essential to transfer this informations as well. We store VSD metadata on Neo4j's object level:

1) A VSD instance's class name is mapped to it's Neo4j node's label,
2) a VSD Ref/List-Property's name is mapped to it's Neo4j relationship's type, and
3) a VSD Val-Property's name is mapped to it's Neo4j property's key.

Val-Property values are handled depending on their data type. If the type corresponds to one of Neo4j's supported basic types (e.g., integer, float, string, boolean, etc.) the value will be transfered directly. More complex data structures (e.g., mathematical vectors, etc.) are serialized to a binary representation and transfered as such.

To store additional meta information about VSD Ref/List-Properties, we take advantage of Neo4j's feature to add properties to relationships. Currently, every relationship gets a boolean property with the key *autodelete* as introduced above. Additionally, a RefList-Property entry's order is stored as an index in a relationship property.

B. Synchronization Component

Figure 5 depicts the structure of the synchronization component (based on [2]). Its core is the (object) mapper managing mappings between pairs of VSD instances and Neo4j nodes. Each mapping is stored in form of a so-called ObjectState (OS) holding all relevant information. The OS contains both objects' ids, all collected (but not executed) transactions and the state of the relation between the two. This state indicates whether the pair is synchronous, i.e., equal, or whether one of them has been changed and differs from its counterpart. An exemplary list of object states of the mapper is given in Figure 6.

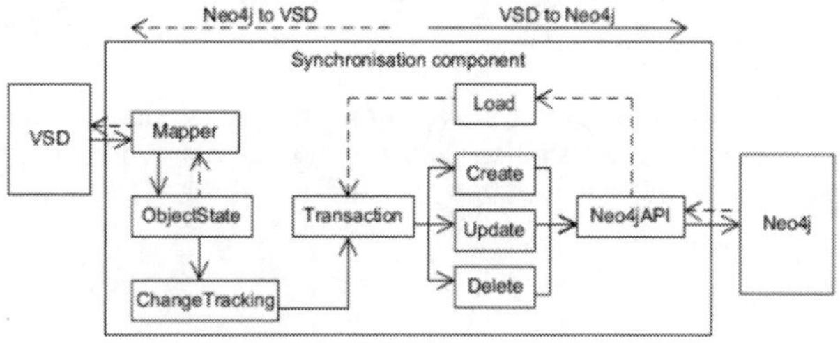

Figure 5. Synchronization component.

VSD-Id	Neo4j-Id	State	Pending-Transactions
...			
6049	0	SYNCED	-
6050	1	PENDING_UPDATE	Update-Transaction1, Update-Transaction2
6051	2	PENDING_DELETE	Delete-Transaction
...			

Figure 6. Exemplary list of object states of the mapper.

Each change to a VSD instance is encapsulated in a transaction stored in the appropriate OS. Subsequently, they can be executed. Depending on the change's type, a create, update, or delete transaction is generated. Furthermore, a separate load transaction is used to load Neo4j contents into VSD. Each transaction comprises all type specific information necessary for its execution. For example, a create transaction contains the names and values of all Val-Properties, the class name, and information on Ref/List-Properties like target ids, reference names and *autodelete* values.

The last part of the synchronization component is the Neo4jAPI, which interacts with Neo4j's Java API.

1) VSD to Neo4j: VSD is an active database. One aspect of this activity is that changes to its instances are notified to registered components like the synchronization component presented in this work. Notifications include all relevant information about the modification like the instance's id or the changed property. The synchronization component encapsulates this information in an appropriate transaction. Using the instance id, the mapper is able to identify the corresponding OS and retrieve the mapping's state. A change tracking mechanism is used to filter redundant transactions as mentioned above (more details are given in Section V-C).

When the user or some automatic mechanism (e.g., a timer) triggers a resynchronization, all collected transactions are executed modifying Neo4j's contents accordingly.

2) Neo4j to VSD: When loading a Neo4j database's contents to VSD, the Neo4jAPI traverses the graph and generates a load transaction for each visited node. All data is read from Neo4j before entries are stored in the mapper. Load transactions contain the respective node's id, all its property keys and values and the ids of adjacent nodes of outgoing relationships and their respective properties (*autodelete* and index for RefList-Properties). Subsequently, the synchronization component executes all load transactions. For each, a new VSD instance with appropriate properties is created and its id is stored in an OS with the corresponding node's id.

C. Change Tracking

As mentioned above, when collecting transactions, newly created ones may cancel out older ones. A change tracking mechanism performs the necessary filtering of such redundant transactions.

Change tracking is based on the current state of the considered OS. Depending on the incoming transaction's type, the state changes and the list of collected transactions is updated.

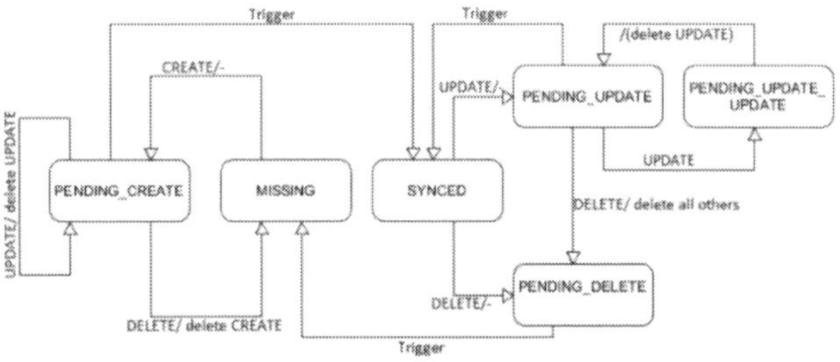

Figure 7. State machine of the change tracking mechanism.

Change tracking is modeled as a state machine as depicted in Figure 7. Here, the input (triggering state transitions) is represented by the incoming transaction type and the output (emitted during state transitions) describes the transaction list's modification. The initial state of any OS for a newly created VSD instance is the *MISSING* state as there is no corresponding Neo4j node. This intermediate state is left as soon as the corresponding create transaction is generated and the state changes to *PENDING_CREATE*. If this VSD instance is deleted before the transaction of type create has been executed, both transactions (create and delete) are removed and the whole OS is deleted. Else, upon a resynchronization trigger, a corresponding Neo4j node is generated, the state changes to *SYNCED*, and all executed transactions are removed from the list. The *SYNCED* state means that a Neo4j node and its VSD instance counterpart are in sync. It is reached every time a resynchronization was performed and is left when the VSD instance is modified (*PENDING_UPDATE*) or deleted (*PENDING_DELETE*).

In *PENDING_UPDATE* state, the changed property of an additional update transaction is compared to existing update transactions to avoid multiple updates of the same property. If two transactions modify the same property only one of them needs to be stored. This is represented by the intermediate *PENDING_UPDATE_UPDATE* state.

VI. Evaluation

Finally, the interface's effectiveness and performance have been evaluated using two simulation models of an industrial robot and a satellite shown in Figure 8. Given the current functional range of the presented prototype, further tests do not appear to provide more insights. Initially, both models are stored in a Neo4j database and, subsequently, loaded back into an (empty) VSD. The robot model yields 170 Neo4j nodes and 209 relationships. The more complex satellite about 20,000 nodes and 25,000 relationships. The highly connected nature of the 3D simulation data is apparent making a GDB ideally suited for its storage.

Figure 8. Robot and satellite (data: [16]) simulation model.

Figures 9 and 1 give an impression of the interface's effectiveness. Figure 9 shows an excerpt of the robot model data within Neo4j. Figure 1 shows the same data loaded into the VSD in-memory simulation database. The data mapping operates generically, i.e., independent from the actual data, making the whole synchronization component very flexible. The interface can synchronize arbitrary VSD contents to a Neo4j database.

In Section V, we present the interface's functionality to selectively resynchronize changes to VSD instances. This feature has been tested by changing some VSD instance's properties (e.g., name or postion of a component). In the Neo4j browser, we verified that these modifications were transferred correctly. Inversely, changes to node properties from the Neo4j browser show up in VEROSIM when the model is reloaded.

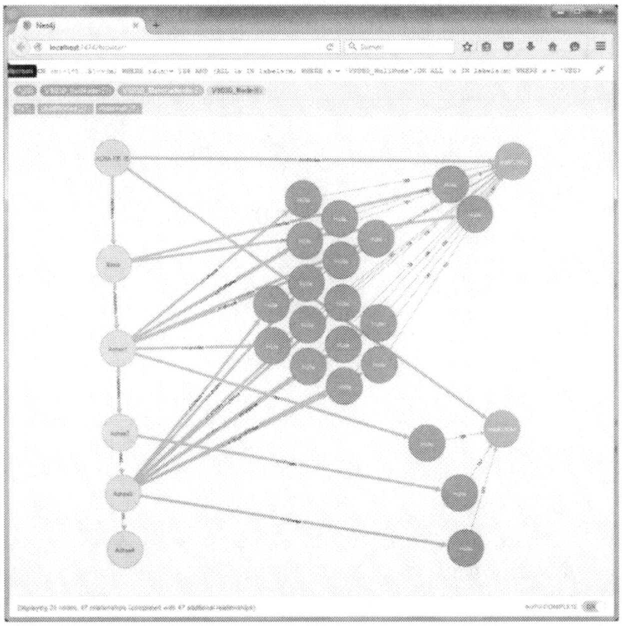

Figure 9. 3D simulation model data (excerpt) of an industrial robot stored within Neo4j.

TABLE I. LOADING AND SAVING TIMES OF THE PROTOTYPE.

	Neo4j		File	
	Robot	Satellite	Robot	Satellite
Loading	0.14	3.99	0.1	2.8
Saving	2.63	10.53	1.8	9.9

This also shows the advantage of selectively modifying data within a database in contrast to a file-based approach.

Another important aspect of the evaluation is the interface's performance. Here, the initial storage of a simulation model into Neo4j and the loading of a whole simulation model from Neo4j were examined and compared to saving and loading models to and from the native VEROSIM file format. Results are given in Table I. The access operations to the GDB are only somewhat slower than the native file operations. For a prototypical implementation from a student project, these results are very promising. First of all, compared to the highly optimized code for reading and writing the native file format, the current prototype is only optimized to a certain degree. Furthermore, the more high-level database access operations will always remain a little more complex than simple, sequential file reading or writing. Yet, the additional benefit from a full-fledged database (providing security, multi-user support, etc.) more than compensates for this small drawback.

Altogether, this shows that a GDB like Neo4j is well suited for highly connected 3D simulation model data and can be handled fast.

VII. CONCLUSION AND FUTURE WORK

Our approach to connect the GDB Neo4j with VEROSIM's simulation database VSD is motivated by the hierarchical structure of 3D simulation models that matches well with a graph structure. The presented interface encapsulates all VSD modification in independent transactions. A mapper maps individual VSD instances to single VSD nodes so that modifications can be processed individually and there is no need to save the complete VSD contents to Neo4j every time a single VSD instance changes. The stored data (as shown in Figure 9) indicates the highly linked structure of the simulation data so that GDBs are an ideal storage back end.

As future work, further performance optimizations and evaluations beyond the results from the student project could be performed. For instance, better traversal algorithms might improve loading speed. Another idea is to use Neo4j's batch inserter in contrast to the transactional structure to reduce resynchronization time. Furthermore, Neo4j might be used as a central database in a distributed simulation scenario with several VEROSIMs and VSDs. Here, an equivalent notification mechanism is needed for Neo4j to be able to track modifications in the central database.

REFERENCES

[1] I. Robinson, J. Webber, and E. Eifrem, Graph Databases-New Opportunities For Connected Data, 2nd ed. O'Reilly, 2015.

[2] M. Hoppen and J. Rossmann, "A Database Synchronization Approach for 3D Simulation Systems," in DBKDA 2014,The 6th International Conference on Advances in Databases, Knowledge, and Data Applications, A. Schmidt, K. Nitta, and J. S. Iztok Savnik, Eds., Chamonix, France, 2014, pp. 84–91.

[3] R. Diestel, Graph Theory, 2nd ed. Springer, 2000.

[4] M. Hunger, Neo4j 2.0 A graph database for everyone (orig.: Neo4j 2.0 Eine Graphdatenbank für alle), 1st ed. entwickler.press, 2014.

[5] Neo4j Team, "The Neo4j Manual v2.2.5," 2015, URL: http://neo4j.com/docs/stable/ [retrieved: May, 2016].

[6] J. Rossmann, M. Schluse, C. Schlette, and R. Waspe, "A New Approach to 3D Simulation Technology as Enabling Technology for eRobotics," in 1st International Simulation Tools Conference & EXPO 2013, SIMEX'2013, J. F. M. Van Impe and F. Logist, Eds., Brussels, Belgium, 2013, pp. 39–46.

[7] N. Martinez-Bazan, S. Gomez-Villamor, and F. Escale-Claveras, "Dex: A high-performance graph database management system," in Data Engineering Workshops (ICDEW), 2011 IEEE 27th International Conference on, April 2011, pp. 124–127.

[8] R. Kumar Kaliyar, "Graph databases: A survey," in Computing, Communication Automation (ICCCA), 2015 International Conference on, May 2015, pp. 785–790.

[9] Microsoft, "Graph engine 1.0 preview released," 2016, URL: http://research.microsoft.com/en-us/projects/trinity/ [retrieved: May, 2016].

[10] B. Shao, H. Wang, and Y. Li, "Trinity: A distributed graph engine on a memory cloud," in Proceedings of the 2013 ACM SIGMOD International Conference on Management of Data. ACM, 2013, pp. 505–516.

[11] B. Iordanov, "HyperGraphDB: A Generalized Graph Database," in Web-Age information management. Springer, 2010, pp. 25–36.

[12] InfoGrid Team, "Infogrid: The web graph database," 2016, URL: http://infogrid.org/trac/ [retrieved: May, 2016].

[13] J. Peilee, "A survey on graph databases," 2011, URL: https://jasperpeilee.wordpress.com/2011/11/25/a-survey-on-graph-databases/ [retrieved: May, 2016].

[14] "Allegrograph," 2016, URL: http://franz.com/agraph/allegrograph/ [retrieved: May, 2016].

[15] M. Hoppen, M. Schluse, J. Rossmann, and B. Weitzig, "Database-Driven Distributed 3D Simulation," in Proceedings of the 2012 Winter Simulation Conference, 2012, pp. 1–12.

[16] J. Weise et al., "An Intelligent Building Blocks Concept for On-Orbit-Satellite Servcing," in Proceedings of International Symposium on Artificial Intelligence, Robotics and Automation in Space (i-SAIRAS), 2012, pp. 1–8.

Subgraph Similarity Search in Large Graphs

Kanigalpula Samanvi

Dept. of Computer Science and Engineering
Indian Institute of Technology Hyderabad, India
Email: cs13m1001@iith.ac.in

Naveen Sivadasan

TCS Innovation Labs Hyderabad, India
Email: naveen@atc.tcs.com

Abstract—**One of the major challenges in applications related to social networks, computational biology, collaboration networks, etc., is to efficiently search for similar patterns in their underlying graphs. These graphs are typically noisy and contain thousands of vertices and millions of edges. In many cases, the graphs are unlabeled and the notion of similarity is also not well defined. We study the problem of searching an induced subgraph in a large target graph that is most similar to the given query graph. We assume that the query graph and target graph are undirected and unlabeled. We use graphlet kernels to define graph similarity. Our algorithm maps topological neighborhood information of vertices in the query and target graphs to vectors and these local information are combined to find global similarity. We conduct experiments on several real world networks and we show that our algorithm is able to detect highly similar matches when queried in these networks. Our implementation takes about one second to find matches on graphs containing thousands of vertices and million edges, excluding the time for one time pre-processing. Computationally expensive parts of our algorithm can be further scaled to standard parallel and distributed frameworks.**

Keywords–Similarity Search; Subgraph Similarity Search; Graph Kernel; Nearest Neighbors Search.

I. INTRODUCTION

Similarity based graph searching has attracted considerable attention in the context of social networks, road networks, collaboration networks, software testing, computational biology, molecular chemistry, etc. In these domains, underlying graphs are large with tens of thousands of vertices and millions of edges. Subgraph searching is fundamental to the applications, where occurrence of the query graph in the large target graph has to be identified. Searching for exact occurrence of an induced subgraph isomorphic to the query graph is known as the subgraph isomorphism problem, which is known to be NP-complete for undirected unlabeled graphs.

Presence of noise in the underlying graphs and need for searching 'similar' subgraph patterns are characteristic to these applications. For instance, in computational biology, the data is noisy due to possible errors in data collection and different thresholds for experiments. In object-oriented programming, querying typical object usage patterns against the target object dependency graph of a program run can identify deviating locations indicating potential bugs [1]. In molecular chemistry, identifying similar molecular structures is a fundamental problem. Searching for similar subgraphs plays a crucial role in mining and analysis of social networks. Subgraph similarity searching is therefore more natural in these settings in contrast to exact search. In subgraph similarity search problem, induced subgraph of the target graph that is 'most similar' to the query graph has to be identified, where similarity is defined using some distance function. Quality of the solution and computational efficiency are two major challenges in these search problems. In this work, we assume that both the underlying graph and query graph are unlabeled and undirected.

Most applications work with a distance metric to define similarity between two entities (graphs in our case). Popular distance metrics include Euclidean distance, Hamming distance, Edit distance, Kernel functions [2]–[5], etc. We use graph kernel functions to define graph similarity.

Kernels are symmetric functions that map pairs of entities from a domain to real values which indicate their similarity. Kernels that are positive definite not only define similarity between pairs of entities but also allow implicit mapping of objects to a high-dimensional feature space and operating on this space without requiring to compute explicit mapping of objects in the feature space. Kernels implicitly yield inner products between the feature vectors without explicit computation of the same in feature space. This is usually computationally cheaper than explicit computation. This approach is usually referred to as the kernel trick or kernel method. Kernel methods have been widely applied to sequence data, graphs, text, images, videos, etc., as many of the standard machine learning algorithms including support vector machine (SVM) and principle component analysis (PCA) can directly work with kernels.

Kernels have been successfully applied in the past in the context of graphs [6]–[8]. There are several existing graph kernels based on various graph properties, such as random walks in the graphs [9][10], cyclic patterns [11], graph edit distance [12], shortest paths [13][14], frequency of occurrences of special subgraphs [15]–[17] and so on.

Graphlet kernels are defined based on occurrence frequencies of small induced subgraphs called graphlets in the given graphs [18]. Graphlet kernels have been shown to provide good SVM classification accuracy in comparison to random walk kernel and shortest path kernel on different datasets including protein and enzyme data [18]. Graphlet kernels are also of theoretical interest. It is known that under certain restricted settings, if two graphs have distance zero with respect to their graphlet kernel value then they are isomorphic [18]. Improving the efficiency of computing graphlet kernel is also studied in [18]. Graphlet kernel computation can also be scaled to parallel and distributed setting in a fairly straight forward manner. In our work, we use graphlet kernels to define graph similarity.

A. Related Work

Similarity based graph searching has been studied in the past under various settings. In many of the previous works, it is assumed that the graphs are labeled. In one class of problems, a large database of graphs is given and the goal is to find the most similar match in the database with respect to the given query graph [19]–[24]. In the second class, given a target graph and a query graph, subgraph of the target graph that is most similar to the query graph needs to be identified [25]–[28]. Different notions of similarity were also explored in the past for these classes of problems.

In [29], approximate matching of query graph in a database of graphs is studied. The graphs are assumed to be labeled. Structural information of the graph is stored in a hybrid index structure based on B-tree index. Important vertices of a query graph are matched first and then the match is extended progressively. In [30], graph similarity search on labeled graphs from a large database of graphs under minimum edit distance is studied. In [25], algorithm for computing top-k approximate subgraph matches for a given query graph in a large labeled target graph is given. In this work, the target graph is converted into a set of multi-dimensional vectors based on the labels in the vertex neighborhoods. Only matches above a user defined threshold are computed. With higher threshold values, the match is a trivial vertex to vertex label matching. In [26], algorithm NeMa was proposed which uses a combination of label similarity and local structural similarity to search for subgraph similar to query graph in large labeled graphs. Their query time is proportional to the product of number of vertices of the query and target graph. Subgraph matching in a large target graph for graphs deployed on a distributed memory store was studied in [27]. In [28], efficient distributed subgraph similarity search to retrieve matches whose number of missing edges is below a given threshold is studied. It looks for exact matching and not similarity matching. Though different techniques were studied in the past for the problem of similarity searching in various settings, to the best of our knowledge, little work has been done on subgraph similarity search on large unlabeled graphs. In many of the previous works, either the vertices are assumed to be labeled or the graphs they work with are small with hundreds of vertices.

B. Our Contribution

We consider undirected graphs with no vertex or edge labels. We use graphlet kernel to define similarity between graphs. We give a subgraph similarity matching algorithm that takes as input a large target graph and a query graph and identifies an induced subgraph of the target graph that is most similar to the query graph with respect to the graphlet kernel value.

In our algorithm, we first compute vertex labels for vertices in both query and target graph. These labels are vectors in some fixed dimension and are computed based on local neighborhood structure of vertices in the graph. Since our vertex labels are vectors, unlike many of the other labeling techniques, our labeling allows us to define the notion of similarity between vertex labels of two vertices to capture the topological similarity of their corresponding neighborhoods in the graph. We build a nearest neighbor data structure for vertices of the target graph based on their vertex labels. Computing vertex label for target graph vertices and building the nearest neighbor data structure are done in the pre-processing phase. Using nearest neighbor queries on this data structure, vertices of the target graph that are most similar to the vertices of the query graph are identified. Using this smaller set of candidate vertices of target graph, a seed match is computed for the query graph. Using this seed match as the basis, our algorithm computes the final match for the full query graph. By using vertex level vector labels based on graphlet distribution in the local neighborhood of vertices, we are able to extend the power of graphlet kernels, which was shown to perform well for graph similarity search on smaller graphs, to subgraph similarity search on much larger graphs.

We study the performance of our algorithm on several real life datasets including facebook network, google plus network, youtube network, road network, amazon network provided by the Stanford Large Network Dataset Collection (SNAP) [31] and Digital Bibliography & Library Project (DBLP) network [32]. We conduct number of experimental studies to measure the search quality and run time efficiency. For instance, while searching these networks with their communities as query graphs, the computed match and the query graph has similarity score close to 1, where 1 is the maximum possible similarity score. In about 30% of the cases, our algorithm is able to identify the exact match and in about 80% of the cases, vertices of exact match are present in the pruned set computed by the algorithm. We validate our results by showing that similarity scores between random subgraphs and similarity scores between random communities in these networks are significantly lower. In other words, similarity score obtained by chance is significantly lower. We also query communities across networks and in noisy networks and obtain matches with significantly high similarity scores. We use our algorithm to search for dense subgraphs and identify subgraphs with significantly high density. We also conduct experiments to compare performance of our algorithm with NeMa [26], which is a subgraph similarity search algorithm that uses both structural and label similarity. We use graphs with uniform label for this purpose.

Computationally expensive parts of our algorithm can be easily scaled to standard parallel and distributed computing frameworks such as map-reduce. Most of the networks in our experiments have millions of edges and thousands of vertices. We use multi-threaded implementation for the one time pre-processing phase. Single threaded implementation of our search algorithm takes close to one second. This excludes time taken by the pre-processing phase.

C. Paper Organization

In Section II, we present the preliminaries including graphlet kernels and the problem statement. In Section III, we present the details of the vertex labeling technique. In Section IV, we present the details of our algorithm including the pre-processing phase and the matching phase. In Section V, we present the experimental results. In Section VI, we present our conclusions and directions for future research.

II. Preliminaries

Graph is an ordered pair $G = (V, E)$ comprising a set V of vertices and a set E of edges. To avoid ambiguity, we also use $V(G)$ and $E(G)$ to denote the vertex and edge set. We consider only undirected graphs with no vertex or edge labels.

A subgraph H of G is a graph whose vertices are a subset of V, and whose edges are a subset of E and is denoted as $H \subseteq G$. An induced subgraph G' is a graph whose vertex set V' is a subset of V and whose edge set is the set of all edges present in G between vertices in V'.

DEFINITION 1 (Graph Isomorphism). Graphs G_1 and G_2 are isomorphic if there exists a bijection $b : V(G_1) \to V(G_2)$ such that any two vertices u and v of G_1 are adjacent in G_1 if and only if $b(u)$ and $b(v)$ are adjacent in G_2.

DEFINITION 2 (Subgraph Isomorphism). Graph G_1 is isomorphic to a subgraph of graph G_2, if there is an induced subgraph of G_2 that is isomorphic to G_1.

DEFINITION 3 (Graph Similarity Searching). Given a collection of graphs and a query graph, find graphs in the collection that are closest to the query graph with respect to a given distance/similarity function between graphs.

DEFINITION 4 (Subgraph Similarity Searching). Given graphs G_1 and G_2, determine a subgraph $G^* \subseteq G_1$ that is closest to G_2 with respect to a given distance/similarity function between graphs.

A. Graphlet Kernel

Graphlets are fixed size non isomorphic induced subgraphs of a large graph. Typical graphlet sizes considered in applications are 3, 4 and 5. For example, Figure 1 shows all possible non isomorphic size 4 graphlets. There are 11 of them of which 6 are connected. We denote by D_l, the set of all size l graphlets that are connected. The set D_4 is shown in Figure 2.

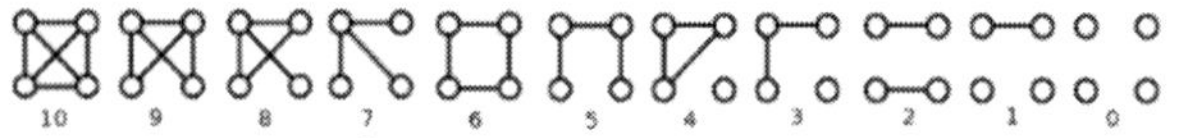

Figure 1. Set of all non isomorphic graphlets of size 4

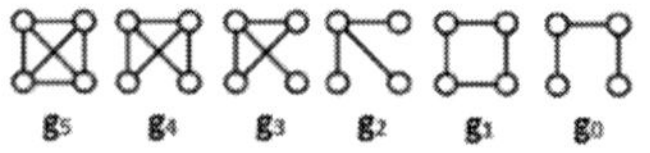

Figure 2. Non isomorphic connected graphlets of size 4

DEFINITION 5 (Graphlet Vector). For a given l, the graphlet vector f_G for a given graph G is a frequency vector of dimension $|D_l|$ where its ith component corresponds to the number of occurrences of the ith graphlet of D_l in G. We assume the graphlet vector f_G to be normalized by the L_2 norm $||f_G||_2$.

If graphs G and G' are isomorphic then clearly their corresponding graphlet vectors f_G and $f_{G'}$ are identical. But the reverse need not be true in general. But, it is conjectured that given two graphs G and G' of n vertices and their corresponding graphlet vectors f_G and $f_{G'}$ with respect to $n-1$ sized graphlets D_{n-1}, graph G is isomorphic to G' if f_G is identical to $f_{G'}$ [18]. The conjecture has been verified for $n \leq 11$ [18]. Kernels based on similarity of graphlet vectors provide a natural way to express similarity of underlying graphs.

DEFINITION 6 (Graphlet Kernel). Given two graphs G and G', let f_G and $f_{G'}$ be their corresponding graphlet frequency vectors with respect to size l graphlets for some fixed l. The graphlet kernel value $K(G, G')$ is defined as the dot product of f_G and $f_{G'}$. That is, $K(G, G') = f_G^T f_{G'}$

Graphlet vectors are in fact an explicit embedding of graphs into a vector space whose dimension is $|D_l|$ if size l graphlets are used. Graphlet kernels have been shown to give better classification accuracies in comparison to other graph kernels like random walk kernel and shortest path kernel for certain applications [18]. Values of $K(G, G') \in [0, 1]$ and larger values of $K(G, G')$ indicate higher similarity between G and G'. In this work, we use kernel function $K(G, G')$ to represent similarity between graphs G and G'. Exact problem statement is given below.

PROBLEM STATEMENT. Let $K(\cdot, \cdot)$ be graphlet kernel based on size l graphlets for some fixed l. Given a large connected graph G of size n and a connected query graph Q of size n_q with $n > n_q$, find a subset V^* of vertices in G such that its induced subgraph G^* in G maximizes $K(Q, G^*)$.

III. GRAPHLET VECTOR BASED VERTEX LABELING

Computing vertex labels that capture topological neighborhood information of corresponding vertices in the graph and comparing vertex neighborhoods using their labels is crucial in our matching algorithm. Our vertex labels are graphlet vectors of their corresponding neighborhood subgraphs.

Given a fixed positive integer t and graph G, let $N(v)$ denote the depth t neighbors of vertex v in G. That is, $N(v)$ is the subset of all vertices in G (including v) that are reachable from v in t or less edges. Let H_v denote the subgraph induced by vertices $N(v)$ in G. We denote by f_v, the graphlet vector corresponding to the graph H_v, with respect to size l graphlets for some fixed l. We note that for defining the graphlet vector f_v for a vertex, there are two implicit parameters l and t. To avoid overloading the notation, we assume them to be some fixed constants and specify them explicitly when required. Values of l and t are parameters to our final algorithm.

For each vertex v of the graph, its vertex label is given by the vector f_v. Given vertex labels f_u and f_v for vertices u and v, we denote by $s(u, v)$ the similarity between labels of f_u and f_v, given by their dot product as

$$s(u, v) = f_u^T f_v \tag{1}$$

Values of $s(u, v) \in [0, 1]$ and larger values of $s(u, v)$ indicate higher topological similarity between neighborhoods of vertices u and v. Computing the vertex labels of the target graph is done in the pre-processing phase. Implementation details of the vertex labeling algorithm are discussed in the next section.

IV. OUR ALGORITHM

Our subgraph similarity search algorithm has two major phases: one time pre-processing phase and the query graph matching phase. Each of these phases comprise sub-phases as given below. Details of each of these subphases is discussed in the subsequent sections.

A. Pre-processing Phase: This phase has two subphases:

1) In this phase, vertex labels f_v of all the vertices of the target graph G are computed.
2) k-d tree based nearest neighbor data structure on the vertices of G using their label vectors f_v is built.

B. Matching Phase: This phase is further divided into four subphases:

1) Selection Phase: In this phase, vertex labels f_v for vertices of the query graph Q are computed first. Each vertex u of the query graph then selects a subset of vertices from the target graph G closest to u based on their Euclidean distance.
2) Seed Match Generation Phase: In this phase, a one to one mapping of a subset of query graph vertices to target graph vertices is obtained with highest overall similarity score. Subgraph induced by the mapped vertices in the target graph is called the seed match. The seed match is obtained by solving a maximum weighted bipartite matching problem.
3) Match Growing Phase: The above seed match is used as a basis to compute the final match for Q.
4) Match Completion Phase: This phase tries to match those vertices in Q that are still left unmatched in the previous phase.

A. Pre-processing Phase

1) Computation of vertex labels f_v: In this phase, vertex label f_v for each vertex v of the target graph G is computed first. To compute f_v, we require parameter values t and l. These two values are assumed to be provided as parameters to the search algorithm. For each vertex v, a breadth first traversal of depth t is performed starting from v to obtain the depth t neighborhood $N(v)$ of v. The graph H_v induced by the vertex set $N(v)$ is then used to compute the graphlet vector f_v as given in [33]. The algorithm is given in Figure 3.

Major time taken by the pre-processing phase is for computing the graphlet vector for H_v. In [18], methods to improve its efficiency including sampling techniques are discussed. We do not make use of sampling technique in our implementation. We remark that finding the graphlet frequencies can easily be scaled to parallel computing frameworks or distributed computing frameworks such as map-reduce.

Algorithm 1
Input: Graph G, vertex v, BFS depth t, graphlet size l
Output: Label vector f_v

1: Run BFS on G starting from v till depth t. Let $N(v)$ be the set of vertices visited including v.
2: Identify the induced subgraph H_v of G induced by $N(v)$.
3: Compute graphlet vector f_v for graph H_v.
4: Normalize f_v by $||f_v||_2$.
5: **return** f_v

Figure 3. Algorithm for computing label f_v for vertex v

2) Nearest neighbor data structure on f_v: After computing vertex labels for G, a nearest neighbor data structure on the vertices of G based on their label vectors f_v is built. We use k-d trees for nearest neighbor data structure [34]. k-d trees are known to be efficient when dimension of vectors is less than 20 [34]. Since the typical graphlet size l that we work with are $3, 4$ and 5, the dimension of f_v (which is $|D_l|$) does not exceed 10.

B. Matching Phase

In the following we describe the three subphases of matching phase.

1) Selection Phase: The vertex labels f_v for all vertices of the query graph Q are computed first using Algorithm 1. Let R_v denote the set of k vertices in G that are closest to v with respect to the Euclidean distance between their label vectors. In our experiments, we usually fix k as 10. For each vertex v of Q, we compute R_v by querying the k-d tree built in the pre-processing phase. Let R denote the union of R_v for each vertex v of the n_q vertices of Q. For the subsequent seed match generation phase, we will only consider the vertex subset R of G. Clearly size of R is at most $k.n_q$ which is typically much smaller than the number of vertices in G.

2) Seed Match Generation Phase: In this phase, we obtain a one to one mapping of a subset of vertices of the query graph Q to the target graph G with highest overall similarity score. We call the subgraph induced by the mapped vertices in G as the seed match. To do this, we define a bipartite graph $(V(Q), R)$ with weighted edges, where one part is the vertex set $V(Q)$ of the query graph Q and the other part is the pruned vertex set R of G obtained in the previous step. The edges of the bipartite graph and their weights are defined as follows. Each vertex v in the part $V(Q)$ is connected to every vertex w in $R_v \subseteq R$, where R_v is the set of k nearest neighbors of v in G as computed in the previous step.

The weight $\lambda(v, w)$ for the edge (v, w) is defined in the following manner. Let $0 < \alpha < 1$ be a fixed scale factor which is provided as a parameter to the search algorithm. We recall that vertex v belongs to query graph Q and vertex w belongs to target graph G and $s(v, w)$ given by equation (1) denote the similarity between their label vectors f_v and f_w. Let V_w denote the neighbors of vertex w in graph G including w. Let Q' denote the subset of $V(Q)$ excluding v such that each vertex in Q' is connected to at least one vertex in V_w in the bipartite graph $(V(Q), R)$. In particular, for each vertex $u \in Q'$, let $s(u)$ denote the maximum $s(u, z)$ value among all its neighbors z in V_w in the bipartite graph. Now the weight $\lambda(v, w)$ for the edge (v, w) of the bipartite graph is given by

$$\lambda(v, w) = \frac{\left(s(v, w)^\alpha + \sum_{u \in Q'} s(u)^\alpha\right)^{1/\alpha}}{(|Q'| + 1)} \quad (2)$$

We now solve maximum weighted bipartite matching on this graph to obtain a one to one mapping between a subset of vertices of Q and the vertices of G. Defining edge weights $\lambda(v, w)$ to edge (v, w) in the bipartite graph in the above fashion not only takes into account the similarity value $s(v, w)$, but also the strength of similarity of neighbors of w in G to remaining vertices in the query graph Q. By assigning edge weights as above, we try to ensure that among two vertices in G with equal similarity values to a vertex in Q, the vertex whose neighbors in G also have high similarity to vertices in Q is preferred over the other in the final maximum weighted bipartite matching solution.

Let M denote the solution obtained for the bipartite matching. Let Q_M and G_M respectively denote the subgraphs induced by the subset of matched vertices from graphs Q and G under the matching M. The connectivity of Q_M and G_M may differ. For instance, the number of connected components in G_M and Q_M could differ. Therefore, we do not include all the vertices of G_M in the seed match. Instead, we use the largest connected component of G_M as a seed solution. That is, let $S_G \subset V(G)$ denote the subset of vertices in G_M corresponding to a maximum cardinality connected component. Let S_Q denote their corresponding mapped vertices in Q_M. We call S_G as a seed match. The pseudo code for seed match computation is given in Algorithm 2.

Algorithm 2

Input: Vertex sets $V(Q)$, R and R_v for each $v \in V(Q)$ and their labels f_v, parameter α

Output: S_G and S_Q

1: Construct bipartite graph $(V(Q), R)$ with edge weights given by $\lambda(v, w)$.
2: Compute maximum weighted bipartite matching M on $(V(Q), R)$
3: Let Q_M and G_M respectively denote the subgraphs induced by vertices from Q and G in the matching M.
4: Compute largest connected component in G_M. Let S_G denote the vertices in that component. Let S_Q denote its mapped vertices in Q_M under the bipartite matching M.
5: **return** S_G and S_Q

Figure 4. Computing seed match S_G in G and its mapped vertices S_Q in Q

3) Match Growing Phase: After computing the seed match S_G in G and its mapped vertices S_Q in Q, we use this seed match as the basis to compute the final match. The final solution is computed in an incremental fashion starting with empty match. In each iteration, we include a new pair of vertices (v, w) to the solution, where v and w belongs to G and Q respectively. In order to do this, we maintain a list of candidate pairs and in each iteration, we include a pair with maximum similarity value $s(v, w)$ to the final solution. We use a max heap to maintain the candidate list. The candidate list is initialized with the mapped pairs between S_G and S_Q as obtained in the previous phase. Thus, the heap is initialized by inserting each of these mapped pairs (v, w) with corresponding weight $s(v, w)$.

We recall that the mapped pairs obtained from previous phase have stronger similarity with respect to the modified weight function $\lambda(v, w)$. Higher value of $\lambda(v, w)$ indicates that not only $s(v, w)$ is high but also their neighbors share high $s()$ value. Hence, they are more preferred in the solution over other pairs with similar $s()$ value. By initializing the candidate list with these preferred pairs, the matching algorithm tries to ensure that the incremental solution starts with these pairs first and other potential pairs are considered later. Also, because of the heap data structure, remaining pairs are considered in the decreasing order of their similarity value. Moreover, as will be discussed later, the incremental matching tries to ensure that the partial match in G constructed so far is connected. For this, new pairs that are added to the candidate list are chosen from the neighborhood of the partial match between G and Q.

The incremental matching might still match vertex pairs with low $s()$ value if they are available in the candidate list. Candidate pairs with low $s()$ values should be treated separately as there could be genuine pairs with low $s()$ value. For instance, consider boundary vertices of an optimal subgraph match in G. Boundary vertices are also connected to vertices outside the matched subgraph. Hence, their local neighborhood structure is different from their counterpart in the query graph. In other words, their corresponding graphlet vectors can be very dissimilar and their similarity value $s()$ can be very low even though they are expected to be matched in the final solution. In order to find such genuine pairs, we omit pairs with similarity value below some fixed threshold h_1 in this phase and such pairs are handled in the next phase.

In each iteration of the incremental matching, a pair (v, w) with maximum $s(v, w)$ value is removed from the candidate heap and added to the final match. After this, the candidate list is modified as follows. We recall that v and w belong to G and Q respectively. We call a vertex unmatched if it is not yet present in the final match. The algorithm maintains two invariants: (a) the pairs present in the candidate list are one to one mappings and (b) a query vertex that enters the candidate list will stay in the candidate list (possibly with multiple changes to paired partner vertex) until it is included in the final match. Let U_v denote the unmatched neighbors of v in G that are also not present in the candidate list. Let U_w denote the unmatched neighbors w in Q. For each query vertex y in U_w, let x be a vertex in U_v with maximum similarity value $s(x, y)$. We add (x, y) to the candidate list if y is absent in the list and $s(x, y) \geq h_1$. If y is already present in the candidate list, then replace the current pair for y with (x, y) if $s(x, y)$ has a higher value. The incremental algorithm is given in Algorithm 3. The candidate list modification is described in Algorithm 4.

Algorithm 3

Input: Seed match S_G and its mapped vertices S_Q, threshold h_1

Output: Partial match F

1: Initialize F to empty set.
2: Initialize the candidate list max heap with mapped pairs (v, w) of the seed match where $s(v, w) \geq h_1$.
3: **while** candidate list is not empty **do**
4: Extract maximum weight candidate match (v, w)
5: Add (v, w) to F
6: **updateCandidateList**(candidate list, (v, w), h_1,F)
7: **end while**
8: **return** F

Figure 5. Incremental Matching Algorithm.

4) Match Completion Phase: In this phase, vertices of the query graph Q that are left unmatched in the previous phase due to similarity values below the threshold h_1 are handled. Typically, boundary vertices of the final matched subgraph in G remain unmatched in the previous phase. As discussed earlier, this is because, such boundary vertices in G and their matched partners in Q have low $s()$ value as their local neighborhood topologies vastly differ. Hence, using neighborhood similarity for such pairs is ineffective. To handle them, we try to match unmatched query vertices with unmatched neighbors of the current match F in G. Since the similarity function $s()$ is ineffective here, we use a different similarity function to compare potential pairs. Let X denote

Algorithm 4

Input: candidate list, (v, w), h_1 and F

Compute U_v which is the set of unmatched neighbors of v in G that are also not present in candidate list.
Compute U_w which is the set of unmatched neighbors of w in Q.
for all vertex $y \in U_w$ **do**
  Find $x \in U_v$ with maximum $s(x, y)$ value.
  if y does not exist in candidate list **then**
    Include (x, y) in the candidate list if $s(x, y) \geq h_1$.
  else
    Replace existing pair for y in the candidate list with (x, y) if $s(x, y)$ has higher value.
  end if
end for

Figure 6. Algorithm for updateCandidateList

the set of unmatched neighbors of the current match F in G. Let Y denote the set of unmatched query vertices. Let $v \in X$ and let $w \in Y$. We define the similarity $c(v, w)$ as follows. Let Z_v denote the matched neighbors of v in target graph G and let Z_w denote the matched neighbors of w in query graph Q. Let Z'_v denote the matched partners of Z_v in Q. We now define $c(v, w)$ using the standard Jaccard similarity coefficient as

$$c(v, w) = \frac{|Z'_v \cap Z_w|}{|Z'_v \cup Z_w|} \tag{3}$$

We use a fixed threshold h_2 that is provided as parameter to the algorithm. We now define a bipartite graph (X, Y) with edge weights as follows. For each $(v, w) \in X \times Y$, insert an edge (v, w) with weight $c(v, w)$ in the bipartite graph if $c(v, w) \geq h_2$. Compute maximum weighted bipartite graph matching on this bipartite graph and include the matched pairs in the final solution F. In our experiments, size of Y (number of unmatched query graph vertices) is very small. The pseudo code is given in Algorithm 5.

Algorithm 5

Input: Partial match F and threshold h_2

Output: Final match F

Let X denote the set of unmatched neighbors of the match F in G.
Let Y denote the set of unmatched vertices in Q.
Construct bipartite graph (X, Y) by introducing all edges (v, w) with edge weight $c(v, w)$ if $c(v, w) \geq h_2$.
Compute maximum weighted bipartite matching.
Add each of these matches to F
return F

Figure 7. Match completion algorithm

We remark that our searching algorithm finds the matched subset of vertices in G and also their corresponding mapped vertices in the query graph Q.

V. Experimental Results

In this section, we conduct experiments on various real life graph datasets [31] including social networks, collaboration networks, road networks, youtube network, amazon network and on synthetic graph datasets. We also conduct experiments to compare performance of our algorithm with NeMa [26], which is a subgraph similarity search algorithm that uses both label similarity and structural similarity to find subgraph similar to query graph in large labeled graphs.

A. Experimental Datasets

Social Networks: We conduct experiments on facebook and google plus undirected graphs provided by Stanford Large Network Dataset Collection (SNAP) [31]. Facebook graph contains around 4K vertices and 88K edges. In this graph, vertices represent anonymized users and an undirected edge connects two friends. google plus graph contains 107K vertices and 13M edges. google plus graph also represents users as vertices and an edge exists between two friends. The dataset also contains list of user circles (user communities), where user circle is specified by its corresponding set of vertices. We use these user circles as query graphs and they are queried against the entire facebook network. We also query facebook circles against google plus network to find similar circles across networks. We also experiment querying facebook circles against facebook network after introducing random noise to the facebook network.

DBLP Collaboration Network: We use the DBLP collaboration network downloadable from [32]. This network has around 317K vertices and 1M edges. The vertices of this graph are authors who publish in any conference or journal and an edge exists between any two co-authors. All the authors who contribute to a common conference or a journal form a community. The dataset provides a list of such communities by specifying its corresponding set of vertices. We use such communities as query graphs.

Youtube Network: Youtube network is downloaded from [31]. Network has about 1M vertices and 2M edges. Vertices in this network represent users and an edge exists between two users who are friends. In youtube, users can create groups in which other users can join. The dataset provides a list of user groups by specifying its corresponding set of vertices. We consider these user-defined groups as our query graphs.

Road Network: We use the road network of California obtained from [31] in our experiments. This network has around 2M vertices and 3M edges. Vertices of this network are road endpoints or road intersections and the edges are the roads connecting these intersections. We use randomly chosen subgraphs from this network as query graphs.

Amazon Network: Amazon network is a product co-purchasing network downloaded from [31]. This network has around 334K vertices and 925K edges. Each vertex represents a product and an edge exists between the products that are frequently co-purchased [31]. All the products under a certain category form a product community. The dataset provides a list of product communities by specifying its corresponding set of vertices. We use product communities as query graphs and we query them against the amazon network.

The statistics of the datasets used are listed in Table I.

TABLE I. DATASET STATISTICS

DataSet	#vertices	#edges
Facebook	4039	88234
Google Plus	107614	13673453
DBLP	317080	1049866
Amazon	334863	925872
Youtube	1134890	2987624
Road Network	1965206	2766607

B. Experimental Setup

All the experiments are carried out on a 32 core 2.60GHz Intel(R) Xeon(R) server with 32GB RAM. The server has Ubuntu 14.04 LTS. Our implementation uses Java 7.

The computationally most expensive part of our algorithm is the computation of vector labels for all vertices of a graph. The pre-processing phase that computes label vectors for each vertex of the graph is multi-threaded and thus executes on all 32 cores. Similarly, in the matching phase, computing label vectors for all vertices of the query graph is also multi-threaded and uses all 32 cores. Remaining phases use only a single core.

C. Results

To evaluate the accuracy of the result obtained by our similarity search algorithm, we compute the graphlet kernel value $K(Q, G^*)$ between the query graph Q and the subgraph G^* of G induced by the vertices V^* of the final match F in G. We use this value to show the similarity between the query graph and our obtained match and we refer to this value as *similarity score* in our experiments. We recall that similarity score lies in the range $[0, 1]$ where 1 indicates maximum similarity.

There are six parameters in our algorithm: (1) graphlet size l, (2) BFS depth t for vertex label computation, (3) value of k for the k nearest neighbors from k-d tree, (4) value of α in the edge weight function λ and (5) similarity thresholds h_1 for match growing phase and h_2 for match completion phase. In all our experiments we fix graphlet size l as 4. We performed experiments with different values of k, α, h_1 and h_2 on different datasets. Based on the results, we chose ranges for these parameters. The value of k is chosen from the range 5 to 10. Even for million vertex graphs, $k = 10$ showed good results. We fix scaling factor α to be 0.3 and the thresholds h_1 and h_2 to be 0.4 and 0.95 respectively.

Experiment 1: This experiment shows the effect of bfs depth t on the final match quality. We performed experiments with different values of t. We observed that after the depth of 2, there is very little change in the similarity scores of the final match. But as the depth increases the time to compute graphlet vectors also increases. Thus, the bfs depth t was taken to be 2 for most of our experiments. Table II shows the similarity scores of querying amazon communities on amazon network and and DBLP communities on DBLP collaboration network for different values of t. These results are averaged over 150 queries.

Experiment 2: For each of the datasets discussed earlier, we perform subgraph querying against the same network. For each network, we use the given communities as query graphs and measure the quality of the search result. That is, we query facebook communities against facebook network, DBLP communities against DBLP network, youtube groups against youtube network and amazon product communities against amazon network. For road network, we use randomly chosen induced subgraphs from the network as query graph. Second column of Table III shows the similarity score of the match. All the results are averages over 150 queries. The average community (query graph) size is around 100 for facebook, around 40 for DBLP, around 50 for youtube and around 300 for amazon. Query graphs for road network have about 500 vertices.

TABLE II. EXPERIMENT 1 : SIMILARITY SCORE VS. t

Dataset	t=2	t=3	t=4
Amazon	0.9999823	0.9999851	0.9999858
DBLP	0.9999942	0.9999896	0.9999917

To validate the quality of our solution, we do the following for each of the network. We compute the similarity score between random induced subgraphs from the same network. These random subgraphs contain 100 vertices. We also compute the similarity score between different communities from the same network. All results are averaged over 150 scores. Table III shows these results. Second column in the table shows the average similarity score between query graph and the computed match. The query graphs are the given communities. Third column in the table shows the average similarity score between random subgraphs. Fourth column shows the average similarity score between communities. The results show that the similarity score of our match close to 1 and is significantly better than scores between random subgraphs and scores between communities in the same network. For road network, the third column shows the average similarity between its query subgraphs.

TABLE III. EXPERIMENT 2 : SIMILARITY SCORES.

DataSet	Query graph & Final Match	Between Random Subgraphs	Between Communities
Facebook	0.944231	0.702286	0.787296
DBLP	0.975137	0.443763	0.6144779
Amazon	0.999982	0.663301	0.624756
Youtube	0.998054	0.311256	0.524779
Road Network	0.899956	0.770492	0.599620

Table IV shows the $\#exactMatches$ which is the number of queries that yielded the exact match out of the 150 queries (query graph is a subgraph of the network), and $\#inPruned$ - the percentage of queries where the vertices of the exact target match are present in the pruned subset of vertices R of target graph G obtained after the selection phase. Table IV shows that, for about 30% of the query graphs, our algorithm identifies the exact match. Also, for about 75% of the queries, vertices of the ideal match are present in our pruned set of vertices R in the target graph after selection phase.

Table V shows the timing results corresponding to *Experiment 2*. The timing information is only for the matching phase and it excludes the one time pre-processing phase. Here δ denotes time taken (in secs) to compute the label vectors for all vertices of the query graph and τ the time taken (in secs)

TABLE IV. EXPERIMENT 2 : EXACT MATCH STATISTICS

Dataset	$\#exactMatches$ out of 150 (percentage)	$\#inPruned$ (percentage)
Facebook	53 (35.3)	83
DBLP	47 (31.3)	82
Amazon	60 (40.0)	72

for the entire matching phase (including δ). We recall that the label vector computation is implemented as multi-threaded on 32 cores and the remaining part is executed as a single thread. It can be seen that the label vector computation is the computationally expensive part and the remaining phases take much lesser time.

TABLE V. EXPERIMENT 2 : TIMING RESULTS

DataSet	δ(in sec)	τ(in sec)
Facebook	0.213596	0.253706
DBLP	0.159492	0.777687
Amazon	0.199767	0.781500
Youtube	0.225131	0.989452
Road Network	0.216644	1.437619

Experiment 3: In all previous experiments, query graphs were induced subgraphs of the target network. In this experiment, we evaluate the quality of our solution when the query graph is not necessarily an induced subgraph of the target graph. For this, we conduct two experiments. In the first experiment, we use facebook communities as query graphs and query them against google plus network. To validate the quality of our solution, we measure the similarity score of the query graph with a random induced subgraph in the target graph with same number of vertices. In the second experiment, we create a modified facebook network by randomly removing 5% its original edges. We use this modified network as the target graph and query original facebook communities in this target graph. Here also, we validate the quality of our solution by measuring the similarity score for the query graph with a random induced subgraph of same number of vertices in the target graph. Table VI shows these results. Second column in the table shows the similarity score between query graph and match. Third column shows the score between query graph and a random subgraph. Values shown for both experiments are averaged over 150 scores. The results show that similarity score of our match is close to 1 and is significantly better than a match by chance.

TABLE VI. EXPERIMENT 3 : SIMILARITY SCORES

DataSet	Final Match	Random Subgraph
Google Plus	0.912241	0.600442
Facebook with random noise	0.933662	0.701198

Experiment 4: We use our matching algorithm to identify dense subgraphs in large networks. In particular, we search for dense subgraphs in DBLP and google plus networks. For this, we first generate dense random graphs using the standard $G(n,p)$ model with $n = 500$ and $p = 0.9$. We now use these random graphs as query graphs and query them against the DBLP and google plus networks. We use the standard definition of density ρ of a graph $H = (V, E)$ as

$$\rho = \frac{2|E|}{|V| * |V - 1|} \in [0, 1] \quad (4)$$

The average density of our random query graphs is 0.9. We queried these dense random graphs against DBLP and google plus networks. Table VII shows the results. Column 2 shows the similarity score between query graph and obtained match. Column 3 shows the density ρ for the obtained match. The results are averaged over 150 queries. Results show that the similarity score with matched result is close to 1 for google plus. For DBLP the score is close to 0.8 primarily because DBLP does not have dense subgraphs with about 500 vertices. Also, the density of the obtained match is close to that of the query graph, which is 0.9.

TABLE VII. EXPERIMENT 4 : DENSE SUBGRAPH MATCH RESULTS

DataSet	Similarity Score	ρ for the match
Google Plus	0.926670	0.812
DBLP	0.799753	0.730

Experiment 5 - Comparison with NeMa: We conducted experiments to compare performance of our algorithm with NeMa [26]. NeMa uses combination of label similarity and structural similarity to search similar subgraphs in large labeled graphs. NeMa was shown to find high quality matches efficiently compared to state-of-the-art graph querying algorithms. Similarity search using structural similarity alone is harder as label similarity helps in pruning the search space considerably. For comparing performance of NeMa with our algorithm, we considered query and target graphs with same label for all vertices, which is similar to unlabeled setting. In particular, we used YAGO and IMDB datasets for our experiments which were used also for experimental evaluation of NeMa in [26]. Both datasets were modified to make all vertices to have the same label and all edges unlabeled. IMDB (Internet Movie Database) dataset consists of relationships between movies, directors, producers and so on. YAGO entity relationship graph is a knowledge base containing information from Wikipedia, WordNet and GeoNames. IMDB dataset consists of about 3 million vertices and 11 million edges and YAGO dataset consists of about 13 million vertices and 18 million edges. Induced subgraphs from target graphs were used as query graphs. Query graph size was restricted to 7 vertices as in [26].

We considered only search time for comparison and excluded time taken for one time pre-processing/indexing from our comparison. For a single query, NeMa ran for more than 13 hours and aborted on these datasets. This is in contrast to fraction of a second that NeMa takes for similar queries in the labeled setting. For our algorithm, we considered 50 queries separately on IMDB and YAGO. For IMDB, average similarity score achieved by our algorithm was 0.91 and 41 out of 50 results were exact matches. For YAGO, average similarity score achieved was 0.89 and 37 out of 50 results were exact matches. Average search time in both cases was less than 0.5 seconds. Upon restricting target graphs to 1000 node induced subgraphs of IMDB and YAGO graphs, NeMa took 2.5 hours for searching. We finally used 100 node induced subgraph of IMDB graph as target graph for NeMa. For 50 queries, average search time for NeMa was 8 minutes and 23 out of 50 results were exact matches. For same experiment, our algorithm achieved average similarity score of 0.93 and 40 out of 50 results were exact matches. Average search time for our algorithm was 0.03 seconds.

D. Scalability

Computationally most expensive parts of our algorithm are the vertex label computation for vertices of query and target graphs. Since this is a one time pre-processing for the target graph, it can be easily scaled to a distributed framework using the standard map-reduce paradigm. Vertex label computation for each vertex can be a separate map/reduce job. Vertex label computation for query graph is performed for every search. This can also be parallelized using the standard OpenMP/MPI framework as each vertex label computation can be done in parallel. As shown in the experimental results, remaining phases take much lesser time even with serial implementation. Parts of them can also be parallelized to further improve the search efficiency. Our algorithm can also support dynamic setting since computation of vertex level label vectors uses only local structural information. Edge and vertex modifications can therefore affect only label vectors of vertices in their local neighborhood and these label vectors can be recomputed efficiently and the pre-computed index can be modified accordingly.

VI. Conclusions

In this paper, we propose an algorithm that performs subgraph similarity search on large undirected graphs solely based on structural similarity. In the pre-processing step, our algorithm computes multi-dimensional vector representation for vertices in the target graph based on graphlet distribution in their local neighborhood. These local topological information are then combined to find a target subgraph having highly similar global topology with the given query graph. We tested our algorithm on several large real world graphs and was shown to obtain high quality matches efficiently. Size of these graphs ranged from thousand vertices to million vertices. By using vertex level vector labels based on graphlet distribution in the local topological neighborhood of vertices, we are able to extend the power of graphlet kernels, which was shown to perform well for graph similarity search on smaller graphs, to subgraph similarity search on much larger graphs. Local nature of vector label pre-computation of vertices makes our algorithm amenable to parallelization and to handle dynamic setting. Efficient parallel/distributed implementations of label vector pre-computation and matching to handle massive graphs on billions of vertices, large query graphs and massive graph streams would be future work.

References

[1] T. T. Nguyen, H. A. Nguyen, N. H. Pham, J. M. Al-Kofahi, and T. N. Nguyen, "Graph-based mining of multiple object usage patterns," in Proceedings of the the 7th joint meeting of the European software engineering conference and the ACM SIGSOFT symposium on The foundations of software engineering. ACM, 2009, pp. 383–392.

[2] D. Haussler, "Convolution kernels on discrete structures," University of California at Santa Cruz, Tech. Rep., 1999.

[3] F. Desobry, M. Davy, and W. J. Fitzgerald, "A class of kernels for sets of vectors," in ESANN, 2005, pp. 461–466.

[4] R. Kondor and T. Jebara, "A kernel between sets of vectors," in ICML, vol. 20, 2003, pp. 361–368.

[5] S. Vishwanathan and A. J. Smola, "Fast kernels for string and tree matching," in Kernel methods in computational biology. MIT Press, 2004, pp. 113–130.

[6] S. Hido and H. Kashima, "A linear-time graph kernel," in ICDM. IEEE, 2009, pp. 179–188.

[7] D. K. Hammond, P. Vandergheynst, and R. Gribonval, "Wavelets on graphs via spectral graph theory," Applied and Computational Harmonic Analysis, vol. 30, no. 2, 2011, pp. 129–150.

[8] N. Shervashidze and K. M. Borgwardt, "Fast subtree kernels on graphs," in Advances in Neural Information Processing Systems, 2009, pp. 1660–1668.

[9] T. Gärtner, P. Flach, and S. Wrobel, "On graph kernels: Hardness results and efficient alternatives," in Learning Theory and Kernel Machines. Springer, 2003, pp. 129–143.

[10] H. Kashima and A. Inokuchi, "Kernels for graph classification," in ICDM Workshop on Active Mining, 2002.

[11] T. Horváth, T. Gärtner, and S. Wrobel, "Cyclic pattern kernels for predictive graph mining," in Proceedings of the tenth ACM SIGKDD international conference on Knowledge discovery and data mining. ACM, 2004, pp. 158–167.

[12] M. Neuhaus and H. Bunke, "Edit distance based kernel functions for attributed graph matching," in Graph-Based Representations in Pattern Recognition. Springer, 2005, pp. 352–361.

[13] K. M. Borgwardt and H.-P. Kriegel, "Shortest-path kernels on graphs," in ICDM. IEEE, 2005, pp. 74–81.

[14] R. C. Bunescu and R. J. Mooney, "A shortest path dependency kernel for relation extraction," in Proceedings of the conference on Human Language Technology and Empirical Methods in Natural Language Processing. Association for Computational Linguistics, 2005, pp. 724–731.

[15] H. Fröhlich, J. K. Wegner, F. Sieker, and A. Zell, "Optimal assignment kernels for attributed molecular graphs," in Proceedings of the 22nd international conference on Machine learning. ACM, 2005, pp. 225–232.

[16] J. Ramon and T. Gärtner, "Expressivity versus efficiency of graph kernels," in First International Workshop on Mining Graphs, Trees and Sequences, 2003, pp. 65–74.

[17] S. Menchetti, F. Costa, and P. Frasconi, "Weighted decomposition kernels," in Proceedings of the 22nd international conference on Machine learning. ACM, 2005, pp. 585–592.

[18] N. Shervashidze, T. Petri, K. Mehlhorn, K. M. Borgwardt, and S. Vishwanathan, "Efficient graphlet kernels for large graph comparison," in International conference on artificial intelligence and statistics, 2009, pp. 488–495.

[19] D. Shasha, J. T. Wang, and R. Giugno, "Algorithmics and applications of tree and graph searching," in Proceedings of the twenty-first ACM SIGMOD-SIGACT-SIGART symposium on Principles of database systems. ACM, 2002, pp. 39–52.

[20] X. Yan, P. S. Yu, and J. Han, "Graph indexing: a frequent structure-based approach," in Proceedings of the ACM SIGMOD international conference on Management of data. ACM, 2004, pp. 335–346.

[21] S. Zhang, S. Li, and J. Yang, "Gaddi: distance index based subgraph matching in biological networks," in Proceedings of the 12th International Conference on Extending Database Technology: Advances in Database Technology. ACM, 2009, pp. 192–203.

[22] M. Mongiovi, R. Di Natale, R. Giugno, A. Pulvirenti, A. Ferro, and R. Sharan, "Sigma: a set-cover-based inexact graph matching algorithm," Journal of bioinformatics and computational biology, vol. 8, no. 02, 2010, pp. 199–218.

[23] S. Zhang, J. Yang, and W. Jin, "Sapper: Subgraph indexing and approximate matching in large graphs," Proceedings of the VLDB Endowment, vol. 3, no. 1-2, 2010, pp. 1185–1194.

[24] X. Wang, A. Smalter, J. Huan, and G. H. Lushington, "G-hash: towards fast kernel-based similarity search in large graph databases," in Proceedings of the 12th international conference on extending database technology: advances in database technology. ACM, 2009, pp. 472–480.

[25] A. Khan, N. Li, X. Yan, Z. Guan, S. Chakraborty, and S. Tao, "Neighborhood based fast graph search in large networks," in Proceedings of

the 2011 ACM SIGMOD International Conference on Management of data. ACM, 2011, pp. 901–912.

[26] A. Khan, Y. Wu, C. C. Aggarwal, and X. Yan, "NeMa: Fast graph search with label similarity," in Proceedings of the VLDB endowment, 2013, pp. 181–192.

[27] Z. Sun, H. Wang, H. Wang, B. Shao, and J. Li, "Efficient subgraph matching on billion node graphs," Proceedings of the VLDB Endowment, vol. 5, no. 9, 2012, pp. 788–799.

[28] Y. Yuan, G. Wang, J. Y. Xu, and L. Chen, "Efficient distributed subgraph similarity matching," VLDB journal, vol. 24, 2015, pp. 369–394.

[29] Y. Tian and J. M. Patel, "Tale: A tool for approximate large graph matching," in ICDE. IEEE, 2008, pp. 963–972.

[30] W. Zheng, L. Zou, X. Lian, D. Wang, and D. Zhao, "Graph similarity search with edit distance constraint in large graph databases," in Proceedings of the 22nd ACM international conference on Conference on information & knowledge management. ACM, 2013, pp. 1595–1600.

[31] J. Leskovec and A. Krevl, "SNAP Datasets: Stanford large network dataset collection," http://snap.stanford.edu/data, [retrieved: May, 2016].

[32] "DBLP Network," http://dblp.uni-trier.de/db/, [retrieved: May, 2016].

[33] N. Przulj, D. Corneil, and I. Jurisica, "Efficient estimation of graphlet frequency distributions in protein-protein interaction networks," Bioinformatics, vol. 22, no. 8, 2006, pp. 974–980.

[34] G. T. Heineman, G. Pollice, and S. Selkow, Algorithms in a Nutshell. O'Reilly Media, Inc., 2008.

Implementing Semantics-Based Cross-domain Collaboration Recommendation in Biomedicine with a Graph Database

Dimitar Hristovski
Faculty of Medicine
Ljubljana, Slovenia
dimitar.hristovski@gmail.com

Andrej Kastrin
Faculty of Information Studies
Novo mesto, Slovenia
andrej.kastrin@guest.arnes.si

Thomas C. Rindflesch
National Library of Medicine
Bethesda, MD, USA
trindflesch@mail.nih.gov

Abstract— **We describe a novel approach for cross-domain recommendation for research collaboration. We first constructed a large Neo4j graph database representing authors, their expertise, current collaborations, and general biomedical knowledge. This information comes from MEDLINE and from semantic relations extracted with SemRep. Then, by using an extended literature-based discovery paradigm, implemented with the Cypher graph query language, we recommend novel collaborations, which include author pairs, along with novel topics for collaboration and motivation for that collaboration.**

Keywords- Research collaboration; Recommendation system; Literature-based discovery; Semantic MEDLINE; Graph database; Neo4j.

I. INTRODUCTION

Nowadays, high quality science requires collaboration, as demonstrated by studies reporting that higher levels of collaboration correlate with higher productivity [1]. Current systems for recommending scientific collaboration are largely based on statistical analysis of co-occuring terms (e.g., ArnetMiner [2]); they provide a list of potential collaborators, but do not give motivation for the recommendations. Our methodology enhances previous work by providing a list of potential collaborators and topics for collaboration, in addition to compelling motivation for the collaboration. This innovative approach is based on a semantic implementation of literature-based discovery (LBD) methodology.

LBD is a methodology for automatically generating research hypothesis by uncovering hidden, previously unknown relationships from existing knowledge [3]. For example, suppose a researcher has studied the effect of substance X on gene Y. Further suppose that a different researcher has found a relationship between gene Y and disease Z. The use of LBD may suggest a relationship between X and Z, indicating that substance X may potentially treat disease Z. For a recent review of LBD tools and approaches see [4].

The relationships on which this project is based are semantic predications. A semantic predication is a formal structure representing part of the meaning of a sentence. For example, "Metformin TREATS Diabetes" represents part of the meaning of "Metformin is commonly used as first-line medication for management of diabetes." A semantic predication consists of a predicate ("TREATS" in this example) and arguments ("Metformin" and "Diabetes"). We used predications extracted by SemRep [5] from all of MEDLINE (titles and abstracts). SemRep is a rule-based, symbolic natural language processing system that extracts 30 predicate types expressing assertions in clinical medicine (e.g., TREATS, ADMINISTERED TO), substance interactions (e.g., INTERACTS WITH, STIMULATES), genetic etiology of disease (e.g., CAUSED, PREDISPOSES), and pharmacogenomics (e.g., AUGMENTS, DISRUPTS). The extracted predications are stored in a MySQL database (SemMedDB) which is publicly available [6]. The expressiveness inherent in semantic predications enhances the value of our system over that of the majority of LBD systems. Such systems are largely based on simple co-occurrence of phrases or concepts, which does not express the meaning of the relationship between the co-occurrences.

This work is a continuation and extension of our previous work. In [7] we described the basic cross-domain collaboration recommendation methodology, and in [8] we explained how to implement LBD with Neo4j graph database [9]. In this paper, we describe the implementation of the cross-domain collaboration recommendation methodology with the Neo4j graph database and its query language Cypher [9].

The paper is structured as follows. In Section II, we present the methods used to construct the graph database and the prediction algorithm, in Section III we present the results, and in Section IV we preset the conclusions .

II. METHODS

We first construct a large network and load it into the Neo4j graph database. We have used the Neo4j graph database because our data can be naturally expressed as a large graph and because Neo4j is well suited for storing and working with graphs. The network (graph) consists of two major types of nodes: authors and biomedical concepts. We extract the authors from the full MEDLINE bibliographic database. We extract the biomedical concepts from the set of arguments (subjects or objects) of semantic relations extracted from all MEDLINE titles and abstracts with SemRep. Each biomedical concept has a subtype, such as Disease or Syndrome or Pharmacologic Substance. We call the node subtypes semantic types and they come from Unified Medical Language System (UMLS). We use 126 semantic types. Our network contains several types of arcs and edges. `co_author` edges link any two authors that have been co-authors in at least one paper. We use this edge type to determine which authors already know each other. `writes_about` arcs link authors to biomedical concepts.

These arcs are derived from the semantic relations extracted from the articles written by the authors. We use the writes_about arcs to represent the expertise of the authors. Finally, we have 30 types of semantic relations extracted with SemRep that link the nodes representing biomedical concepts. These relations represent current biomedical knowledge.

The large network of nodes, arcs and edges described is the foundation on which the algorithm for recommending research collaboration operates. We implement the algorithm with the Cypher query language and it operates as follows. For a given input author (last and first names), we first compile the author's topic (concept) profile, which represents both the authors interests and expertise, by following the `writes_about` arcs as described above. The concepts from the author's profile are input to the LBD phase. For each input concept we perform an open LBD discovery. Here the methodology of discovery patterns can be used to improve the precision of the LBD process [10]. LBD proposes target concepts as novel collaboration (research) topics that are not yet published in the literature. For all target concepts found by LBD, we find authors who have these concepts in their profiles and eliminate those authors who are already co-authors with the starting author. The output is a list of the remaining authors as potential collaborators and topic(s) for collaboration. Shown in Figure 1 is a generic implementation with a Cypher query, which can be made more specific as needed.

```
MATCH (author1:author)-[:WRITES_ABOUT]->
(X:Concept) -[Rel_XY]-> (Y:Concept)
-[Rel_YZ]-> (Z:Concept) <-[:WRITES_ABOUT]-
(author2:author)
WHERE NOT (X)-[RelXZ]->(Z)
AND NOT (author1)-[CO_AUTHOR]-(author2)
RETURN author1, X, Rel_XY, Y, Rel_YZ, Z,
author2;
```

Figure 1. Generic implementation of the collaboration recommendation algorithm with a Cypher query.

We provide an illustration for this discovery process (Figure 2). In this example we use the "inhibit the cause of the disease" LBD discovery pattern [11] which states that a drug X maybe treats disease Z (new hypothesis) if the drug X inhibits gene(s) Y which causes disease Z. We have all the necessary information for this discovery pattern in our network. Also from the network we can find that authors A and B are experts for drug X and disease Z, respectively, because they write about these topics. The explanation goes as follows: If author B wants to find a novel way to treat disease Z she should collaborate with author A, because she is an expert for drug X which might be beneficial for disease Z.

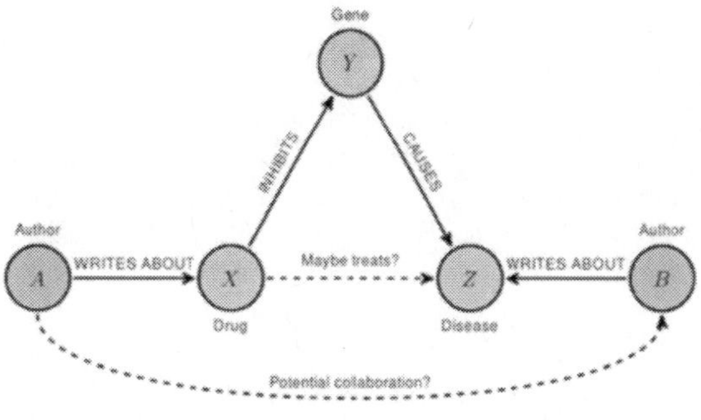

Figure 2. Illustration of the recommendation process. Based on the current biomedical knowledge (solid arcs) we recommend novel collaboration (dashed arcs).

Shown in Figure 3 is a Cypher query for the collaboration recommendation based on "inhibit the cause of the disease" discovery pattern.

```
MATCH (author1:author) -[:WRITES_ABOUT]->
(drug:phsu)-[:INHIBITS]->(gene:gngm)
-[:CAUSES]-> (disease:dsyn)
<-[:WRITES_ABOUT]- (author2:author)
WHERE NOT (drug)-[:TREATS]->(disease)
AND NOT (author1)-[CO_AUTHOR]-(author2)
RETURN author1, drug, gene, disease,
author2;
```

Figure 3. Implementation of the collaboration recommendation algorithm with a Cypher query based on the "inhibit the cause of the disease" discovery pattern.

III. Results

The network we constructed consists of 69333420 semantic relations extracted from 23657386 MEDLINE bibliographic records using SemRep. The characteristics of the network are as follows: There are 9516106 author nodes and 269047 biomedical concept nodes. Regarding edges, there are 181664746 `co_author` edges between the authors, 189294999 `writes_about` arcs between the authors and biomedical concepts, and 69333420 arcs that come from SemRep semantic relations between the biomedical concepts.

We applied the collaboration recommendation algorithm using the LBD discovery pattern "inhibit the cause of the disease," which returned 275661539 unique pairs of authors. 1817 distinct drugs, 3218 distinct genes, and 8698 distinct diseases were included in the topics for collaboration; these recommendations need to be evaluated from the biomedical point of view.

Future work includes development of a user interface and visualization module. Author name ambiguity currently introduces considerable noise into the discovery process, and we need to address disambiguation in this area.

IV. Conclusions

Using a graph database such as Neo4j for storing the large network data structure needed for semantics-based cross-domain collaboration recommendation is more natural and efficient than using a relational database. Implementing collaboration recommendation algorithms is conceptually easier and more simple when using a graph query language such as Cypher when compared to standard SQL.

ACKNOWLEDGMENT

This work was supported by the Slovenian Research Agency and by the Intramural Research Program of the U.S. National Institutes of Health, National Library of Medicine.

REFERENCES

[1] J. Katz and B. R. Martin, "What is research collaboration," Research Policy, vol. 26, no. 1, pp 1-18, 1997.

[2] J. Tang, J. Zhang, L.Yao, J. Li, L. Zhang, and Z. Su, "ArnetMiner," in Proceedings of the 14th ACM SIGKDD international conference on Knowledge discovery and data mining – KDD 08. New York, NY: ACM Press, pp. 990-998, 2008.

[3] D. R. Swanson, "Fish oil, Raynaud's syndrome, and undiscovered public knowledge," Perspectives in Biology and Medicine, vol. 30, no. 1, pp. 7-18, 1986.

[4] D. Hristovski, T. Rindflesch, and B. Peterlin, "Using literaturebased discovery to identify novel therapeutic approaches," Cardiovascular & Hematological Agents in Medicinal Chemistry, vol. 11, no. 1, pp. 14-24, 2013.

[5] T. C. Rindflesch and M. Fiszman, "The interaction of domain knowledge and linguistic structure in natural language processing: Interpreting hypernymic propositions in biomedical text," Journal of Biomedical Informatics, vol. 36, no. 6, pp. 462-477, 2003.

[6] H. Kilicoglu, D. Shin, M. Fiszman, G. Rosemblat, and T. C. Rindflesch, "SemMedDB: A PubMed-scale repository of biomedical semantic predications," Bioinformatics, vol. 28, no. 23, pp. 3158-3160, 2012.

[7] D. Hristovski, A. Kastrin, and T. C. Rindflesch, "Semantics-bsed cross-domain collaboration recommendation in the life sciences: Preliminary results," Proceedings of the 2015 IEEE/ACM International Conference on Advances in Social Networks Analysis and Mining, pp. 805-806, 2015.

[8] D. Hristovski, A. Kastrin, D. Dinevski, and T. C. Rindflesch, "Towards implementing semantic literature-based discovery with a graph database," Proceedings of the GraphSM 2015, The Second International Workshop on Large-scale Graph Storage and Management, pp. 180-184, 2015.

[9] Neo4j website. Available at: http://neo4j.com. Last accessed June 20th 2016.

[10] D. Hristovski, C. Friedman, T. C. Rindflesch, and B. Peterlin, "Exploiting semantic relations for literature-based discovery," AMIA Annual Symposium proceedings, pp. 349-353, 2006.

[11] C. B. Ahlers, D. Hristovski, H. Kilicoglu, and T. C. Rindflesch, "Using the literature-based discovery paradigm to investigate drug mechanisms," AMIA Annual Symposium proceedings, pp. 6-10, 2007.